... in Psy... ... an
... Psychology. She ha... ...rie... e in
... ...elling and psychotherap... ...h... ...men,
and in running women's therapy groups. Since 1980,
she has been working as a Clinical Psychologist in the
National Health Service.

Gerrilyn Smith has a degree in Psychology and English
Literature from Canada. She moved to London in
1976, where she obtained an M.Phil in Clinical
Psychology. She has worked in a number of settings,
including voluntary agencies, the health service, local
authorities and the private sector. Gerrilyn Smith
currently works as a freelance trainer, consultant and
clinician.

Also by Gerrilyn Smith from The Women's Press:

*The Protectors' Handbook: Reducing the risk
of child sexual abuse and helping children
recover* (1995)

KATHY NAIRNE & GERRILYN SMITH

Dealing
with
Depression

SECOND EDITION
FULLY REVISED AND UPDATED

THIS EDITION EDITED

BY KATE MOSSE

First published by The Women's Press Ltd, 1984
A member of the Namara Group
34 Great Sutton Street, London EC1V 0DX

Reprinted 1984, 1985

Reprinted and revised 1995

British Library Cataloguing-in-Publication Data.
A catalogue record for this book is available from
the British Library

ISBN 0 7043 4443 2

Typeset in Sabon & Franklin Gothic by Contour
Printed and bound in Great Britain by Cox & Wyman Ltd,
Reading, Berks

Foreword
About Ourselves

This book has come out of our life experiences. We did not want to write this book as experts, but as women who have shared a lot of experiences with other women. All involved with this book, and there are many, are convinced that sharing their thoughts and feelings – about depression – will ultimately help other women.

We did not want to write about women as if *we* weren't women or about *them* as 'objects' of study. Yet, we could not be every woman described in this book. In the end, we decided to start with *us*, as individual women writing this book.

Without the support, encouragement, cajoling and criticism of each other and friends, the book would not have grown. It comes out of our experiences as women, feminists and psychologists. These three roles in themselves involve us in considerable contradictions.

We are both white, unmarried and working in a profession. Neither of us has children at home. Research has shown that these factors make it less likely that we will become clinically depressed. For both of us, our present positions have been gained by a combination of some inherent privileges and personal choice.

We understand women's experiences within a feminist perspective. This means we see issues relating to women as separate from, and different to, those relating to men. We recognise and experience the oppression of women by men and feel very strongly that any psychology of women must begin by accepting this fact. We believe in change and work towards it both personally and professionally.

Our routes to psychology were very different. Together we bring a wealth of experiences and previous occupations. These include, mother's helper, big sister, daddy's girl, babysitter, waitress, van driver, squatter, switchboard operator, unemployment benefactor, astrologist, tarot card reader.

Psychology is a good 'feminine' occupation. It is profesionalisation of what most women do all of their lives: look after other people's feelings. We are paid to listen, to be sympathetic and to care. It could be said that we make our living from other people's emotional suffering and pain. We could also be seen as agents of state control, helping women to fit in rather than to change. Sometimes we are asked by others to do this – 'Make my wife better'; 'Talk to my children and make them behave'. Other times women ask us themselves – 'Teach me to have orgasms through penetration'; 'Help me to like men'. These are very difficult dilemmas and we by no means have all the answers. We try to provide a service that works towards our own redundancy and that maximises individual women's freedom of choice. There are some 'treatments' we refuse to give.

We use a variety of psychological models, as appropriate. We try to discuss with the women and girls we work with what the best approach is for them. We recognise that in our work with women, we are in the position of power. We try to acknowledge that imbalance, and to work constructively within it.

Part of our motivation to become psychologists stems from an awareness of our own vulnerabilites. We have both, in our different ways, struggled with depression. We do feel that our knowledge of ourselves and others has been deepened not only by our own personal experiences but also by those of other women. We are aware of the pressures most women are under to be happy with life as it is and to be able to cope, whatever the demands and stresses put on them.

In our work we encourage women to acknowledge their own feelings and needs as valid, to share feelings both of strength and weakness, and to believe in their right to *want* more, even if it cannot be achieved. We do not forget that opportunities in life may be different for different women. But we feel we can support someone else in establishing her own goals, and in moving towards them. Neither of us has had experience of working with women of colour. We can only hope that our own experiences will help us to respect their different cultural background and social context.

In writing this book the connection between the colour black and depression is something we have reconsidered. Depression is constructed as a negative experience. White women will often use expressions like 'a black mood', 'a dark cloud', or make other references to blackness when discussing or describing depression. Where possible, this has been avoided in the book. The association of blackness with death, depression and other assumed 'negative' images must be changed. Our language is not only inherently sexist but also racist.

We have tried to explore the possibility of seeing depression as a positive experience. Intuitively, we believe this to be true.

We believe in humour. To be able to laugh at yourself is a gift. Humour is so often funny because it captures the irrational side of yourself that in retrospect you can laugh at. This doesn't mean that we don't see the serious side of life or of depression.

We have to balance our own needs with the needs of others. Our job encourages us to feel enormously responsible for others. We are not immune to the image of the strong woman – trying to be the one who always copes and provides the 'answers'. We are both aware of how important it is that we care for ourselves. As the carriers of many women's most painful experiences, we have had to learn ways of taking care of ourselves that help us to continue in our work. Our support networks have been invaluable in this respect. No doubt, there have been times when we have been less active and less open in our work.

Working in a psychiatric unit, we have to sit in ward meetings and watch how doctors decide to treat many women who are in-patients with depression. Here we are confronted by our own impotence, as doctors prescribe drugs or ECT when we know that the cause of the depression is connected to a woman's personal circumstances. We are frustrated and angry that we cannot provide all the counselling and support we would like to and which women may want to use.

Working with children and families means operating either with no feminist theories of child development or, at the other extreme, with feminist theories of 'mothering' that are so removed from most mothers' realities that it seems difficult to see their relevance.

Yet, regardless of the setting, we have brought our feminism with us. Being together in the same department and knowing other feminist mental health workers has helped.

We recognise that all women have a right to feelings of regret and anger about lost opportunities, or the restrictions on their lives. But even if the choices we can make now are limited, we can work towards a future where we will have greater freedom of choice.

Foreword to the Second Edition
About Ourselves Ten Years On

Revising a book written ten years ago is not an easy task. So much has happened, not least of which involves personal changes and life experiences. We used to work together and with that intimate proximity, that daily contact, we were able to establish the degree of consensus needed to work collaboratively on a book. We now work in different places and rarely see each other except recently to talk about the revision!

In many ways we have followed the predicted path of development as we moved through our thirties and entered our forties. We both have partners and children. This superficially common ground conceals a host of differences that ten years ago we would have been able to manage perhaps more openly. We don't have that same intimacy and the choices we have made in our lives have moved us farther apart rather than brought us closer together. So in some ways the task of revising this book was very daunting to us personally.

Our life experiences have included the deaths of significant people in our lives, some of them untimely. In ten years, we have both learned to take better care of ourselves and the frantic pace of work has been dramatically modified by other equally absorbing aspects of our lives. For Kathy, the experience of developing chronic arthritis and coping with a degree of disability has been a catalyst for changing priorities.

The context for providing psychological services has also changed dramatically over the last ten years. There have been massive re-organisations of all the major providers of pastoral care including both the health service and social services. Access to these services often isn't easier but harder. Paradoxically, issues regarding the quality and accessibility of services and user-involvement have simultaneously come to the fore, and this has led to opportunities for new and innovative services in some places. For example, counselling services have been set up in some General Practice surgeries; there are now more support groups for survivors of sexual abuse; and services do exist to provide support for people with long term mental health problems. By and large, however, these developments are patchy and their overall impact difficult to summarise.

Our professional involvement in these changes is very different. Kathy continues to work within the NHS and is involved in the development and management of new services, while Gerrilyn now works privately after years within both the NHS and Social Services.

Our approach to work is marked by much clearer theoretical differences. Kathy has kept her psychodynamic orientation and works predominantly with an adult mental health population. Gerrilyn has a systemic orientation and works with children and their families.

We have both had the privilege of working alongside Black and Asian colleagues who have helped in our thinking around issues of race, culture and gender. These very significant people, Maria Mars, Sandy Da Silva, Marcia Spencer, Maxine Dennis and Nimisha Patel, have given us the confidence to work across race and culture whilst recognising that some issues remain which need to be dealt within a different context.

There has been an explosion of self-help guides on many different topics, including depression. When comparing what we did to what exists now, our efforts seem inadequate at times. So many issues were dealt with only in passing or not at all. Yet the original purpose of the book – its primary focus on women – continues to be its great strength. The premise that depression is one feeling among many, shared unevenly throughout the population, is still one we hold. We also very much believe that depression can have its positive side, making time for reflection and recovery.

There are still 'treatments' we wouldn't give or do. When we first wrote the book we had arguments with colleagues over the use of pornography in the treatment of sexual dysfunction and the use of vaginal dilators in the treatment of vaginismus. Our position on this has not changed, although whether these methods are still used is difficult to assess. Our current concerns mirror the present focus in our work. Gerrilyn has been involved in the field of child protection for many years and has concentrated on working with survivors of abuse and their primary caregivers, usually mothers. She is committed to services for girls and women and is hesitant about mixed residential provisions for young women – particularly when helping them recover from the effects of male violence. She continues to have these debates with her colleagues. For Kathy, the issue of protection for women on in-patient psychiatric wards is an ongoing concern. The general practice has been for wards to accommodate both genders, with little thought being given to the issue of women's safety from sexual harassment or overt coercion.

In addition to dramatic organisational changes, the past ten years have witnessed equally dramatic social changes. Recent research on educational attainment indicates that girls are out-performing boys at all levels. This news was packaged into a television documentary with the byline 'the future is female'. The young women in the programme were assertive and eager to demonstrate that they were as, if not more, competent than boys in all areas of achievements. There are now more women who have chosen not to get married and to have children without living with the father of the child. Many working women are the sole wage-earners for their families – and some men have become house-husbands. Men are receiving more encouragement to be involved with their children, and many more advertisements show fathers as care-givers to their children.

Yet against this backdrop of welcome social change are other more frightening changes. The discovery of HIV and AIDS infections, including their modes of transmission, has provided a sobering lesson in personal freedom, sexual values and un-relenting discrimination. The rise of the right politically has resulted in policy attacks on lone parents and outspoken support for a return to traditional, nuclear families. There has also been a rise in biological/organic explanations for behaviour, including the resurrection of the IQ debates about innate levels of intelligence in different racial groups, and the search for physio-logical reasons for homosexuality. Given these trends, we will need to guard against a growing intolerance of difference and the enforcement of higher levels of conformity within our society.

The need for information and knowledge to be able to manage and care for yourself is therefore much greater. For those people who do not have a voice, the likelihood that services will be provided is very small. The homeless, for instance, are often deprived of services because they have no address. General Practices have the right to refuse treatment to individuals they deem difficult or problematic.

The safe refuges for people unable to cope with day-to-day living that we felt we needed ten years ago are still not widely available today. Although many long-stay in-patient facilities, which are often oppressive and almost certainly abusive, have closed, sufficient alternatives have not been provided. This is particularly true for people who need either a temporary respite or a gradual rehabilitation. The general public's awareness regarding mental illness remains very low. In London and other inner city areas, the shortage of hospital beds for people having an acute mental health crisis has left vulnerable people without the support and accommodation they may need.

All in all, there is still a lot of be depressed about. In fact, that may be the most appropriate response. But social changes are broad and generalised whereas depression is an individual experience. This book still has relevance in exploring why women get depressed more often than men, which they do. Importantly, it suggests ways of dealing with a depression when you have one that are creative. At the simplest level, we trust it will help to make you feel better about yourself and your life.

Contents

Acknowledgments

The authors gratefully acknowledge permission from the following to reprint material in this book:

Fontana Books for the extract from *Postnatal Depression* by Vivienne Welburn, 1980;

The Guardian, London, for permission to use the interview by Penny Junor, *The Guardian*, 17 June 1982;

Caroline Halliday and Onlywomen Press, London, for The Birth from *Some truth, Some Change*, 1983;

David Higham Associates, London, for the extract from *The Wise Wound* by Peter Redgrove and Penelope Shuttle, Gollancz, London, 1980;

National Council for Civil Liberties, London, for the quotation from *Sexual Harassment at Work* by Ann Sedley and Melissa Benn, 1982;

Penguin Books, Harmondsworth, and George Borchardt, New York, for the extracts from Jean Baker Miller's *Towards a New Psychology of Women*, 1978;

Release, London, for the quotation from *Trouble with Tranquillisers*, 1982;

Spare Rib, London, for the quotations from 'Little Box Living' by Jane Smith, and an article by Ginny Cook;

Spare Rib, London, and Spinsters Ink, New York, for the extract from *The Cancer Journals* by Audre Lorde, 1980;

Tavistock Press, London, for the extracts from *Social Origins of Depression* by George Brown and Tirril Harris, 1978;

Virago Press, London, for the extracts from *Mirror Writing* by Elizabeth Wilson, 1982;

The Women's Press, London, for the quotations from *In Our Own Hands* by Sheila Ernst and Lucy Goodison, 1981; and *Pornography and Silence* by Susan Griffin, 1981.

And many thanks to Paula Youens, who drew the cartoons.

Author's Note: In the text, quotations from some women have dates and some do not. The dated entries are from diaries and journals; the undated ones are from interviews.

1
Depressing Business

How do we make a book on depression come alive when the very topic we are writing about can be so deadly? Depression is a common word and a common experience. It can last an hour, a day, a week, a month or a lifetime. It can deny us the basic pleasures of life: eating, sleeping, loving. It wears away at us – a grinding monotony of despairing, hopeless thoughts or a frenzied agitation that leads nowhere.

> In spite of having my children, the feeling that I couldn't go on battling with life any longer remained. Each time I attempted suicide I admitted defeat. All I wanted was peace of mind and death was the only way I could think of in which I might find it.
> *Chris*

Depression is like defeat. When things are too much we can give up.

> Depression . . . well, you just feel you can't do anything, you can't do anything right and it doesn't seem to matter how hard you try you just can't seem to get to where you want to get . . . you try and you try and you try . . . you have fits of tears and just feel utter despair. *Elizabeth*

Despair is considered by the Christian churches to be a grave sin, a loss of faith – the beginning of eternal condemnation. Despair is psychic murder. To live with depression, we need to overcome despair. This requires a faith in ourselves. We also need our family, friends and lovers to care for us, to support, coax, encourage and sometimes to hold us. It is especially difficult for women to get others to care, as we are so often expected to do the 'caring' for others.

3

What should be a mutual activity, is often one-sided. When we are feeling bad about ourselves, it takes an enormous amount of courage and trust to *ask* to be cared for. Unfortunately, all too often, women have to *ask* – care is not given unless we request it. Asking presupposes there is someone to ask and that they will respond. Frequently, it is our depression that gives us voice and only the supposed 'caring agencies' that respond.

Depression is something that happens to us. We rarely talk about depressing somebody. More often discussions centre on our own state of mind. The statement 'I am depressed' omits the action agent – depressed by whom or what?

If we are going to deal with depression then we must try to understand it, both as an individual experience and a political process.

It's unfortunate I didn't keep a diary during my depressions as I feel so much like a different person then. Because of the culmination of emotions and events that manifest themselves in depression, I wonder who I really am. *Janet*

A dictionary definition of the verb 'to depress' will help us come to a more political understanding.

1. To put down by force, or crush in a contest or struggle; to overcome, subjugate, vanquish (now obsolete!).
2. To press down; to force, bring, move or put in a lower position by any physical action; to lower.
3. To lower in station, fortune, or influence; to put down, bring low, humble. Now rare.
4. To keep down, repress, restrain from activity; to put down, suppress; to oppress. Obsolete.
5. To bring down in estimation or credit; to depreciate, disparage. Obsolete.
6. To lower, bring down in force, vigour, activity, intensity or amount; to render weaker or less; to render dull or languid.
7. To bring into low spirits, cast down mentally, dispirit, deject, sadden – the chief current use.[1]

This lengthy list of past and present meanings is presented because we feel there are connections between them. Mary Daly suggests we look at obsolete meanings of words to recover their

true meaning.[2] This book is about making connections because no one else will make them for us. Depression *is* connected to oppression. In effect, women are forced down to be kept down; depressed to be oppressed.

Depression is well known. It is considered the 'common cold of psychiatry'. This innocuous analogy belittles the deadliness of some depressions. Those who catch this 'cold' are not randomly distributed. Research from many different countries indicates that women are at least twice as likely *to be* depressed as men.[3] It would be easier to write that more women 'get depressed' (as if we seek it out) or 'suffer from depression' (as if it were a physical illness), but the fact remains that women are depressed by their life experiences in greater numbers than men.

We want to examine what is that makes us vulnerable; that encourages and maintains depression in women; and ways in which we can protect ourselves from deadly depression and integrate less serious forms into our everyday lives. This is a book written by women for women whether depressed or not. We need to ask not 'Why am I depressed?' but 'How do I manage *not* to be depressed?' As Ruth Elizabeth puts it:

> We need to examine mental *health* as well as mental illness if those of us who have been labelled mentally ill are going to be able to stop seeing *ourselves* as the problem, as victims of an unfortunate personal failure setting us apart from all 'normal' women around us.[4]

5

Depression is so tied up with the medical model of illness, it is hard to imagine.it in anything but a negative light. As women feel alienated from medicine, so too do we feel alienated from and by depression.

> You're doing what you should be doing but you are so far away that nothing seems to touch you until someone physically touches you and then it gives you a shake. *Janice*

This book is about living with depression. It attempts to touch *you*.

Theories of Depression

The strength of feminist theory is that it gives power and credence to the individual woman's experience while also making connetions with other women's experiences. It draws from them to create its theoretical framework. We do not want to take an existing analysis, of which there are many, and force women's depression into it. This violates our experience, and will inevitably keep us both depressed and oppressed.

This does not mean that other theories on depression have no relevance. Although this book does not aim to provide a review of the theories currently being used in clinical practice, reference will be made to those that have had an influence on our thinking.

The medical model sees depression as a 'mental illness'. This way of understanding would suggest something is wrong in our brains. The treatment would be a drug that rights a chemical imbalance. Medicine really does not know very much about the chemistry of moods, although some drugs do make us feel 'better'. Understanding depression as an 'illness' can be helpful if it means it is taken more seriously. Unfortunately, this isn't always the case.

A mental illness is not considered as legitimate as a physical illness. Something that is 'all in your head' is crazy. A 'loony bin' or 'nuthouse' are hardly neutral names for a highly specialised hospital!

Sympathy and helpfulness is much more forthcoming for 'real illnesses'. 'Mental patients' are tolerated and often viewed with fear. Depression is really the wallflower of mental illnesses, lacking the romanticised 'wildness' and 'passion' of mania or schizophrenia.

As an illness, depression undoubtedly affects our body chemistry. Diet can play a part in helping lift our mood. We feel a medical model is too focused on biological explanations. It is ineffective in explaining depression. It doesn't help our understanding. Psychological models seem to provide more satisfactory explanations of what is essentially an emotional experience, and social phenomenon.

Behavioural psychology understands depression in terms of reinforcement or rewards. You become depressed when you are not getting enough rewards (!). This notion is also coupled with a 'learned helplessness' model of depression. Martin Seligman developed this model with dogs.[5] Despite the obvious incongruity, the experiments demonstrated that having no control over your life contributes to a feeling of helplessness that can lead to depression. We learn our actions have no effect on consequences. Over time we cease to act, because there does not seem any point. If we are not acting we are less likely to get any rewards. And hence a vicious circle begins.

This model is too simplistic. It does not take into account how our feelings, thoughts or past experiences influence our behaviour. There is no social perspective. There needs to be a more detailed discussion of what is rewarding to whom and who gives out these rewards. Although women may have learned to be helpless, we are, at times, rewarded for being precisely that.

On the other hand, we often feel obliged to do a great many things that have no obvious payoff.

Cognitive behaviour therapy was developed by Aaron Beck specifically with humans in mind rather than extrapolating from animal behaviour. There are three principles in this model:

1. All your moods are created by your thoughts.

2. When you are depressed your thoughts are dominated by negativity.

3. 'Twisted thinking is the exclusive cause of nearly all your suffering.' (!)[6]

There are ten types of 'twisted thinking;. This model sees the 'normal' mind working according to rational principles. As with behaviour therapy, it does not take into account historical factors or a sociological perspective. Neither model was developed specifically for women, nor do they have any political or social

7

understanding. Both of these models are based in learning theory. This is perhaps their greatest strength in that there is an emphasis on assuming personal responsibility and a positive approach to change. Because they see depression as a learned response to either environmental events or thought processes, behaviourists believe we can learn new ways to behave or think that will lift our mood.

Psychoanalytic theorists are not so concerned with behaviour. Theirs is the realm of feeling. While behaviourists stick to the dominion of the observable, the analysts are quite comfortable dealing with assumptions and speculations. At its most simplistic, psychoanalysis has claimed that women feel inferior because they do not have penises. This grave lack is supposed to make us more prone to envy, depression, hysteria and other signs of neurosis.

Yet, contained within this simplistic summary, is a partial truth. Women may well feel inferior because they lack penises but not in the literal sense. The penis is the symbol (possibly the reality) of male power. Perhaps if women were more powerful we would be less prone to be depressed. However, this does not mean we want penises. Freudian theory has been criticised for its phallocentric approach (i.e. its concern/obsession with the male experience). Its usefulness for women is limited. It does describe, inadvertently, the situation women must live with, in this male-dominated world. Shulamith Firestone stated: 'Freud was merely a diagonistician for what feminism purports to cure.'[7]

Another analytic concept that is useful in the understanding of depression is direction of hostility. According to psychoanalytic theory, depressed people direct their hostile feelings inwards, on to themselves. It is not surprising that women feel depressed when we live in a women-hating world. What is more puzzling is why some of us are not depressed. Perhaps there are ways of hating yourself that do not manifest themselves as depression.

Analysis, like feminism, does give priority and importance to the individual's experience. A man of his time, Freud chose to believe childhood sexual abuse was fantasy rather than fact when he encountered it in many of the women he treated.[8] He developed a psychological theory of development without examining the cultural context in which it occurred.

Sociological research aims to do just that. It examines the impact of social systems on the individual. George Brown and

Tirril Harris did a large survey of depression in women in Camberwell, South London.[9] They were attempting to examine social factors that influence the likelihood of an individual developing a psychiatric disorder.

They found that 15 per cent of their sample were suffering from what they termed a 'definitive affective disorder', while a further 18 per cent were considered borderline. Together this means 33 per cent of the women interviewed were suffering from a measurable amount of depression. They also listed vulnerability factors, which included the lack of an intimate relationship, three or more children at home and the loss of the mother before the age of eleven. These factors did not in themselves produce depression, but they increased the likelihood of it developing if women experienced further stresses. Having a job acted as a protection against depression.

Brown and Harris' research is still considered essential reading when studying the social factors underlying depression. There have been many refinements to their model, mostly in terms of recognising that early childhood adversity – including physical and sexual abuse – increases the risk of depression in later life. This seems to be not only the result of adverse experiences themselves but equally a result of the consequences of such experiences, including the support – or lack thereof – received.

The model currently being developed from the original Brown and Harris research suggests there is a continuity between childhood and adult adversity. This continuity may reflect a restriction of life choices which often follows negative early experiences. If you feel bad about yourself you are less likely to choose good things for yourself and less able to prevent more bad things from happening. This seems to be more true in cases of chronic or recurrent depression.

Brown and Harris noted that a close confiding relationship, usually assumed to be with the partner reduced the risk of depression. It has also been noted in other research that the good qualities of partners exert a powerful ameliorating effect on those women who have had adverse early experiences (in this study defined as being raised away from the family of origin).[10] As a result, a theme of protectiveness derived from strong and positive intimate relationships has been developed. However the research focusing on women has not been matched by similar research on men. The necessary gender comparisons have not been made, and

9

it is difficult to assess if the same model is as appropriate for men as it is for women.

It is worth noting that all the models we have discussed have been developed without *any* concept of a separate women's psychology. Even though George Brown and Tirril Harris used a women-only sample, they did this for reasons of convenience, and not to *understand* why most *women* are depressed.

The aim of their research was not an examination of the depressing reality of many women's lives but to demonstrate that social factors play a large part in any one *person's* predisposition to a psychiatrtic condition. Indeed, they explained their study's concentration on women as follows:

We also needed as many *people* as possible to agree to co-operate in what we knew would be a lengthy interview . . . Such an interviewing programme is expensive and one way to reduce its cost was to study women only, as they probably suffer from depression more often than men . . . we would need to approach only half as many women as men to obtain the same number with depressive disorders. It also seemed likely that women, who are more often at home during the day would be more willing to agree to see us for several hours.[11]

Ten years ago most of the popular books on depression were written by male doctors.[12] Although some very good practical advice and useful information was offered, the tone was often patronising (doctor knows best), or written to the average person – he – when the average depressed person is more likely to be a woman.

Encouragingly, since this book was first published, there has been a huge expansion of self-help books written by and for women (see Appendix 4). Male theories and books will always remain disconnected from our experiences. Men may understand women but it will always be from the point of view of difference – otherness. For too long 'the male experience' has been accepted as the norm. Women need the space to develop and document their own experience.

The need for a separate and distinct psychology of women has in recent years received some recognition with, for example, the formation of the Psychology of Women section of the BPS and the launching of the journal, *Feminism and Psychology*. At the

10

same time, the ongoing debates regarding the impact of sexual orientation, disabilities and race and culture on the impact of mental health indicate that the broad brush differences based on gender alone need to be refined and made more complex to reflect the multiplicity of experience within society today. However research, which often lags behind common knowledge or confirms things we have always suspected, is likely to confirm that for those who occupy less privileged positions in society, the likelihood of suffering depression is greater.

The need for resources and projects that address issues specific to certain groups of women is essential because it is not always possible to use the services designed for the majority group. Melba Wilson addresses this issue very clearly and powerfully in her book *Crossing the Boundary: Black Women Survive Incest*, for black female survivors of child sexual abuse.[13]

This book is essentially a self-help manual. The discussions and ideas are meant to spark rather than burn. The sparks may set alight the kindling of recognition. It is written in the belief that we are depressed not because of inherent badness, weakness, sickness or craziness, but that there is a good reason for our depression even if we don't always understand or know it. Understanding the reasons gives us hope of coming through the experience stronger and more resilient.

The limitationss of this book are the limits of our experience. Many women's experiences will not be described or given enough space. The experiences quoted in this book come from black and white women living in the West. However, we believe that some of the issues we have raised are common to all women's experiences of depression.

Living in a racist society is depressing at the very least, but much more so for those women who have no choice about when or where they must deal with it. The same is true for women of all oppressed groups. Many women feel alienated from the dominant culture. We believe that feminist theory must address itself not only to sameness but also to differences in women's experience. This book concentrates on the former because we have drawn on our own experience and that of the women we work with, and we hope this limitation is not detrimental or seen as a negation of some women's lives.

There is not one tyrannical identity to which all must approximate, but a group insistence on the value of difference. The testimony of consciousness raising and of those 'women's' literary forms of diary, autobiography and confession, do not suggest an identical experience of the world, although the testimony has made possible the identification of points of similiarity which have formed the basis for collective politics.[14]

The book began with us and our experience coupled with the experience of other women; from there it moved to written work by professional researchers and women who write to share their thoughts. It has been like sewing a patchwork, piecing personal account to public speculation. It reaches out for a balance between these different approaches.

The first Part of the book is about the journey. A brief description of how we can arrive depressed and despairing. The second Part of the book concentrates on ways out, through, or around a depression. It is like a map, which each of you can follow as you want.

There are no simple answers or 'cures' for depression. Examining why you feel the way you do, may give you clues on how to deal with it. Understanding yourself will help you choose what will be most effective for you. For some, depression can pass quickly.

Depression is a funny thing. One minute you will be wallowing in its depths and the next you are miles away from it. *Marie*

For others, it seems a lifetime struggle.

I suppose everybody's got to find peace of mind in their own way. Someone like me, where do I find it?
I really do believe that some of us are born to go through life in the same way . . . *Chris*

For all of us it is at present an essentially lonely experience.

For me, a lot of it is loneliness. If I'm on my own, I get these feelings of being low. *Lyn*

12

To quote the words of a song:

> Sweet misery, she loves her company
> but she is most happy
> When she's all alone.
> (*source unknown*)

The loneliness and alienation of depression can be fatal. This thought gives an urgency to the book. In researching depression, we must also reconsider our ideas about strength and where it lies.

> Women have fallen back on to the notion of the 'strong woman'. But however good it is to be strong, we feel ambivalent about the strong, powerful woman, since this too is an image that allows for no moment of weakness and cannot reflect the diversity and complexity of our desires.[15]

The myth of the strong woman is especially potent for black women. This stereotype has been described in Michele Wallace's book, *Black Macho and the Myth of Superwoman* as 'a woman of inordinate strength, with an ability for tolerating an unusual amount of misery and heavy distasteful work'.[16]

> As black women, we are often taught to keep our emotional hurt carefully suppressed and hidden within ourselves, and to ignore the emotional signals that we are hurting until the problem has become so bad we can no longer conceal it. *Jackie*

Strength is often defined as a denial of feeling. To be an 'emotional woman' is to be seen as hysterical. This implies weakness and inferiority.

> I used to think that to be an independent strong woman meant to be autonomous and to deal with one's own oppression or depression. I think that it's really important to share those sorts of feelings with other women. It's only very recently for me that I've been able to do that. I should have learnt that years ago in consciousness raising groups, but I was too terrified.
>
> I used to think that to be autonomous meant to be self-

13

contained and to take care of my own feelings. OK, that's fine – but not really. I think you have to share. *Betsy*

There are many definitions of strength. As feminists, we must make our own. As Marge Piercy says in a poem, a strong woman is one 'who loves strongly and weeps strongly; is strongly terrified and has strong needs'.[17]

We need to reconceptualise depression. It can be seen as a potentially positive experience. This can be evidenced in recent books which commend a more spiritual approach to life such as *Sisters of the Yam*[18] and *Women Who Run with the Wolves*[19]. 'Natural cycles forced into unnatural rhythms to please others'[20] describes most accurately the lives of many women. Depression can push us to look at ourselves or our pasts differently. The tiredness and fatigue so often felt as part of depression can help us slow down and get the rest we so obviously need. It is partially our fear of this side of ourselves that contributes to our perception of the depressed experience as being ultimately negative. Frequently, the natural connection between sadness and depression is lost.

In struggling to free ourselves from 'psychiatric depression', we may be able to create life styles where being alone with our depression will not be so terrifying or lonely. Our desire must be for all women to live with the vigour and intensity we should have as our birthright.

> You must be strong but not hard, soft but not weak. You must be open when it is called for and closed when it is not. You must act on your intuitions. Let your feelings be your guide and your intellect protect you . . . your suffering is your experience. Use it, to help yourself understand. *Marie, May 1978*

14

2
The Experience

Janice: For me, to be depressed means a cold empty feeling, that I haven't been nice enough to be happy. Sometimes to feel depressed also made me feel guilty. It made me feel guilty because it made me think that if people saw me depressed, they might take pity on me, notice me, maybe even love me, and to me this was a confusing time, as I wasn't sure if I was genuinely depressed or just seeking attention. I felt something was wrong, but my mother said that crying and being depressed and unsure of things was all part of growing up. I tried to believe her but somehow I still didn't feel right.

As a teenager I found that I daydreamed a lot. I'd find somewhere as quiet as possible and shut my eyes and daydream. I dreamed mostly of being seriously ill in hospital. I can remember laying in bed at night, propping myself up as I'd imagine myself to be after an accident and suddenly in would come the man who loved me and he'd try and give me the will to live. My escape from depression would be dreams of someone (always a male) who loved me more than anything. Unfortunately the dreams didn't always help me as it depressed me more to realise that in reality this person just didn't exist.

As I got older the depressions got harder to cope with. I found it harder to daydream. So to cope, for me, was to go to work, do my job as best as possible, which I'm now told wasn't very good, keep myself as distant from my boyfriend as possible – by that I mean if in the same house to try and do things in a different room to him, and with my family I'd put on a brave face for the one day a week that I visited them. They never saw me in a very bad state of depression. I guess as I got older the more I tried to hide it from them.

The things that made me feel worse were people telling me to snap out of it, grow up, or think of those worse off than yourself.

15

When you're depressed none of this makes any sense, because when feeling down you don't think that anyone can possibly understand how you feel, and to you, you is all that counts.

Elizabeth: To start off with, say at school work, if you don't get the marks you want . . . you're a perfectionist and you want to get A's and you can't get A's 'cause you haven't got that in you – you want to get A's but you get C's, perhaps a B occasionally – sometimes you might even get a D which is really annoying and you get depressed and there are these other people saying 'Ohhh I got an A, I got an A, I got an A, I got an A' and you're thinking 'Get lost' . . . but you think 'If they got an A so should I' and that's a danger sign really. Really you should think 'I did my best'. It's like telling yourself off. You don't tell anyone else off, just yourself – and then you punish yourself – make yourself work harder to get A's – maybe you get slightly higher marks but you still don't get the A's – your social life gets smaller 'cause you're working so hard and then you realise you have no social life and you're still not getting A's . . . it gets worse 'cause you may have no one to talk to. I'm lucky I've got my mother but it can be important to have someone outside the family.

16

It's like you start thinking 'I can't seem to get on with boys. I can't seem to get on with my family. They're always saying how awful I am.' You start getting ratty 'cause you can't get what you want. By this time you're low. 'I'm not good at anything. Oh crumbs is this right?' How do you switch off a light – and that's stupid. That is getting very low.

The grammar school girls used to walk past and I'd look up and I'd think 'They passed the eleven-plus and I didn't. I'm a failure.' I used to think that every day.

If you continually fail, you fail more.

I know when I was depressed, I thought I'd never get rid of it . . . that it would never go away.

Shareen: Depression is helplessness. When I feel depressed I feel hollow and empty. When I am feeling down I don't want anyone to see me – how I really am. There is a different side of me that pretends to be friendly and warm but inside I am really in pain. I remember being really depressed when my dad died. There was a sense of loss. This depression took away my confidence and motivation. I am a fighter but when I am depressed there is no fight in me. I lose control and play the victim. Depression is different for me now. When I am feeling low, I can talk about this feeling with someone I trust and try to reflect on the positive things in my life.

Margaret: Depression is quite a horrific thing. It's very crippling emotionally and physically – desolate despair, loneliness. In my case, a great need to be understood, needing to be loved and needing to give my feelings to someone else. The inability to feel is very frightening.

The fear is that something has happened to yourself which you don't understand. You know it is a mental thing, which again is frightening. If it was measles, you could accept it. It's fear of not being able to cope, of feeling so remote, of feeling so strange, so withdrawn. And at the same time not having the ability to do anything about it. The feeling is completely one where I want to curl up and hibernate because there's nothing out there for me. The frightening things is that one has experienced this desolation that one didn't know could exist.

I think 'Why can't I make this thing go away on my own?' I don't even know myself anymore because I thought I could have

17

fought this, pushed it away – but is like an enormous blanket that completely covers you. Although you fight you don't always win. Some days you do, but some days you don't.

I have realised that for me the most frightening thing was the lack of feeling – the lack of warmth or enthusiasm – desperately trying to feel nice about something that I'd got. Not being able to enjoy even the simplest things, like a cup of tea or you own front room. Not finding comfort even in bed or sleep. It was completely raw and frightening.

Patricia: Depression overcomes your whole being. You seem to be enveloped by feeling low. It erodes your confidence and your motivation. You want to withdraw into a world of your own and opt out of the ordinary world. You can't cope with fairly straightfoward things. Certainly when you're very depressed you can't work. You tend to alienate yourself from people, even the closest to you and I found from my experience that I cut myself off. I hardly spoke to anyone and went around in a world of my own. It's only in retrospect, when you're out of it, that you realise that it's such a frightening state to be in. You feel very lost and at times rather hopeless because you don't know how you're going to get yourself out of it.

Penny: I feel as though I am at a fancy dress party wearing a sack. Nobody can guess who is inside it and I cannot explain who I am.

Elizabeth: Mild depression you need to face and be positive by going ahead and doing something about it like going out and meeting people ... As it gets worse you start to feel a failure all the time, you might get rid of it for a while, like when your friends are there, but you feel it again when they go away, then you feel it every few minutes. Gradually you begin to not sleep at night; you start crying for what seems to be no reason, you sort of feel why on earth was I meant to live? Why on earth was I meant to be here at all? Why God did you let it happen? Why do you let me live? ... it's ridiculous, if you believe in God that is ... Why am I here? I'm no use to anybody. I'm an absolute failure; I feel as if I'm going mad!

Theresa: Depression feels like I can't handle anything anymore. It feels like things are not in my control. At the moment my

18

depression seems to be linked to where I am in my menstural cycle. About two weeks before I start a period I begin a slow process of winding up. I feel like I am being stretched and I get tired and I just feel I can't cope. And that makes me feel like I'll never be able to cope. It will always be bad. I can't imagine things being different. I can't see a way out of it, even though I tell myself that my body is going through changes.

Caroline: The negativeness of depression is something which is absolutely common no matter what level it seems to be at. It's appallingly negative. It can turn absolutely everything into the negative state. I am capable of looking at a brilliantly sunny morning with the crocuses coming up at the end of the garden and turning it into 'How intolerable it all is, because it's not as it was'. I have no ability to use things which on other occasions you can look at and welcome and say 'What a beautiful day' and allow yourself to be lifted.

That doesn't convey what it really feels like. When you start using words it distances you from the actual experience of dragging yourself around. I don't mean physically. I mean the mental feeling of dragging yourself out of some kind of pit or pulling against something that's restraining you – you don't know what it is.

There are times when you can say that being depressed is feeling weighed down. People use words like clouds or blankets and so on. But it's like fighting your way through something – almost marshmallow, which is far too yielding an image – something thick and enveloping and cloying. Even with clouds and blankets, those have boundaries and you know where they end, whereas it's a sense of pushing your way through something which has no boundary, which you cannot conceive of as ending.

One of the most difficult things is when you're feeling really low and you talk to perhaps a wise old friend or someone else who has been depressed, and there is a tendency for them to say 'Well, hang on – you know it will pass.' And one of the worst feelings for me is that however much that is said, or even if you wrote it up on the wall and had it there as a motto, however much you might want to believe that, in fact you don't believe it. If only there was some way that you could convey to someone who is depressed that it will pass, that it will go – then it would be like finding a cure for cancer – because the most destructive element, it seems to me,

19

is that when you're feeling truly depressed you can't *conceive* of any other state. You can't conceive of what it would be like not to be depressed.

Margaret: The fear of other people's reactions. Indeed the experience of other people's reactions. I think that unfortunately many people are afraid of depression. Although I had been an accepted person for many years, the very fact that I was depressed seemed to make people shy away. The worst thing is when you desperately need to talk or to reach your friends and they push you away. They seem to feel you are in a predicament which you shouldn't necessarily be in. 'Why are you depressed? Pull yourself together.' They will perhaps listen for ten minutes and then want to get out of it. They don't want to be involved. They don't understand. They tend to think that it's something which one should be left to deal with. They don't want to help. It's not like flu and very alien to them. So let's leave it. So I feel pushed away.

If they do want to help, they usually suggest that you go somewhere with them – to the cinema or something, but somehow that's not what you want. You desperately want to talk but you're frightened of possible hurt. Going to the cinema doesn't do any good at all because you're not the same person who could enjoy the cinema. You come away having not taken the film in one little bit. And you would have been much better cuddling your pillow.

It makes me feel much worse to be dragged out into society when I can't cope. If I could cope, I wouldn't be away from it. They don't understand that I wouldn't be sitting here if I *could* be out there. It's not my choice. I feel I have been blamed for sitting around being self-indulgent, when they don't know how desperate and horrible and terrifying the whole experience is.

Caroline: My experience is that anyone in a social relationship, by which I mean colleagues and people who live in the area, are quite unable to see now that there may be times when I can't see any point in continuing to live; because of what feels like a sense of horror that however much the individual struggles, partly to express themselves, but also to genuinely communicate with other people, there is this recognition that an awful lot of people can't hear – and a great many people don't want to hear.

That they can't hear is to me very, very depressing. However hard I try, I feel there are people who cannot understand. That worries me and distresses me intensely. That I can want so much to communicate – and sometimes it's to communicate an immense sense of outrage about life, about evil, pain and things of that kind. There are people who have no way of understanding that and *that* I find terrifying. It makes me feel very isolated. It shouldn't because there *are* people who *can* hear.

Elizabeth: Depression comes on very gradually and when you've been through it once – you know what the signs are and you can say 'Whoops, you are getting depressed . . . now you go out and meet somebody or do something you like before you get depressed again'.

Marie, 29 October 1980: Feeling my journey inwards being interrupted by outside demands, or perhaps my inability to let go of reality or my outward self. Trust and feelings of security . . . almost overwhelming feelings of vulnerability. Last night in my dreams I coughed up this great ugly blob – throbbing with my anger, my hostilities, my fear. I did this only while held. This person held me in such a way that I could examine my fears. They did not force me to do so but contained me, gave me the security and support I needed to examine this revolting blob.

Betsy: Usually for me depression starts with some sort of desperation. In the past I used to panic – therefore I never felt it. Depression is helplessness and feeling stuck in myself. And the image I have is a deep hole. Despair and anguish – that's the feeling.

Depression is different for me now, because I allow myself to feel it; whereas before I didn't allow myself to feel it. So the feeling then was 'I can't cope'. Then I would panic and I wouldn't allow myself to feel loss. There was a cut-off on the feeling level. Now when I go into it I can actually talk about it; talking about it in a different way: not looking for sympathy, but for support and sharing.

I was very depressed today. So I left early from work. I drove and I wanted some quiet, so I went to the park and I knew that I was going to go over what I was feeling. I waited there for a bit and I said to myself 'OK you can feel those things and later you are going to talk about it, because she's your friend'. I knew I could share those feelings without thinking I was a burden. I trust my friends enough now to tell me if it's too much.

Depression comes on in two ways. Either when I get really angry about something and don't allow myself to feel that – then it goes inwards and it becomes self-destructive. The other way is when it's about a sense of loss. Lots of times I'm aware of feeling a sense of loss about a change going on inside me, connected with an image of myself of which I have to let go. I'm changing and moving forward but I'm looking back and seeing this image of myself that no longer fits. It's just not right. I'm changing and moving forward to something else and feeling more open to life. That's what's happened to me recently. I have felt depressed but I haven't felt that desperation.

I think depression is normal and a part of life. It can be positive if you use all your resources and take responsibility for the feeling. The only way to get out of depression is to allow yourself to feel it. For instance, a year ago I was in excruciating agony and pain – psychic pain. When I fought I got totally immobilised. When I allowed myself to feel it I got energy. Right now I can still feel pain and anguish but I have energy. A year ago I would have felt I couldn't cope. Now I can use depression more positively and be angry and direct my energy. I still feel a sense of loss that there isn't that special person in my life but I can cope with it.

Elizabeth: You go through hell but you do come out of it. Gradually the signs wear off . . . you gradually come out with a sympathetic person guiding you perhaps.

Marie, July 1978: In my dream, I am colouring in a landscape sketch. It is a valley with rolling hills. There is one large tree in the foreground. The whole sketch is in black ink on white paper. I am not satisfied with this picture. It is barren, sterile. I search for colour pencils. I find a green felt tip and start to fill in leaves on the branches of the tree. The leaves are very tiny new ones and the green is a new green, very pale and shiny. The tree is unfolding.

Margaret: Fortunately I am coming to terms with my feelings. I'm beginning to treat myself in a different way. I now accept that I'm fragile at the moment and I try to be nice to myself. Although the feelings of desperation are still there, I'm a bit less frightened. The frightening thing is that you don't want to accept depression but in the end you have to. As soon as you accept it you probably start to come through.

It's important to talk to someone who doesn't mind if you burst into tears and say how awful you feel. It helps to know that someone else knows how you feel. I think it helped that I wanted to hang on. I'm not sure if I hoped for a better future or not but I've often had the feeling that I'm going to hang on regardless. When I was at my most foul, I always wanted to live – goodness knows why – I could be sitting in a heap in a dressing gown at lunchtime, not wanting to get dressed.

The real me is lost but it's got to be found. I don't think it will be an un-injured me, because it's an experience that I've gone through, but it's going to be a different me. As long as I can face and cope with my feelings.

PART ONE

So often I come into contact with sisters of all ages who are ready to give up on themselves because they believe they are not worthy of love and their lives are worthless. *Jackie*

Why do more women than men get depressed?[1] Is it because women are fundamentally weak? Doctors and 'professional carers' have tended to see it that way: either it is the weakness of individual women that is to blame or it is some weakness of women as a sex.

This approach to women's depression makes us angry because we know that women are not weak. We see women all the time who have survived through the most appallingly difficult circumstances, with their courage, compassion and humour intact. Most women are survivors rather than victims. It is amazing that, often in spite of depression, women are able to continue working both inside and outside the home.

During the last decade there has been an increasing awareness within the helping professions and certainly within some voluntary ogranisations, such as MIND, of the social pressures and roles which may contribute to women's 'vulnerability'.[2] There have also been some research studies showing that when women and men are in very similar social situations and occupations, there is no gender difference in risk of depression.[3]

However, it is still controversial within psychiatry as to whether the fact that more women than men get depressed can be ascribed to some inherent biological difference.[4] Somehow theories about women's moods being controlled by their hormones are very appealing, perhaps because they allow people to ignore differences in social roles and issues about inequality.[5]

We do not believe that there is any one theory that is sufficient on its own to explain why women get depressed. Such a theory could not do justice to the variety of our experience. But in Chapters 3, 4 and 5 we explore some of the influences which seem to make us vulnerable to depression. We make connections between depression and oppression: between our internal, sometimes unconscious, feelings and the very real external factors in the world which can inhibit us from being fully ourselves.

In Chapters 6 and 7 we discuss some of the events and phases in our lives when we are most likely to get depressed. In Chapter 8 we describe how women stay depressed. We have tried to explain the institutions and processes which can work to keep women depressed to the point where it becomes a permanent lifestyle.

The ways women develop and the opportunities that are available to them are changing gradually in our society, even though the changes may seem frustratingly slow and erratic. When we generalise about the reasons why we get depressed, some women will feel that what we are saying is outdated while others will feel that their struggles are not described adequately. However, all of us are under the influence of a culture which still degrades, exploits and abuses women. It is worth reminding ourselves of how persistent some of the forces are which lead us to feel undervalued and unconfident.

3
Early Relationships

From childhood I have had a feeling that I belonged nowhere and belonged to nobody – a childhood of wanting to be loved and continually being rejected. It is hard to think of a child suffering from depression or to use my own word, despair. It is hard to think of a child who wishes they were dead; to try to find a place where they can cry alone because nobody was there to understand them or even care why they were crying. Even after all these years I can still not explain the feelings of loneliness I was brought up with. *Chris*

I seem to associate depression with an image of my mother as non-active, as not able to control her own destiny; and also with the loss of my father, when he left the family, which made me feel I had to try to win him back. *Sally*

Why is that our experiences of growing up as girls often leave us with such a fragile sense of our own worth? We are all profoundly influenced by our early relationships with mothers, fathers, sisters, brothers or whoever were the important people in our lives as children. Our view of ourselves and of the world outside is determined at first by our place in the small world at home; although it may be modified or even radically altered by later experiences.

Not all of us grow up in the conventional family of mother, father and two or three children. Yet we are all influenced by this institution. Without any prior experience of it we can desire it for ourselves. Children may long for the happy family they do not have. Adult women often try to create the family in which they would like to have grown up, through caring for their own children.

We all have a basic need for closeness and intimacy which is most often met by 'the family'. Many girls find and develop strong relationships with other adults outside the family. The importance of these significant others is often unnoticed. In discussing early relationships we have referred to mothers and fathers. However, it is probable that some of the issues raised were experienced in other relationships that were important to you, such as with an older sister, a close friend, a school teacher, grandparents.

We carry around with us inside our heads and hearts many of the feelings we had in childhood. Some of our experiences as adults can seem to reactivate these old feelings. Feelings from childhood can affect the way we experience life later on, without us fully realising it.

A psychoanalytic model assumes that unconscious fantasies connected with childhood experiences influence our adult relationships. In trying to explain women's depression we feel that this model can be used to give us some of the clues but not the whole story. We have also to take into account the very immediate circumstances of women's lives which affect us on an all too conscious level.[1]

Girls are Second Best

'Mine is a girl but I don't mind *really* because you can dress 'em pretty.' Vivienne Welburn quotes this as said to her by a young mother in a maternity ward.[2] It is very often assumed that most parents would prefer a son to a daughter, if they had the choice. To the extent that this is true, many women must grow up feeling fundamentally inferior because they are female. A woman may feel that she was always second best and that she cannot be fully loved for what she is.

> In some ways I think I was competing with my older brother for my parents' attention. I felt he was favoured by my parents. He was seen as highly significant. That certainly fed into me.
>
> *Caroline*

This feeling can be confirmed in many ways. For example, there may be a lack of encouragement for a girl's education in comparison to a boy's.[3] This implies that she is not destined to be so important as an individual in the outside world.

30

My parents always seemed to take more notice of what my brother did. Even now they seem to think that what he is doing is more interesting that anything I could do. *Janey*

My mother had a son who died before I was born. She made me feel that she had lost the one she really loved. I have always felt unloved because I knew that, whatever I did for her, I just couldn't be the son she really wanted. *Maureen*

In many cultures the value placed on boys has to be understood within the context of a life where economic survival may be very difficult. For example, Amrit Wilson describes the situation in rural India:

In this life of stress there was only one source of hope – having sons . . . The social structure in the villages was based on patriarchal families, where the daughter is invariably given away in marriage and where, because a woman's chief economic role is a producer of labour power (her sons), she is not considered of any economic value before she is married.[4]

It is strange that the preference for sons, which may have originally been rooted in economic necessity, still prevails when the original reason for this *preference* is no longer valid. Because of the need for population control, China introduced a one-child per family policy. As a result the preference for boys became very stark and the anti-female ethos was heightened. There have been significant social repercussions, such as more baby girls being put up for adoption; an increased divorce rate, since men often divorce women when they produce girls; and even many deaths of baby girls.[5]

In Western society, where we are not under such extreme pressures, it is difficult to know how much the preference for sons may be changing. In a recent research survey of pregnant women, the majority said that they did not mind what sex their baby would be, and amongst the rest, there was very little difference in the preference for girls or boys.[6] However, even though there may be less of a tendency to consciously favour boys over girls, it is still true that many women feel that somehow their brothers are of more importance to their parents than they are.

Women who are mothers also sometimes talk about how

differently they feel about sons and daughters. Rachel Billington, author of a book about the mother-daughter relationship, has described how she sees her son as miraculous and special whereas the bond between herself and her daughters is valued but taken for granted. 'A son is perfect for his mother, whatever he does, and a daughter is expected to work at it.'[7] If women feel that their self-esteem has to come through their achievements or through what they do for others, rather than being an inherent part of who they are, then they become exceptionally vulnerable, when faced with failure or the loss of important relationships.

Feeling Deprived

> I couldn't understand why the babies were cuddled and not me. I felt jealous and deprived and wondered what was wrong with me. *Kate*

Women can get depressed because they are deprived of much that they need. Sometimes our feelings of deprivation become more intense because old feelings are stirred up which have their roots in childhood.

The concept of 'maternal deprivation' which was popularised in the 1950s made women feel that they should be looking after their children all the time and that any separation was likely to cause irreparable damage. 'Maternal deprivation' as a concept only confirms the sterotype that women care for children and are ultimately responsible for their wellbeing. Many theories about early relationships can be construed as 'blaming' and are often used in this way to make mothers responsible for any bad qualities or problems their children may display. Our discussion of women caring for female children is set within the context of motherhood in our society. We do not subscribe to mother-blaming theories, although we do recognise the importance of these women, our mothers, in our lives.

The popularising of 'maternal deprivation' seems to have coincided with the desire to exclude women from the labour market after the Second World War by returning them to the home. A similar process seemed to be happening in the 1980s when unemployment for men was once again very high. Since the early 1990s, however, the number of women in the labour force has continued to increase rapidly and it is forecast that the number of women with jobs will soon be greater than the number of men with jobs.[8] Many of these jobs are part-time and women are still expected to take the main responsibility for parenting and caring within the family. The blaming of working women and single mothers for society's problems continues, as does the lack of suitable childcare provision.[9]

The ongoing popularity of the 'maternal deprivation' theory in no way reflects its scientific credibility. The evidence for the 'maternal deprivation' theory was based on John Bowlby's work with children reared in orphanages: a rather extreme example of deprivation. Much of this evidence has now been reassessed.[10] It must be recognised that, while children need attachments, these special relationships can be with more than one adult and not necessarily with their mother or a woman at all.

It is important that we re-think the language of child rearing and development. 'Maternal deprivation' really describes nurturance deprivation. The nurture and care of children is not the sole responsibility of mothers. Nurturing is something that women are skilled at. This quality is seen as maternal or as 'mothering'. If men show these qualities they are seen as 'good mothers'. This must make us question what qualities are paternal. What is paternal deprivation? Why has *it* not been researched or documented?[11] If we are going to maintain that *caring for* is mothering then anyone who cares is a mother. This brief discussion highlights the difficulties our language often imposes on us. We have tried to use the words 'nurturing', 'caring' and 'parenting' were possible in place of 'mothering' to indicate the assumptions we as feminists make about childcare issues.

Many women feel that as girls they were not given enough physical affection or holding. There are significant class and racial differences as to the amount of physical contact that is expressed in families. But many research studies have also shown definite differences in the way parents treat their children according to sex.[12] In one of these studies the same baby was given to adults to hold, either dressed in pink and described as a girl or dressed in blue and described as being a boy. The adults handled the baby very differently, according to whether they thought it was a girl or a boy.

There may be some reasons why, at least in white middle-class culture, women are less likely to cuddle their daughters. They may be afraid of the strength of the feelings aroused by physical contact with children. While such feelings are more acceptable in relation to a male child, the feelings women have towards girls may be considered to be lesbian ones and therefore taboo.

Women may find it difficult to respond to the needs of their daughters because to do so reminds them painfully of their own unmet emotional needs. If you are feeling needy yourself, it can be very difficult to put your arms round someone else. Girls can learn quite young not to ask for too much attention or affection from another woman. bell hooks has described how black women often grow up learning to repress the desire to touch and the need to be touched

> . . . the idea that black children must learn to be 'tough' serves as the logic for denying them forms of physical bonding that communicate that their flesh is lovable, that it deserves tenderness and care.[13]

Men also may be afraid of the feelings they have towards children. Whereas with boys their loving feelings can be channelled into a 'rough and tumble' type of play, with girls they may feel a need to hold back. Men tend to feel uncomfortable about expressing tender or affectionate feelings directly. As a result girls may feel deprived both of the affection they would like to have from adults and also of encouragement to be physically active and adventurous.

> Even though I came from the sort of family where feelings are important and both my parents were very volatile, feeling people, we never had the space as children to feel vulnerable. It was too dangerous as a child to show vulnerability. Although I was a gregarious child, I was also withdrawn. *Betsy*

Our need for physical affection does not go away and often makes us too vulnerable when we do receive praise and cuddles.

Our neediness can be exploited and misinterpreted by men, increasing the risk of sexual abuse. Phyllis Chesler describes this process in *Women and Madness*.[14]

> The way in which female children grow up – or learn not to grow up – is initiated by the early withdrawal or relative

absence of the female and/or nurturant body from their lives. Nurturance-deprivation and the sexual abuse of female children are possibly the two most important factors involved in making female children receptive to 'submission conditioning'.

The result of this 'submission conditioning' is that many women grow up feeling they have to be what someone else wants them to be if they are to get the affection and appreciation they need. It is difficult to find a sense of your own worth and identity if you believe that to win the love of others you have to hide your real needs. You can even become so used to doing what others want that you no longer know what you want for yourself. You may feel that you need others to make decisions for you.

This type of dependency makes women vulnerable to depression in later life. We tend to form relationships, often with men, in which we believe we cannot manage without the other person. The paradox is that in a dependent relationship, you feel as though you need the other person so much precisely because you are *not* getting what you need. Feeling deprived makes you feel all the more helpless and tied down.

I am hurt over and over again by his lack of response when I need to talk about something. And yet I can't decide to leave because we've been together so long and I have no other life. I feel I'd be nothing without him. *Penny*

Trying to Separate

I was the youngest in the family with three older brothers. My mother wanted me to be her perfect little girl. She enjoyed dressing me in frilly dresses. I wanted to wear trousers and play games with the boys. You couldn't have fun in a dress. As I grew up she wanted me to do something feminine – be a beautician or hairdresser. I feel I have deeply disappointed her by wanting to be different. I feel guilty and I keep trying to make it up to her. *Mary*

How do we manage to grow into separate people, with our own likes and dislikes, our own opinions, dreams and desires? There are often special difficulties for girls in trying to become separate and different from their mothers. A fundamental difference between the sexes in conventional family life is that girls are reared mainly by a parent of the same sex, while for boys the parent is of the opposite sex. Nancy Chodorow[15] suggests that a mother will push her son into being a separate person. Because he is biologically different, she expects him to be different from herself in personality. A mother sees her daughter as being almost part of herself. Because a daughter is expected to be the same as her mother, she will find it harder to separate, harder to rebel and harder to think of herself as being a different person from her mother with possibly very different feelings and needs.

Many women leave their mothers by forming a new relationship with a lover. If a woman has not already established herself as a separate person, she may find that her sense of herself becomes tied up with her partner's personality in the same way that she previously felt herself to be part of her mother's.

For some women getting married can seem to be the only way to separate from their mothers.

I married very young for the wrong reasons. I wanted so much to belong to somebody who cared for me. The trouble was we were both very young. What I was searching for I might have found in someone more mature. *Chris*

A sexual relationship can be a shortcut to finding an identity. But is it really your own? It may work out all right while life runs smoothly. But when difficulties happen you can feel completely lost.

After I had two miscarriages I was extremely depressed. I realised I had never worked out for myself what I wanted to be or do. I had accepted what my parents thought was best for me and after I married I accepted that my husband knew best. Now I feel I don't know who I really am. I don't feel anybody sees the real me. *Penny*

Nancy Chodorow also argues that girls, through relating so closely to their mothers, come to experience themselves as continuous with others. The boundaries of their sense of self are more flexible. Boys come to define themselves as separate and distinct, wtih a greater sense of rigid boundaries. The result is that in many heterosexual relationships it is the woman who expresses the need for openness and communication, while the man creates emotional distance.

If you are in a heterosexual relationship, it may seem that you are always the demanding one. Your attempts to express feelings may even be labelled as neurotic. If you are not feeling strong it is easy to believe this and judge yourself harshly.

He never seems to want to talk about his anxieties. Am I wrong to want to share mine? *Maureen*

For women in lesbian relationships it may be easier to share inner thoughts and feelings; to feel close and connected. It can be a relief to find that the value you place on keeping the relationship alive is equally shared by your partner. The difficulties in lesbian relationships more often occur in establishing separateness. When closeness is so rewarding, it can feel more threatening to allow yourself to have separate friends, separate activities and some thoughts and feelings which you do not wish to share. But the need to feel separate within a relationship is as important as the need to feel close.[16]

I feel – the woman alone. I do not feel 'a' woman because I feel so many others like myself. I have arrived finally from girlhood to womanhood. The feeling is still new, unusual, frightening. The feeling of aloneness is not new. But perhaps my desire to hold it a little longer is. No flight into partners this time. No need to use someone else to do my talking. *Marie, April 1980*

There are however cultural differences about how much importance is given to having a separate individual identity. This can be confusing when conventional Western ways of viewing identity clash with the culture you have been brought up in.

For most of my life within my family, I grew up with a sense of self which was very different from how my friends who are not black and not Indian defined their sense of self. In my family being Indian and Hindu, one of the key things is that a woman has no sense of self. When she is born she belongs to her father and when she marries she belongs to her husband, and when she is older, she belongs to her oldest son, if she has a son. Your sense of self is always defined as part of a family, as part of a system.

The thing I found most disempowering throughout all of my training is that for the first time in my life, I was discovering that I had a voice . . . But when I started to use it, the comments I would get from my supervisors were always about how I needed to be more assertive and to be clear about what I wanted. There was no recognition of the fact that for twenty years my sense of self had been defined differently from their sense of self. *Gita*

The 'Mother' We Can Never Have

'Little boys fall in love with Mummy and little girls fall in love with Daddy.' This is a stereotyped version of what happens, and only tells part of the truth. It is less often recognised that for girls as well as boys their first love is their mother. Many little girls say 'I want to marry Mummy.' Whereas boys can imagine themselves being loved by someone like Mummy as an adult, girls have to somehow transfer this fantasy to their father and to men in general, if they are to become heterosexual. This is something women are encouraged or even pressurised to do, before they have had a chance to make their own choice.[17]

We all start off by experiencing a complete unity with our mother in the womb and to some extent in the first few months of life. Gradually we have to face the loss of this unity, which is also the loss of the fantasy perfect Mother who will always be there when we need her; an image that no real person can live up to. The awareness of this loss can occur at any stage, such as when a younger brother or sister is born, or when we first realise that our parents cannot always understand us or respond to our needs.

This loss may be the same for girls and boys, but the ways women cope with the loss are different. Boys can protect themselves from its full impact by their fantasy of rediscovering unity with mother through heterosexual love. Many men will find women to 'mother' them throughout their lives. As adult women we have had to give up expecting to be 'mothered'.

Part of the experience of depression is often a desire to be looked after. We want to be cared for at times of crisis or loss and if such support is not available, this can rekindle painful feelings from childhood. Believing we cannot have what we feel we need, we collapse into feelings of helplessness. If you have actually lost your mother through death or separation, then these feelings may be all the more intense.[18]

Many adult women, even if they are actively heterosexual, feel that their more basic emotional needs are satisfied by other women (mothers, sisters, friends). One of our greatest fears can be of losing female friends. It can also be very painful to see that men have their needs met by women more easily than we do. Heterosexual relationships often become so exclusive that we are unable to see much of our women friends. It may be difficult to keep your relationships with women friends as you take on an identity as one of a couple.

Sometimes we look to men to respond to our emotional needs. Often we are disappointed, because as men grow up they are taught to suppress their sensitivity rather than to develop it. Women who are single and working often long for the 'someone to come home to' which women have traditionally provided for men.

All of these experiences can contribute to a sense that our needs are too much for anyone, confirming a belief that the 'real me' is unlovable.

Although I had a happy childhood, I have often felt a loneliness which at times seems overwhelming. It's not so much to do with being alone, although at those times it seems more frightening. It's more to do with feeling unloved or abandoned. *Kate*

Mother's Power

Dorothy Dinnerstein has also discussed the effects of women's role in early childcare.[19] She explains that both girls and boys grow up fearing the power of women and with a desire to put women down. Young children have mixed feelings towards the parent who first looks after them. This parent (usually a woman) has at that stage the power to give or withhold the food and the love they need to survive. The parent can cause important humiliations and defeats in the young child's battle for autonomy. She has the power both to encourage exploration and to limit it. Because this parent is usually a woman both boys and girls direct their primitive feelings of fear, rage and envy towards their mother and thereby towards women in general.

The father is allowed to be seen as the 'good parent'. The little time he does have for the children after working is often structured by his wife in such a way that he may appear to have more time to play and be less likely to reprimand the child. He does not have to deal with the everyday tasks of getting washed, dressed, going to the toilet and feeding which inevitably involve frustration for both parent and child. Children can split their good and bad feelings. They can transfer to 'father – who starts out with a clean slate, so to speak, innocent of association with the inevitable griefs of infancy – much of the weight of these positive feelings, while leaving the negative ones mainly attached to their [mother].'[20]

Adrienne Rich[21] has suggested that the inability of men to forgive their mothers for their power may be one explanation for the way men continually treat women as inferior in our society. The implication for us as women is devastating in another way. Not only we do we direct these feelings towards our mothers but also towards ourselves since we are women like our mothers. By doing, so we undermine our own strength.

What Dorothy Dinnerstein seems to be saying is that because of the primitive fear of our mother's power we find it hard to trust the authority of our own feelings. We are more afraid than men of allowing ourselves to be powerful. We grow up doubting our ability to make good use of our strength, except within the role of mother (and even there it is very hard to believe we are good enough). We deny power in the outside world to ourselves and to other women. Men actively encourage this state of affairs, describing women as 'the weaker sex' and the division of sex roles as being biologically determined. This gives an explanation for some of the ways in which we feel unable to use our strength to achieve what we want. Fear of our own power is reinforced by all the external difficulties in finding recognition and rewards.

It is also quite devastating to discover the lack of real power in the world that our mothers have. Although 'Mummy' seems to be so powerful when we are little, at some stage we discover that she is not. We discover that she cannot protect us from abuse or bullying. We become sensitive to her feelings and needs. Many of

40

us, particularly if we are the eldest daughter, start to feel some responsibility for helping and protecting our mothers at quite a young age. Through sensing our mother's feelings we learn quite early the difficulties for women in getting what they need. This can result in an acceptance of the subordinate role of women; by learning not to expect too much for yourself you will not be disappointed. Or it can lead to rejection of mother; a desire not to be like her which becomes a rejection of part of oneself. Blame seems to get passed around. We want to blame our mothers for not being as powerful as we would like them to be. At the same time we blame ourselves, believing that there must be something wrong with us. The result is great inner conflict about ourselves as women.

Father's Power

Our fathers can affect our feelings about ourselves in very powerful ways. The power is present even if the man or father is absent. A father's approval can seem so much more valuable than a mother's, because he is the one with status in the world outside. A father's authority is given an extra weight in family life by the fact that it is men who are seen to have positions of power in most areas of life.

A mother will say, 'When your Dad says "no" he means it', or 'Wait till your father comes home and ask him', ascribing to him an authority which he may or may not be able to fulfil. Frequently a mother will get more respect from her children if she is seen by them to be respected by her male partner. The implication is that women alone do not command respect.

To a girl, her father's life can seem so much more exciting than her mother's. Consciously or unconciously she may wish to be like him and not like her mother.

He seemed to represent the more positive things. He would talk about life and the broader vision and principles – all gut-stirring stuff – while my mother would winge on about the bills. His life seemed exciting and my mother's seemed depressing. Mind you, I can see now that his life was depressing too, but he was very good at fantasising and not very aware of reality.
Sally

41

There are two main routes, by which women try to win approval from their fathers and subsequently other men. The first way is by appealing to their ideas of how women should look. We can concentrate on making ourselves attractive to men, for example by conforming to an image of 'Daddy's girl' which is titillating but non-threatening to him. The danger is that a woman's sense of identity and worth can become so bound up with being found attractive by men that is hard to take other aspects of herself seriously. A woman is often made to feel that she is nothing if she is not sexually involved with a man.

The other way of trying to win approval is by denying our sexuality and trying to become as like Daddy as possible; to be 'one of the boys'. One way is to gain his interest through being intellectual. Jane Lazarre has written vividly about the contradictions in the relationship with her father.

> My sister, who resembled his fair-haired and blue-eyed family, possessed that envied paternal adoration – she was her father's little girl. But I slowly discovered that there was a way in which I could claim his attention – through my willingness to inherit his ideas and his theories, and through my ability, which I had surely inherited from him, to put thoughts into words.[22]

The problem is that, while gaining approval for your intellect, it can become harder to express yourself as an emotional and sexual being. It can be a girl's active sexual desires which make her father appear uneasy or disapproving. It can also be her emotional spontaneity.

> I used to laugh a lot. I was also very talkative – a chatterbox and a giggly child. My father particularly had what I would now see as a fear but what I felt then as a distaste for a child who laughed a lot and might become hysterical. That was the feeling I was left with as a child; 'It's not good to laugh too much because you might get out of control.' I ended up with a feeling that I was disapproved of if I was spontaneous. *Caroline*

We may go to great lengths to try to please our fathers.

> There were things I was contemplating doing, like riding across South America on a motor-bike, which were for my father –

completely to win his approval. And trying to be a success – I used to send him copies of the first magazines I edited – he never used to read them. A lot of things in my life I did to try to win his approval, rather than for myself. *Sally*

Trying to be like 'father' can make it harder for a woman to show any feelings of weakness or need, since this would threaten her status as a woman who can be like a man. 'Because people expect women to burst into tears every few minutes or throw a wobbler in some way, you feel you can do it even less.' (*Sally*) This is just one example of the price we have to pay for acceptance within a male world.

Sometimes fathers can be more directly destructive.

My father is a miserable person. If I try to talk to him about my worries or look to him for support he is always undermining. He says things like, 'You'll always be the same – you'll never be happy – you're just like me.' *Pauline*

My father was very strict, a frightening person. We had to be on best behaviour when he was there, for fear that his rage would explode. *Sharon*

Men sometimes try to gain a sense of power or gratification through their children.

My father used to beat me when I was sixteen years old. I know it was because of his own frustrations, but the effect was to control my behaviour and to make me rebel all the more violently later. *Frances*

In the last few years the sexual abuse of children has begun to be openly talked about, and it is horrifying to discover how many women were sexually abused as children by fathers, step-fathers, uncles and other male 'friends' or relatives. As women begin to talk about these experiences it is clear that one of the effects is feeling utterly worthless.

I felt disgusted and humiliated. I knew it was wrong but was too terrified to tell anyone. I felt I must be like him – I too must be dirty and dangerous. *Rosemary*

43

This experience is a wound to self-respect which can feel unhealable. The connection with later depression is obvious but until recently was seldom recognised by professionals.[23]

For women who are lesbians the connections with their fathers and other men can be confusing. As a woman loving women, it can seem that you must be like your father. The construction of 'butch' and 'femme' roles heightens the confusion. Questions like 'Which one of you is the man?' make it very clear that love between women is conceptualised in heterosexual terms. Loving women sexually is 'a man's privilege'. To exercise it ourselves may pose the question, 'Am I really a man?' We may see it as a way of affirming our love for ourselves as women. It may be that we have no feelings for men or we may dislike them. But the 'normal' model of sexuality implies that to love a woman means identifying as a man.

Fathers may be more supportive of our choice to relate sexually to women. In some ways it confirms that no man is good enough for his little girl and that the closeness or intimacy in the father-daughter relationship will never be threatening or threatened.

It wasn't until after, that I realised why coming out to my father was so much easier than to my mother. For my mother it meant she had to confront her own lesbian feelings. For my father it meant I would always be Daddy's girl. *Marie*

Father's power has a double edge. On the one hand we may want to experience it vicariously by being connected to powerful men, or directly by succeeding in a man's world. On the other hand we will never have complete access to it. Any power we may acquire in traditionally male arenas in ours because men choose to let us have it. They are capable of taking it away at any time.

The power of paternity is legitimised and protected by law. For instance 'illegitimate' children are defined as such by a lack of a father, regardless of having a mother. Even if a 'father' has had no relationship with 'his' child, he can still apply for access to her/him. Why is fatherhood defined by the giving of sperm?

Whereas maternity is never in doubt, there is no such certainty when it comes to paternity. Perhaps because fatherhood can never be proved, men feel the need to control women.

Most of us have an image of the ideal happy family in our minds, even if our own experience as children was very different. At the same time, it would be difficult not to notice that the structure of families has been changing radically. One in five children are now living in single-parent families. One in three new marriages are predicted to end in divorce. Through remarriage there are also 4-parent or even 5- or 6-parent families. Some women choose to bring up children in situations where they share childcare with other women.

There has been much public debate about the 'state of the family'.[24] The government has even created the title 'Minister for the Family'. There is a desire for a return to traditional family values, and at the same time, much ambivalence about the fact that the traditional nuclear family is no longer the norm. Attempts are being made, sometimes in a misguided way, to make absent fathers take more responsibility for their children.

As sex roles within heterosexual relationships are becoming more flexible, men are gradually becoming more involved with childcare, although from the point of view of some women these changes may not be happening quickly enough.[25] With higher unemployment for men and higher employment for women, men are more often staying at home with their children out of necessity, if not out of choice.

Within the younger generation of women, some will have grown up able to say 'My mother is a feminist' and this must in some way affect their expectations about their own lives.[26] Non-sexist books for children are now produced, which challenge the traditional view of sex roles, the assumption that all children live with biological parents, and that everyone is heterosexual and white-skinned.

We do not yet know how these changes are affecting the experiences of girls.[27] But however much families or approaches to childcare may vary now, we still grow up absorbing certain ideas about the acceptable ways of being female in our society.

4
Images of Women

'I do not feel I'm a proper woman.' This is often said by women who are depressed. What do they mean by it? As we grow up we take in ideas about what women should be from television, books, our teachers and our parents, to name but a few sources. We may try to accept these images or to reject them but either way they influence our feelings about ourselves.

Our relationship with such images can be quite contradictory. Most women have conflicting feelings about, for example, the different images of female beauty. There are now various new stereotypes to contend with: the 'liberated woman', the 'divorcee', the 'dyke', the 'lesbian couple', the 'single parent'. At times we can accept these images, or try to create our own versions.[1] But sometimes the media produce stereotypes so distorted, that we can only reject them as having nothing to do with our own reality. In our discussion of images in this chapter we have ignored much of the complexities. We have chosen just some of the traditional stereotypes in order to bring out the connections between women's vulnerability to depression and the ways women are expected to feel or behave.

The Feminine

To be feminine in our culture is to be dependent, passive and submissive; to be silly and sweet and concerned with clothes and appearance; to be emotional, excitable and cry a lot. These are some of the stereotypes of femininity.

In a classic research study in 1970, Inga Broverman and her colleagues investigated the sort of stereotypes which psychotherapists have as to what it is to be a mature, socially-competent, healthy person in our culture.[2] The results of this study showed that the psychotherapists rated the healthy female as showing more *stereotypically* feminine traits than the healthy male. The healthy female was rated as being more concerned about appearance, more expressive of emotions, less independent, more passive, and so on.

The most interesting result came from asking the psychotherapists to describe the 'healthy, mature, socially-competent adult', no sex specified, who turned out to be described in ways that were identical to the 'healthy adult male'. In other words the masculine qualities seem to be generally seen as being healthy and the feminine qualities as much less so. This implies that to be typically feminine means being seen as potentially less mature and healthy as a person. But at the same time women who display the more 'masculine' traits, who are competitive, ambitious and adventurous, who are less interested in their own appearance, lay themselves open to the accusation that they are not 'feminine' or not 'real women'. This is a 'double-bind': a situation in which you are being given two conflicting messages at the same time. You cannot be a healthy adult and a healthy woman, according to these ideas of mental health. It is no wonder that women get confused by different stereotypes of how they should be, particularly as some seem to prescribe an inability to cope.

Naomi Selig[3] has described how such stereotypes enable a dominant group to keep a subordinate group in their place. Certain personality characteristics are assigned to subordinates which confirm the dominants' belief that they, the dominants, are 'better' in some way. When people in subordinate groups take in these values, they feel ill at ease with themselves, without knowing the reason why.

As long as women are told and continue to believe that the reason they are miserable is because they are 'neurotic', 'hysterical' etc., they will continue to feel individually maladjusted . . . An example of a similar phenomenon which took place recently was a conversation I had with a person I know. I explained that though not at all religious I still felt and identified myself as a Jew. This person told me I was mistaken because Jews are mean and she liked me. She then rationalised this by saying that maybe I was an exceptional Jew. The logical implication of what she was saying was that I was either identifying with a mean, unscrupulous group of people or I was not really a proper Jew. But I was not anything else either. If I were to believe her, the net result for me would be conflict, confusion and alienation.

Perhaps the most damaging aspect of the idea of femininity is the pressure to be nice all the time. As women we are not supposed to be angry. We believe that we can only be loved, if we are continually placating, pleasant and compliant. All the images of angry women are very derogatory ones. An angry woman is seen as a witch, a bitch, a shrew or a vixen, whereas an angry man is considered to be showing admirable strength. One theory of depression suggests that it results from the suppression of aggressive feelings. Instead of being angry with others we turn our anger on ourselves. This leads to an attack on our own sense of worth and so to depression.

If women do allow themselves to be angry they often suffer from feeling they are not as they should be.

I was very angry with my parents as a teenager. Although I could talk about it with my friends, I felt that I was very different from them – that they weren't having the same feelings. So that made me think 'Well, am I normal to feel like this?' and I went through a whole period of thinking: 'Am I mad? If other people don't experience this there must be something wrong with me.' I think that's why I felt depressed – because I did feel so different. *Theresa*

This illustrates the way in which images of femininity can be oppressive. If we conform to them, our ability to be ourselves is damaged. If we do not conform, we feel inadequate or peculiar.

To be feminine is to be passive. To be passive is not to take initiative, not to act for oneself. Girls grow up believing that a relationship with a man will be their main fulfilment in life. They wait to be chosen by men. Girls are not encouraged to be adventurous, or to see themselves as warriors and explorers. Instead they are encouraged to be cautious, clean and tidy and to wait for life to happen.

As women we often do not feel we are at the centre of our own experience, but rather that our experience of life is determined by our attachment to others. In our relationships we are taught to be submissive. We do not learn to assert our own needs. It is important to realise that submission is very different from consent, although the two may look similar. A woman who sticks with her husband in spite of his affairs with other women is probably submitting to this arrangement rather than consenting. To submit implies that we do not feel we have any real choice but go along with what others decide to do. When difficulties occur we are not used to taking action or standing up for ourselves and so we easily feel powerless and helpless: feelings which are a large part of the experience of depression.

> The strange thing on looking back is that I was a married woman. Why did my mind dwell so much on having something of my own to love? I should have known then that my marriage was lacking the things I needed and craved for. That marriage continued for a total of twenty-one years. At least sixteen years of it were spent feeling like a displaced person, with beatings when my husband was drunk and continually being thrown out of his house. *Chris*

In reality we often do have little power but the stereotype of femininity seems to imply that we *should* be powerless. An overtly powerful woman is not usually seen as being a feminine one. She is seen as being like a man. This can result in great conflict. We do not want to lose our sense of being female but we also want to be strong. Sometimes the two seem incompatible. This may be why traditionally women have been seen as devious and manipulative. Some women learn to get what they want by indirect means because to have the power to ask directly is impossible.

To be feminine is to be concerned with clothes and make-up. Concern with appearance can be a form of creative self-expression, a form of play and a means of pleasure. However, so often we feel pressurised by the images of female beauty which we are presented with. Fashions change so often, even to the extent of whether women should have large, or small breasts. Many women see themselves as continually failing to live up to idealised images of how they should look.

> I can remember doubting whether I was a woman sometimes because I didn't have big breasts, for example. I thought, 'Maybe there's some doubt about this?' *Theresa*

The whole image of the female body, what is acceptable and what one has to do in terms of presentation to be acceptable is something which I feel I have bought into completely and even now find very difficult to reject. It's a thing which leaves me feeling uneasy. I often wonder why I dress the way I do. I do have reasons for it. I like colour, texture and shape. I like to be aesthetically pleasing. But I find it difficult to tease out how far I'm still very deeply affected by needing to present myself as an 'attractive' woman, meaning 'attractive' in all the stereotyped senses to the male. *Caroline*

For those women who are more confident about looking good it can still be devastating to find that at certain times in their life they can no longer achieve the same image. Pregnant women can feel very self-conscious and unhappy about their changing shape. As our bodies change through growing older we may feel that we are losing something central to our identity as women. The idealisation of youth is something that particularly affects women. An older man with grey hair may be seen as attractive by virtue of his wisdom and experience. He may be seen as distinguished and dignified. When an older woman is considered glamorous it is usually by virtue of still looking young. The dyeing of grey hair, face lifts and so on are ways in which women desperately try to maintain the image of youthful femininity. Underneath this image may be feelings of despair, based on a lack of confidence about growing into a new view of oneself as a mature woman.

One of the crucial things for me was my image of myself and how I looked was an important part of that image. That affected me more because I'm female. Women are judged more by their looks than are men. I worry about what I want to look like, now that I'm in my forties. I'm afraid of looking ridiculous but I also don't want to look dull. There don't seem to be any attractive images of what a woman over forty should look like. *Margaret*

The images of beauty prescribed by men, the media and by advertising are based on the notion of rarity. As with jewels, the most valued qualities are the least common. At least until recently the most favoured Anglo-Saxon image was of blonde hair and blue eyes. With qualities like these it is easy to spot the non-conformers. Black women who have lived for years in western society have had to put up with images of beauty which are completely alien to them.[4] When their own looks are appreciated by white culture it is as 'exotic'; another example of the value given to the rare or unusual. Melba Wilson has discussed the effects of these stereotypes on black women.

> ... the myths surrounding black women's sexuality are qualitively different from those assigned to white women. White women, for example, are sexy, black women are animals. White women are pretty; black women are exotic. White women are promiscuous; black women are sluts.
> ... It is equally important to point out that a great many black women do not require validation from white norms in order to see the beauty of our bodies. Many of us love, admire and are proud of the way we look. The stereotype is, after all, the problem of those who utilise it; we know who we are. That is not to say that we are unaffected by it.[5]

The images of beauty which all women live with are specifically designed so that they are unattainable for the vast majority of us. We are expected to be hairless, spotless and fatless. Again the paradox is that to be a 'real' woman is to wear make-up, false eye-lashes and to dye one's hair blonde; in other words to conform to a 'false' image of oneself.

Women who are considered beautiful in a conventional sense can feel very insecure as to whether people like them. With men they may wonder 'Does he like me for me or just for my looks?' With other women they may be afraid of envy. An identity based on living up to a certain image can feel fragile and easily threatened. If we achieve the ideal we can still feel empty inside. If we do not achieve it we feel a failure. In rejecting the ideal we have to live with the sense that society sees us as peculiar. All of these feelings can contribute to depression.

While worrying about our appearance can lead to depression it is also true that when we are depressed we tend to worry more about whether we have hairy legs, whether our complexion is spotless, whether we are too fat, or whether our shoulders are too broad. This can lead to a vicious spiral of escalating feelings of self-hate.

When one of my teeth started to go, I felt I was falling apart. It was a natural everyday happening, but to me it had a different meaning. I went and hid for a couple of hours in the bathroom and thought, 'What am I going to tell people? – I may have to have a false tooth!' *Margaret*

To be feminine is to be silly. So often we preface our remarks with 'I know I'm being silly but . . .' We usually say this when we are about to talk about something which is really worrying us. We may have so often been told that we are silly or stupid that it is hard to take ourselves seriously. The fear that we will not be taken seriously can hold us back from talking about our feelings when we most need to do so. Not being able to talk about ourselves seriously makes us more vulnerable to depression.

To be feminine is to be emotional and to cry a lot. On the assumption that to have feelings is an important part of being alive, it is very strange that one half of the human race is supposed to have more feelings than the other half. This stereotype seems to mean that women are expected to show their feelings more than men. The types of feelings we are expected to show are vulnerable ones. We often cry when we want to get angry. We express our feelings in ways which seem weak rather than strong. But whether we cry or shout, we are still liable to be labelled by men as 'hysterical' or 'over-emotional' or 'attention-seeking'. Paradoxically, to be a 'real woman' we are supposed to express feelings, but when we do so we are still likely to be put down either directly or by being ignored.

At work I was scared that if I showed feelings, whether of tears or anger, I would be seen as the little inadequate woman who is not capable of doing anything – or alternatively as another negative version of woman – the virago – a sterile stereotype, sexless, neutered. I found it very difficult to tread between all those different stereotypes and come out with something which in the end I think is me and which is more or less accepted. *Sally*

Jean Baker Miller, in her analysis of women's psychology,[6] has suggested that women have become the 'carriers' for society of certain aspects of the total human experience. Feelings of weakness and dependency are a part of the experience of all

52

human beings. We all have need for emotional connections with others. But women are traditionally more aware of this aspect of life than men and can protect men from the parts of themselves which seem 'weak'. As women we automatically satisfy men's emotional needs, often without them having to ask or even realise that they have such needs. In this way the myth is maintained that men are strong and women are weak.

It is frequently observed in psychiatric clinics that when a woman is referred with problems such as agoraphobia or depression, her husband may appear to have problems of his own. The woman is the one who expresses her vulnerability and sometimes seems to be expressing her husband's as well, enabling him to feel tough and in control. This type of relationship can maintain a woman's depression for years.

The Maternal

The image of the maternal is one of giving out to others. This image affects all of us as women, whether or not we have children. We expect ourselves to be the givers, to family or friends or in our jobs. The ideal of the maternal is to be always giving, always patient, always self-sacrificing, always cheerful and comforting. These maternal qualities are supposed to be inherent in women much more than in men.

As girls we grow up learning that our main value in life comes from caring for men and children. We learn that to be a strong woman is to be a self-sacrificing one. While caring for other people is a quality we may want to nourish, what is damaging to us is the expectation that as women our only worth comes from caring for others and that we should do so at the expense of our own needs.

The idea of always putting someone else first is very central to my belief about the female; that it is the nurturing, appropriate thing to do; that the woman should be caring in a way which means putting someone else first to a point which is quite nonsensical. Even though I know intellectually that it's a pattern which has been handed down to me, I still *feel* 'You as a female should be able to do this'. And that causes very considerable problems. *Caroline*

53

A woman who does not feel any special maternal feelings or desire to have children may feel inadequate or worry about whether she is a 'real woman'. To have children seems to be considered the proof that we are 'real' women. Although many women now do choose not to have children, this is still considered to be a choice that is rather peculiar. We are expected to justify such a choice and are likely to be accused of being selfish.[7]

It is even worse if a woman has children and then leaves them. Some women do decide that this is the best thing to do, often in very painful circumstances. Although their reasons are not usually purely selfish ones, this is seen as a tremendously shameful act; far more so than when a man does the same thing.[8]

Many of us do succeed in being maternal, in the sense of devoting most of our energy to looking after others. We are then in danger of being left feeling empty when people no longer need us. We need people to need us or else we feel are are nothing. We also feel ashamed if we ourselves need something from others. We are terrified of showing how weak and vulnerable we can feel when people are so used to us being strong. Depression can result from giving out for years while never getting much back for ourselves.

I feel that it's my turn to be weak now – I've looked after everyone for so long. But they don't want to let me. They get angry with me for not being the mother I was. They want me to go on being strong when I feel I can't. *Penny*

To be maternal is to be always able to cope. Even if we experience a deep loss, such as the death of a parent, loss of a baby, or break-up of a marriage, or we are faced with great stress at work or home, we still believe that we should cope. This can lead to depression hitting us apparently out of the blue, when suddenly we collapse into terrible feelings of helplessness.

The image I had of myself was that I should be able to cope with everything; that I should take on other people's burdens and also be the life and soul of the party. My first feeling when I got divorced was: 'I have got to cope because I have got Matthew.' It wasn't 'I have got to cope for me!' That's the role of being relied on. And perhaps I tried to cope too much and put too much stress on myself. *Margaret*

54

Depression can be made worse by guilt at not having coped.

> I don't think I can ever forgive myself for letting the family down. I should have been able to cope. I always have done before. *Jackie*

To be maternal is to be sexless. We do not see mothers as being sexual. This is another way in which to be maternal implies not having needs of our own. The image of woman as maternal makes us vulnerable to depression because we are not supposed to have needs, including sexual ones and if it is recognised that we *do* have them, they are considered unimportant.

Women may have different needs at different times. We may need to do things to enjoy ourselves; we may need time alone, we may need affection and attention from other people, or we may need rest and comfort. If we are not encouraged to even ask the question 'What do I need?' then we are most likely to end up feeling empty, angry and depressed, without any understanding of why we feel that way.

> We were brought up with a very strong pattern that we were not to get too big for our boots and that we were not *really* to have a concern for ourselves, that we should always be self-effacing, and recognise that somebody else would be better than us. It wasn't just an occasional remark. It was very consistent, early training. And that has contributed to my attitude now which says 'I will recognise everybody else's worth *before* my own'; what then seems to happen is that you end up without ever being able to recognise your own worth because you're so busy acknowledging everybody else. To change this attitude is fiendishly difficult. The business of asserting myself and owning my needs is very threatening. I suspect that sometimes I get very deep moods of depression because I won't own what it is I really feel and need. *Caroline*

In recent years there has been a growing recognition among many women of the importance of trying to combine looking after others with allowing enough time and space for meeting their own needs as people. But this can lead to a very tricky juggling act, in which women often feel they cannot win. Unless a woman has sufficient support from those around her, the expectation to be a 'successful mother' and a 'successful person' or 'successful career woman' can become just another pressure and another stick to beat herself with when she feels she is failing.[9]

Sexual Object

To be a woman is to be a sexual object for men. This image of woman is presented to us as being the opposite of the maternal. These images are mutually exclusive. The split enters our minds too. We are often confused as to whether it is all right to be sexual. We are expected to be sexual in order to attract a man but, having attracted him, we are not then supposed to be too overtly sexual if we are to be seen as a 'nice girl' or a 'respectable woman'.

To be a sexual object is to be available for men's stimulation. This is something very different from enjoying your own sexual feelings. When a woman is seen by a man as a sexual object, her own feelings do not come into it at all. It is possible to enjoy being found attractive and to enjoy feeling attractive, but we can only enjoy these feelings if we are in a position where we have some control. The essence of the images of heterosexuality with which we are bombarded is that we have no control; that our bodies are something to be used by men for their gratification.

The association between women and machines is constantly being reinforced by advertisements in which the body of a woman is used to advertise a car, a camera, a new tool and so on. Increased economic power amongst some women has enabled pressure to be put on advertisers so that the cruder 'bikini-on-the-car-bonnet' approach to selling occurs less often. However the association between women and cars (both driven and driving) is still connected to images of women's bodies.

Women's bodies are also seen as being property that belongs to men. They can be 'bartered for as in marriage, stolen as in rape or bought as in prostitution'.[10] It is difficult for us to respect the sensuality of our bodies when we see them being used this way.

I can remember feeling really surprised that intercourse involved penetration by the man of the woman. I always thought 'of course the woman does something.' I never imagined that the man did something and the woman lay there

56

passively waiting, which is how it was presented. I remember that being a real surprise. *Theresa*

bell hooks has discussed how black women are affected by society's attitudes to their bodies:

When we consider the uses that this society has made of black women's bodies – as breeding machines, as receptables for pornographic desires, as 'hot pussies' to be bought and sold – surely our collective estrangement from a life-giving eroticism makes sense.[11]

The images in pornography show us extreme versions of the degradation of women as sexual objects. Susan Griffin's analysis of pornography[12] describes how women are completely humiliated and silenced in these images. Pornography shows women as helpless, submissive and wanting to be violated. It gives us a male version of what female sexuality is like.[13]

It is significant that so many women who are used as sex symbols become seriously depressed and even kill themselves. The most obvious example is Marilyn Monroe. Susan Griffin describes how she imagined Marilyn felt in her life.

Increasingly, as she felt empty, she must have decided that if only she could improve her impersonation of a sex symbol, she might finally find her real *self*. All her life, she had been led to believe that it was herself and not the pornographic ideal who was deficient. That she felt herself to be a fraud, that is to be in reality unlike the image she copied, only made her try harder and harder to perfect her impersonation. Finally she became the sex goddess of her age. Now she was the very image she had hoped so desperately to imitate. Yet, even *being* this image, she still *felt* empty. Inside this perfection was the same nothingness and the same numbness she feared.[14]

Although Marilyn Monroe's life is an extreme example, this numbness or nothingness is something many women can recognise as part of their worst experiences of depression. To feel nothing is worse than feeling bad. It is like death. The images of women as sexual objects contribute to this numbness. By treating our bodies as men seem to treat them, we deny the possibility of finding our own ways of feeling sexually alive.

> It seems to be possible to give him what he wants without feeling anything much myself. I do have some sexual feelings but they seem to disappear very quickly because I'm much more aware of his needs than my own. *Sandra*

The sexual liberation movement of the 1960s and 1970s has not altogether helped women. Although the increased availability of contraception has given us more choice in how we express our sexuality, the new images of the 'sexy liberated woman' have been just as oppressive as the old idea that 'good women' were not sexual. In the media, the stereotyped 'liberated woman' has often been portrayed as a woman who can enjoy sex casually 'like a man'; as a woman who can use men as sexual objects. This image has not been liberating at all. Women are now expected to have orgasms to order and start wondering what is wrong with them if they do not feel like making love all the time.

In the 1980s and 1990s the expectation of living up to this pseudo-sexy image has lessened. First of all women themselves have been increasingly questioning what they really want and trying to define for themselves in what sort of contexts they can fully enjoy their sexuality. At the same time, the fear of contracting the HIV virus through sexual contact has provided an added incentive to be more thoughtful about sexual behaviour. But it is still difficult for a woman, particularly if she is inexperienced, to feel she has the right to take some control in a sexual situation; for example, to ask a man to wear a condom if he is going to make love with her, or to ask for some discussion about what forms of sexual behaviour feel safe. In the early 1990s the controversy around 'date rape' and the recent acquittal of a young man on this charge, have increased confusion about women's right to say 'no' to sex.

It is still difficult for a woman to find out what it means to her to be a sexual person; to develop a relationship with her body by discovering her own inner sensations, rather than trying to live up to an external image of how her body should perform. Most women are struggling to find the best ways to enjoy their sexuality and to understand its rhythms.[15] The choice of another woman as lover is still not socially acceptable. It may also be important to

58

have periods of celibacy when sharing your sexuality is not a priority in your life. The choices we make about our sexuality can be very significant moves in our development towards a more self-determined life.

There will always be images of women and some of these will continue to be contradictory. We do not want new images which define what we *should* be. The effect would be just as depressing when we fail to live up to *them*. Women are trying to find a new relationship with images. Stereotypes are always unreal and constraining. But images can be used creatively to express different aspects of ourselves, in ways that may change throughout our lives. We need, for example, new ideas about what it is to be a 'woman on her own', an 'older woman' or a 'working mother'.

There does not have to be one right way for women to be. We need greater freedom of choice in discovering how we *want* to be. In the present era of transition such choices can involve great risks for many of us. This can lead inevitably to times of anxiety and self-doubt.

5
Recognition and Reward

We have looked at ways in which it is difficult for us as we grow up to develop a strong sense of feeling good about ourselves. We have looked at the images of women by which we judge ourselves. We now turn to the external reality of our lives as women. Many of the ways in which society is organised make it difficult for us to develop rewarding lifestyles. As women we often find ourselves in situations where we get little recognition, financial or otherwise for what we do.

A United Nations report on 'Women and the Economic Crisis' states: 'Women account for one half of the world's population, but they put in two-thirds of the world's working hours, receive one-tenth of the world's income, and own one-hundredth of the world's property.'[1]

Behavioural psychology explains depression as being due to a lack of enough rewards in our lives. In order to keep being active, we need reinforcement for what we do. This reinforcement may be in the form of material rewards such as money or more often social rewards. To be socially rewarded means to be recognised and appreciated by other people.

This model of depression is a limited one and we have already discussed it critically in Chapter 1. It ignores the more complex issues about what is experienced as rewarding and why. Many women have rejected or questioned the situations which were traditionally considered to be fitting rewards for being a 'good woman'. The status of marriage has been seen as the reward which all women are waiting for. The success of her children's lives is supposed to be adequate reward for a woman's sacrifice of her own ambitions. Women are often given 'rewards' or recognitions which they do not want when, for instance, men make sexual passes at them, or compliment them on their looks while ignoring their work.

However, this approach to depression does draw attention to the fact that you are likely to get depressed if you feel that what you do goes unrewarded or unrecognised. By looking at women's lives and work we can see how difficult it it for us to get the rewards we need. So much of the work women do inside and outside the home is both unpaid and unacknowledged.

Housework

Housework has perhaps the lowest status of any work. It is not even considered to be 'real work'. It is taken for granted that it has to be done and that women will do it.

In Ann Oakley's study of the sociology of housework[2] she interviewed a sample of 'housewives'. The majority of the women she talked to were dissatisfied with housework. The best aspects of it were their autonomy and lack of supervision. The worst aspects were pressure of time, fragmentation, monotony and social isolation. All the women said they would value a paid job more than housework, since a paid job would give them more money, social contact and social recognition.

Hazel Seidal did a research study[3] exploring the connection between housework and depression. She analysed the ways in which housework is intrinsically unrewarding. First of all the work is unstructured and invisible. If it is done regularly then the results of each individual piece of work are not obvious. When doing housework you have to monitor yourself according to your own standards. It is difficult to know when you have done enough. It is a never-ending job. What you have done is always being undone.

Usually nobody else notices housework and so if you are to be rewarded the reward has to come from yourself. But this is difficult. Working according to a routine seems to be the best way to know that you have done enough and to be able to feel satisfied by what has been achieved. But a routine can be very boring. In addition the work is unrewarding because it is done in isolation without the rewards of social contact that we gain by working with other people.

The attitudes of men and children constantly confirm the assumption that women should have the main responsibility for work in the house. To some extent these attitudes seem to have changed in recent years, in that both men and women will usually say, when asked, that responsibility for household chores should be shared. In practice, however, families in which men and women equally share housework, cooking, washing and ironing are still the minority rather than the norm. This is true even of families in which the woman is working full-time or part-time outside the home.[4] In Spain, people have become so concerned about this situation that the government has launched an advertising campaign to try to persuade men to do their share of housework.

There are particular ways, sometimes subtle ones, in which this assumption about women's responsibility manifests in families. For example, it is expected that 'Mummy knows where everything is' and that 'Mummy will get things done' or 'knows best how to get things done'. Women are seldom left alone by their children, even when sitting on the toilet!

If housework is your main job it is difficult to admit that it is getting you down. It does not seem to be a dramatic enough reason for being depressed.

At one time I hated going out and was glad to shut myself indoors. I got depressed too, and the thought of washing up got me down so that I was crying into the sink. Little things do get you down when you're trapped in the house all day and now that I've got out and mixed with people more, I've found that other women actually felt the same as me. Of course, I really wanted help at the time, but it's difficult to approach people and say you do silly things like that, as you know it sounds ridiculous – you can't tell someone you're depressed without telling them what you're depressed about. Also, I was never keen on housework and always felt that somehow I wasn't up to standard.[5]

Childcare

The work of childcare usually falls on the same person (a woman!) who does the housework and is similarly taken for granted. This is often justified by the fact that women bear and breast-feed children. It does not follow that all childcare arrangements should have to be solely the mother's responsibility. But we are led to believe that motherhood, that is taking care of children at home, is our 'natural' role in life.

This responsibility is legitimised by various economic structures. Women can get 'maternity leave' from work but until recently there was no male equivalent in most countries. Although 'paternity leave' does now exist within some jobs, it is usually for a very short period of time and, in the UK is not a statutory right. In fact, most other countries in the European Community have developed further than Britain in the rights they give to both parents for time off work to look after children.

The huge increase in the availability of part-time work in recent years should have allowed women and men more flexibility in sharing childcare. But in reality, most of the part-time work is low-paid, is often less pro-rata than the equivalent full-time work, and usually doesn't give the same rights to sickness and maternity benefit, unemployment benefit or a full state pension. These jobs are most often in the service industries which traditionally employ more women, whereas in traditional male sectors of employment, such as heavy manufacturing, shift work with paid overtime is still more common. Women fit in their casual part-time jobs around their child-care responsibilities, whereas men are generally still seen, by themselves and others, as available for full-time work.[6]

There has been a lot of publicity about employers unlawfully dismissing women from their jobs because they are pregnant. But there are also other, less direct ways in which women may be edged out of their jobs when they have children. Women may find their jobs have been restructured so that they are in less important positions or new work practices are introduced which make it impossible to combine the job with family commitments. These tactics seem to reflect very traditional attitudes about male and female roles, which are not easily changed. A film editor working for a TV news programme, who felt she'd been forced out of her job by new work practices requiring unlimited overtime, was quoted as saying, 'I think they thought that by having children I'd let down the very macho, hard-drinking world of News and Current Affairs.'[7]

Motherhood in our society is idealised and romanticised. The reality of life as a housebound mother of young children is very different from many women's expectations. The problems of tiredness and the conflict between different demands of children, housework and husband have been described vividly by Vivienne Welburn in the chapter of her book *Postnatal Depression* called 'Cabbage Days'.

> The stresses which form that mountain of sand deposited outside the home of each new mother are intricate and interrelated. Mothering the baby is 'natural' and therefore receives no recognition. Mother is not an occupational category, housewife is. The mother-housewife earns no money and therefore has no status. She does not 'work' but functions alone in her home. Lack of recognition and repetitive work lead to feelings of fragmentation; exhaustion reinforces isolation and low status compound to create feelings of worthlessness.[8]

As Welburn suggests it is surprising not that many women *become* depressed in these circumstances but that so many do not. Indeed, a research study, based on a large sample of British married womens, found that the most important influence on women's mental health in this sample was the age of their youngest child. Women with children under five were most likely to show signs of psychological distress.[9]

Most of the old street communities, within which women gave each other a lot of support, have been broken down as a result of 'improved' housing programmes. Many women now live in bleak housing estates where there is little community life, few shops and poor bus services. In these circumstances depression can stem from isolation.

> I grew up in a big family and took it for granted that there were people close to me. When I married we moved to a different area where I knew no one. I couldn't understand why I became so depressed. Gradually I realised that a lot of it is loneliness. Often a day goes by and I haven't talked to a single adult. When my husband comes in from work, he is usually too tired to talk and that makes me feel worse because I really need someone to take notice of me. When the children go to nursery school I feel even more lonely and bored and I worry about what I shall do when they are at school all day. I miss my mother and sisters and feel jealous that they are still living close together. *Linda*

64

Often a woman moves to a new area because of her husband's job. If you are shy it can feel enormously difficult to break into a new community, if such a community exists at all. Sometimes women meet each other through taking the children to school or nursery but if such friendships are based on talking about the children they can be very unsatisfying. You may feel that people react to you as a mother and that your own identity got lost somewhere along the way.

> I do resent the fact that he can go out to work, see his mates and have a drink with them in the evening. He assumes he can go out as much as he likes and do most of the same things as before, whereas I can't. I feel stuck in the house and however much I love the children I do resent the loss of freedom. What makes it worse is the fact that he doesn't seem to understand what I'm feeling. *Sandra*

Not all communities are supportive. Sometimes they seem to create a pressure to conform or to keep up appearances. Vivienne Welburn quotes a mother describing life in a private housing estate in a pleasant leafy suburb: 'You had to go about with that big smile on your face and people saying, "Aren't you *lucky* to have such a dear little baby!" and you feel utter despair.'[10]

If you have been working before having a child and have had to stop, the change is enormous. There is a loss of status, independent finance and social contacts. Women who are used to being indepedent and coping with lots of demands at work may find it very difficult to understand why they are having difficulty in coping with a child. It may seem like failure. And yet being in isolation, doing repetitive tasks often after a broken night's sleep, is an obvious recipe for breakdown in the strongest person. It sounds like a regime of torture.

The idea that you should only have positive feelings towards a baby or child is one of the most crippling prescriptions of the romantic view of motherhood. If you have to suppress the resentment and irritation which the demands of a twenty-four hour childcare job will inevitably arouse, you are very likely to get depressed.

> When I first felt the fear of harming my baby I thought it was terrible. How could I have such an evil thought? I couldn't tell

anyone how inadequate and awful I felt. It's only now, two years later, that I can see it was the pressure I was under to be the perfect mother which caused me to react that way. *Sandra*

George Brown and Tirril Harris[11] found that among women with children at home, working-class women were four times more likely to suffer from depression than middle-class women. This class difference was only true for married women and not for women who were single, widowed, divorced or separated.

The implication is that women who have more money, or more often whose husbands have it, are to some extent protected from depression when looking after children at home. They may be able to ease the burden of childcare through labour-saving devices and paying for domestic help. They will have better housing and are more likely to have a car and telephone which can reduce the pressure of isolation. But whatever their social or economic status, all women at home are likely to suffer from lack of adult company, from the low status of their role as 'housewife' and 'mother' and from financial dependence on husbands or the state.

It is interesting that is is only now that unemployment for men is increasing so drastically, that a 'psychology of unemployment' is being developed. It is not recognised that women have been coping with the difficulties of living without employment in the sense of *paid* work for a long time. However hard a woman is working in her unpaid roles as parent, cook, cleaner and nurse at home, in our society paid work is given more respect. As well as being deprived of the benefits of earning her own money, it is very difficult for a woman to feel pride in her work in caring for children. It is usually taken for granted by others if done well, but if problems occur the woman is the first to be blamed.

George Brown and Tirril Harris[12] found that having a paid job did give women some protection against depression. Ann Oakley[13] in her study 'Transition to Motherhood' found that employment outside the home was one of the factors which made women less likely to get depressed after childbirth. However, working mothers often suffer from an enormous sense of guilt which is reinforced by society's attitudes to motherhood. There is a sense in which we cannot win as mothers. If we have a job we are blamed for not being with our children enough. If we do not have a job we feel apologetic for being 'just a housewife' or 'just a mother'.

Relationships with children are usually enjoyable and rewarding in themselves. The intense love women often feel for their children can carry them through times of extreme hardship. It is perhaps fortunate that this is so, for otherwise it is difficult to see why women would continue to take on the responsibilities for bearing and looking after children. When we are told that motherhood is our 'natural' function and that we should feel fulfilled by it, this ignores the tremendous difference which our circumstances can make. In our society women are expected to look after children in situations which are generally not rewarding. This undoubtedly increases our vulnerability to depression.

Work Outside the Home

It is always difficult to define women's work. Women's lives are not so easily categorisable in terms of 'public' work life and 'private' home life as are men's. Women do unpaid work in the home as part of so-called private life. Often this includes much unseen work in, for instance, caring for elderly relatives or in being the general organiser and communications 'switchboard' for family life. These roles are simply not recognised at all as being work.

Women usually do paid work which fits in with their unpaid work. The idea that a woman does not need paid work because her husband supports her is so often untrue. Women have always done bits of cleaning, sewing, child-minding and other 'odd-jobs' to support the family's wages. These types of employment are considered secondary to the woman's 'real' occupation at home and are given very low wages and status, even though they're often essential to the family income.

Women do not have equal opportunity to men in work.

Women have worked separately from men, apartheid-style, in low-paid jobs which hold out little hope of advancement. And they have entered the waged labour force on the strict but unspoken condition that this will not interfere with the unwaged work they perform in the home.[14]

67

Anna Coote and Beatrix Campbell describe how between 1911 and 1971 women's share of skilled (higher-paid) manual work dropped by nearly half while over the same period their share of unskilled manual jobs more than doubled. This trend continued in the 1970s and amounts to a near monopoly by men of skilled work. In non-manual work the same trend can be seen, with women dominating the lower-paid jobs. For example, 99 per cent of all typists, shorthand writers and secretaries are women, but only 14 per cent of office managers are women.

It is often difficult for women to find work when they need it. Women are used as a labour force when the country as a whole needs them, as in the Second World War. The film *Rosie the Riveter* has documented how a concerted propaganda programme manipulated women into the labour force during the war and then back home again afterwards, when men returning from the war required the jobs. The availability of work for women is not under our control. Women are expected to stand back and let men have the jobs.

The unions, which exist in class terms to serve the underdog, have until recently very seldom campaigned for women's interests, and even now these campaigns tend to be peripheral rather than central to their work. Cynthia Cockburn has described how:

> Skilled unions were always quite frankly male clubs. But the male-ascendancy principle exists even in general unions. Women cluster in the least skilled and least rewarded sections. Even where women predominate in numbers men have tended to form the leadership and to determine union priorities.[15]

One issue which is particularly relevant for women's lives is that of part-time workers. Many women do work part-time so as to more easily look after families. At times of economic difficulty, it is usually part-time workers who are made redundant first, on the unjustified assumption that their wage is less important. Recently an industrial tribunal in Birmingham ruled that the clause 'part-time workers to be made redundant before full-time workers' was unlawful sex discrimination. As a result a woman worker was reinstated but:

68

She experienced considerable hostility from the work force on her return to work . . . such hostility to part-timers claiming their rights is still being expressed . . . The union did not back the part-time workers' case and as a result of the continued lack of support only three of the women involved in the case are still members of the union.[16]

We wonder how those women felt. It is depressing to realise that even when women do try to assert their rights at work there is often not only a lack of support but also an antagonism from men. Being faced with hostile feelings from other people, when you are only trying to protect yourself, can make you want to give up trying.

Many businesses and organisations now have equal-opportunity policies. But, as Kate Figes has pointed out, often these policies lie in people's drawers, and simply allow a company to feel that they have dealt with the issue of sex discrimination. Sometimes unjust work practices are forced underground, with managers and recruiters being more careful about their choice of language. As a result many women may find it *more* difficult to raise the possibility of discrimination because that sort of thing is not supposed to happen any more.[17]

Ethnic minority women face discrimination on an even greater scale. Skilled and experienced ethnic minority women are twice as likely as white women to be unemployed. Black women frequently work longer hours in poorer conditions for lower pay than white women or men, even though better educated. A recent study showed that even though a higher proportion of African, Indian and Chinese young women go on to further or higher education than do young white women, women from ethnic minorities still tend to be in the lowest status jobs in their occupation, and are more likely to be on government training schemes or unemployed.[18]

Women in mid-life often want to go back to work or start a new career after their children have grown up. These women have a wealth of experience, wisdom and skills gained from managing a family. Sometimes they have educational qualifications as well. Most firms are very unwilling to take on women at this stage even if they have ten years or more of working life ahead of them. So much of what these women have to give will go unrecognised. It is not surprising if women at mid-life feel undervalued and get depressed.

These examples show how very limited women often are in the choices they can make within their working lives. Women's real powerlessness in the external world of work can so easily reinforce an inner sense of helplessness and hopelessness. This can contribute to the 'learned helplessness' syndrome in which we no longer feel is worth trying to get what we want.

I think the things that get me depressed about work are feeling trapped, knowing that I can't do what I want to do and knowing that it has something to do with being a woman, because if I were a man in that situation it would be totally different. First of all I would be perceived as having more status. I would perhaps get more recognition and I would be seen as more of an equal. If I were a man I would have many more alternatives and possibilities to do what I want – and I would probably already be where I want to be. *Betsy*

Another aspect of our powerlessness at work is the frequent sexual harassment to which we are subjected. The personal secretary who does many domestic jobs for her boss such as taking his suit to the cleaner's also has to tolerate having her bottom slapped or even more intrusive sexual advances. When we are exploited sexually by male bosses we are in a position of extreme powerlessness, because we know that our job is under threat if we complain and that men are much more likely to be believed than we are.

Sexual harassment has become much more publically recognised in the last few years. Most trade unions now produce pamphlets discussing the issues involved and giving advice about how to do something about it.[19] There have been a number of successful cases in which women have taken action through industrial tribunals, backed by the Equal Opportunities Commission. However this sort of legal process is normally very lengthy, involving appeals and counter-appeals, and can feel like an extremely daunting prospect.

Many women get depressed as a direct result of sexual harassment at work. Women often think they should be able to take it or laugh it off. They blame themselves for the feelings of anger and disgust they experience. A woman can end up believing

70

that there is something wrong with her, particularly if no one else feels the same.

Various examples of harassment are described by Ann Sedley and Melissa Benn in their booklet *Sexual Harassment at Work*.[20] These highlight the sense of impotence of the women involved. Here are two examples:

It was all so childish . . . what really mattered was the way in which his attitude undermined me in my work. I was also really worried about what he'd say after I'd gone, when I couldn't defend myself.

You would often get a group of men coming into the restaurant and they would think it funny to talk about you and your body while you were serving them. Sometimes they would actually touch you – pinch your bottom . . . and there was nothing you could do about it. It was really a case of grin and bear it. It would have been stupid to complain to the manager . . . he thought it was funny too.

Racism and racial harassment at work can also result in a sense of powerlessness, which can be deeply depressing.

Today I am feeling low. I am fed up with having to cope with racism at work, the lack of support and the hypocrisy. I feel so helpless and powerless, so weighted down that my spirit and energy seem to be seeping from my body – it is a scary feeling. The feeling as a result of racism is not new but every experience is a reminder of old emotional scars. *Jackie*

There are other ways in which a woman may feel she is not seen as being a full person at work: ways in which various aspects of her identity are not recognised.

It's complicated at work, because sometimes I feel that the men there treat me as if I was a man. It's very weird. If they are to see me as an equal they have to see me as a man. And because they know I'm a lesbian, they can see me as a non-sexual being – because it's safer for them to see me more as a competitor at work rather than as a sharer. So that depresses me and I have to face it every day. *Betsy*

The students I teach don't seem to have any expectation of me beyond that I will be a lecturer. Sometimes I get depressed because I need them to see *me* and yet I'm frightened that if they really knew how muddled and confused I am, then I wouldn't be able to communicate anything to them – to make the contribution that I do make. *Caroline*

There often seems to be a taboo on showing feelings of vulnerability at work. Work is a male world where the values of toughness and being in control are seen as the key to success. Feelings and sensitivity are supposed to be kept to the women's world at home.

Often I find that I want to get depressed or upset or cry a lot and I actually stop myself doing that because I have to go to work the next day and I don't want my face to look all puffy and my eyes to be red. *Sue*

On the other hand, women are often expected to play the same role at work as they do at home: to be the ones who look after the emotional needs of others.

I can see myself playing that role at work. I do see it as part of my responsibility as a teacher – to make myself wholly available so that this other person can discover things for themselves. I feel I make a conscious choice to carry on doing this. And yet I also feel that this sort of giving is an integral part of me as a female and certainly the men at work do it much less than I do. *Caroline*

While some women, predominantly white, have now managed to infiltrate most of the professions, they still find enormous discrimination against them, sometimes in subtle forms. Women usually find that they have to work twice as hard as a man to get the same level of promotion, recognition and status. For example, whereas a vast majority of teachers are women, women are often passed over by men when it comes to promotion to head of a school. Although 81 per cent of nursery and primary school teachers are female, only 49 per cent of headteachers of these schools are women; and while in secondary schools the proportion of male and female teachers is almost equal, only 22 per cent of secondary school head teachers are women.

In the Oxford and Cambridge colleges which have recently changed from being single-sexed to mixed, the result has been a decrease in the number of lecturing jobs for women. The reason is that the former women's colleges have been discriminating in favour of men in order to acquire a number of men on their staff, whereas the colleges formerly for men have not done the same for women. So a change which looked like it was aimed at increased equality has in fact not benefited women at the higher levels. The bastions of male power are not easily penetrated.

There is now a phrase, 'the glass ceiling', which refers to the invisible barrier, caused by covert discrimination, which prevents most women from advancing beyond a certain level in their chosen profession. A recent survey of men and women in various lines of work about the necessary ingredients for professional success highlighted some of the factors involved. Half the women surveyed agreed that 'men don't take women's roles at work seriously' whereas only 31 per cent of men felt this was true. Fifty-four per cent of women agreed that men still resent women for taking 'their' jobs, compared to 38 per cent of men. However, a high proportion of both women and men (71 per cent and 63 per cent respectively) agreed that men in general do not like working for women.

While the men and women surveyed both rated ability and intelligence as important determinants of professional success, women saw these qualities as being even more important for themselves than for their male colleagues. Ninety-five per cent of women thought that women needed ability in order to get to the top. But only 75 per cent of women felt men needed ability to achieve the same degree of success. Women also rated being well-dressed and looking physically attractive as more important for women than men. In short, most women felt they needed to be more able and intelligent than men, *and* better dressed and attractive, to succeed.

On this basis, it's not surprising that women feel daunted by the task of succeeding in what is still perceived to be a man's world – nor that their self-esteem in relation to their jobs is affected. Only 44 per cent of women – compared to 62 per cent of men – thought they were in the top third of their peer group in terms of ability; and only 39 per cent of women – compared to 49 per cent of men – could see themselves getting to the top in their chosen field.[22]

The Health Service provides a good example of the way in which men dominate even in areas of work in which women were previously recognised as having skills. Women recognised as wise women, midwives and witches were traditionally consulted for help with health problems.[23] Gradually men took over by turning medicine into a science in which men have the most powerful positions. Most doctors who have the highest status in hospitals are men and most nurses who have low status are women. Even in the newer professions such as social work and clinical psychology, women outnumber men at the lower levels while the opposite is true at the higher levels.

Two women doctors, interviewed in the *Guardian* in 1982, described the prejudice against women which they had experienced. Abayomi McEwen is a Nigerian woman who became a GP, although she really wanted to be a paediatric surgeon.

> I think there is certain prejudice towards women in the Health Service. If you're young and in the lower echelons you'll be taken on because you'll be fun for a bit of bottom-pinching and not running home to your kids. You'll be more devoted to your career. If you're older and not married then there's got to be something wrong with you. And if you're in the middle then you've had it.[24]

Margaret Ghilchick is a consultant general surgeon.

> There is appalling prejudice against women in medicine. It's been a difficult and hard road to get where I've got, much more so than if I had been a man. In general medicine as well as general surgery in the staffs of the London teaching hospitals there are very, very few women. There's only one woman Professor of Medicine in the country and there has never been a woman Professor of Surgery.[25]

Margaret Ghilchick was interviewed again in 1991 in another article in the *Guardian* about the shortage of women at the top of the medical profession.[25] Not much it seems had changed. Margaret Ghilchick remained one of only 11 women consultant general surgeons in the country (a mere one per cent of the total) and only 15 per cent of all consultants were women, even though women formed half the intake of medical schools. Once again, she spoke of the blatant prejudice and discrimination against women which she had observed when sitting on selection committees.

Both women, when interviewed in 1982, had their own families as well as their careers, and said that they appreciated that things were easier for them than for most women. Both enjoyed some flexibility in the hours they worked and they had been able to pay for help with their children. In 1991, Margaret Ghilchick said that she now felt a strong commitment to helping other women.

When I was younger, all my efforts were directed towards being as much like the men as possible and catching up with them. I didn't have the confidence I have now that I do my job better for being a woman.[26]

The real practical problems of combining families with careers, if women are to have equal work opportunities, have not as yet been faced by society as a whole. Men would have to give something up in terms of their own career advancement if they were to share equal responsibility for childcare and work in the home. Most of them are not yet prepared to do this.

As a result women are expected to take the main responsibility for their traditional role in the home and for developing their own career, trade or work skills. Often this double role is too much and it is not surprising that we become exhausted, tense and more vulnerable to depression. We expect so much of ourselves and then punish ourselves if we feel we have failed in any degree.

My depression began with a build-up of strain and anxiety unbeknown to me. I had left my old job where I felt secure and knew the people. I started a new job where there was a high-powered, competitive atmosphere which I didn't like. At the same time I was trying to create a home for myself and my husband. The house was hardly decorated. Over the months I had stripped this whole room in order to start decorating. I got more and more depressed doing it, because it took a hell of a long time. It was very lonely night after night on my own, stripping wallpaper. I got myself terribly overtired and coupled with the state of anxiety I was in about the job and about trying to make everything go well, I just became extremely depressed. I didn't realise how depressed I was. *Patricia*

There are many ways in which it is made difficult for a woman to do two jobs, even though it is so often expected of her. There are no provisions for parents to have leave if their child is sick. Women are often fired from their jobs if they get pregnant, even though this is against the law. With an increasing elderly population and an emphasis on 'community care', which in practice means care by women at home, even more unpaid nursing work will be expected of women.

While it is obvious that women go unrewarded for much of what they do, the issues concerning recognition are more complex. Traditionally women have been given recognition for their physical appearance, their sexuality and their relationship with men as wives, mothers and daughters. Now women are struggling to find new forms of recognition. We think about how to recognise ourselves. Can we give each other the recognition we need? The process of change can be painful, as we meet resistance from others and within ourselves. Perhaps depression is a necessary phase in the search for new meaning in our lives.

6
Process and Points

'Growing up' implies moving through stages to *higher* phases of development. It is a concept rooted in notions of hierarchy – a system of classifying things one above the other. It is common knowledge that the best place to be in a hierarchy is at the top. In this example that would mean 'grown-up'. The definition and age of 'grown-ups' varies in different cultures. In white western society the 'elderly' are not treated with the respect other cultures bestow on them. Developmental theories do not give equal weight and value to each stage. Often the continuity of experience is sacrificed for clarity of a particular model. For instance, it would seem one day we reach puberty. Puberty can be both an endpoint and a process. Growing up is as well. In order to recognise the connectedness of our total life experiences and to eliminate the notions of development that intimate one stage is better than another, we would like to refer to this life process as 'growing on'. 'Growing on' has no conclusion. It implies we will never finish this process.

We will all need to find our own rhythm to live by. It will be a constant search, for there is no one pattern that will work for a lifetime. There are common themes. One of them is the need for control or 'mastery' over life. This can be gained by making choices. For women, choices often seen limited. Sometimes they actually are. By asserting our right to choose, we are taking responsibility for ourselves and our lives. We also become clearer about those situations where we have no choice. Although we have to accept that situation in the short term we can fight for choices in the future.

A lot of the so called 'choices' in our lives really happen by default. There are also social pressures that influence, even determine, our decisions. We have come to know the power of advertising whether we support the ideas behind the 'ads' or not.

We, as women, are offered a blueprint (perhaps we should say pinkprint) for our lives. This is summarised not only in developmental theories, but also in the countless ads, books, films, magazines, and so on, we live with.

Until recently developmental psychology stopped when we reached adulthood. Babyhood, childhood and adolescence were considered the training for 'becoming an adult'. A lot of us couldn't wait to be one. Being an adult has status and gives me access to power. At some arbitrary point in our lives we become 'grown up'.

In growing we can forget the strengths we had as girl children and young women. As very young girls, we learned to comfort ourselves. We did what felt good and made ourselves feel better. We could have sucked our thumbs, brought out a teddy or a blanket, or whatever it was that gave us comfort. We would go to others for cuddles. We cried, laughed, screamed and shouted our feelings. What we could not control in real life, we controlled in our fantasies. We would use the resources around us creatively. We trusted our own feelings and our physical selves. We were encouraged to grow out of these strategies and find more 'acceptable' (i.e. adult) ways to deal with life.

Gail Sheehey popularised adult developmental psychology in her classic book *Passages*.[1] Although her book is descriptive and the first of its kind, it can at times seem *prescriptive*. It can seem to say 'this is what you *should* be doing'. Such prescriptions can be very powerful. Even when we are trying to be different, we can still be plagued by the 'norm'. Elisabeth Wilson describes life with her lesbian lover in the early 1960s: 'On the contrary we set out to prove that we were as nice, as ordinary, as stable and as normal as the straightest heterosexual couple.'[2]

Passages described the themes that predominate in ten-year chunks of our lives. This kind of chunking and summarising offers a crude kind of measure that reflects dominant cultural expectations. Unfortunately difference is not highlighted. The underlying assumptions of this developmental model is that we are all western, white, middle class and heterosexual.

Adolescent concerns are said to revolve around separation from the family and a preoccupation about our changing bodies. But leaving our families is for some an impossibility though a necessity for others. We are constrained in our choices by the economic dependence we have on our parents.

I had a lot of traumas as I was growing up between the ages of sixteen and eighteen years, which were basically to do with my mother and her wanting to keep control over me, not wanting to let me go. I was the oldest and the first one to leave the nest. She wanted to hang on to me and control what I was doing. I didn't want to live at home – it was crowded and I needed space. I wanted to move out and didn't want to stay at the school I was at. I needed to get away. *Sue*

Psychologically we remain tied up with our families for most of our lives. Trying to be separate is not only an adolescent crisis.

There was tension between my husband and my mother. She was never particularly keen on the idea of me going to England. I wanted her to come over to England and see that all was going well, and in efforts to make everything go well, I completely overdid things. *Patricia*

The reality of bodily changes is undeniable. We can exert some control over them often at great cost to ourselves. Compulsive eating and anorexia, part of a similar continuum, are ways of controlling physical development. More subtle ways are walking hunched over so new breasts don't look so conspicuous, or conversely stuffing bras. However, this preoccupation with our physical appearance does not stop at adolescence.

The transition from girl to woman is what our childhood preparation is about. We are allowed to rebel in adolescence. It is considered 'normal'. Tomboyishness will be indulged for a time. Falling in love with another woman or girl is also a perfectly natural *phase* (to be grown out of).

Our twenties are supposed to be focused on searching for intimacy and commitment – with a man, although this is unsaid. If not, then it is acceptable for women to focus on their careers, which is something denied the vast majority of women. However, concentrating on career prospects will not let us off the hook regarding 'Mr Right'. If you haven't found him, by thirty, you will be in a panic.

When I was in my mid-twenties, I would wake up feeling a sense of futility – even though on so many judgements I would have been said to have achieved a lot. And I myself was very pleased that I'd got the job I'd wanted, that I'd got promotion. I was running a unit of my own. In many ways I was doing a lot of things I wanted to do. I had a relationship with someone I was very close to. The marriage was based on a good friendship and was my first real sexual experience. So the whole thing was very comfortable. But there was a level of depression, in the sense that I felt this hopelessness. I felt anxiety about whether this was all there was to life, and couldn't I change something in it. *Caroline*

The thirties are said to be evaluation time. Have you succeeded? By whose standards? If not, then you are allowed this time before your looks totally fade and your womb and ovaries cease to function, to get it together, so to speak, with Mr Right. Mr Wrong will do. By thirty, you may, in your evaluation, decide decisions you made in your twenties (like about Mr Right) were wrong. The emphasis on male partners *only* should not go unnoticed. It is also an indication that other relationships we make, like our childhood friendships, are not taken seriously as the one relationship with Mr Right! No doubt some of these dilemmas about choice and commitment in relationships affect all of us regardless of our age and the sex of our partners and friends.

Wider societal changes have also begun to erode the notion of Mr Right. There are more and more women who are opting to have children outside of marriage and positively choosing single parenthood. Women who have never married have become the biggest single group of lone parents, representing 40 per cent of lone mothers and exceeding the numbers of divorced, separated or widowed women.[3] The age at which women are choosing to have children is also getting older with many women waiting until they are in their thirties or forties before starting families. Medical technology now enables post-menopausal women to have children through egg donation and artificial insemination.

This fluidity on the one hand has been matched by a tightening of social policy aimed at one parent woman-headed households. Specific laws prohibit certain fertility treatments for unwed women – including, but not acknowledging, lesbians.

Despite the gradual decline of such labels as 'spinster' and 'maiden aunt', and the wider life choices available to women, beyond forty remains relatively unknown territory. After years of being premenstrual, we are now simply labelled menopausal. Some high profile older women have put issues such as the menopause and hormone replacement therapy very much on the agenda. Gail Sheehy,[4] Germaine Greer[5] and Kate Millett[6] have all continued to write and talk about issues that concern them, which include but are not exclusively about the issues facing women getting older. However, personal experience may show that the attitudes of those around you remain fundamentally unchanged.

> Having moved through a number of menopausal stages in the last decade, I am very aware of how little has changed in attitudes towards women and ageing; from both men and women. *Caroline*

Yet despite the welcome intervention of feminist writers, this type of analysis or chunking still serves to reinforce stereotyped patterns. It is based on a waxing and waning type of life. It emphasis the values prescribed by our society. The most valued phase of development varies depending on the popular image of the day. 'Don't trust anyone over thirty', 'Life begins at forty'. Both reflect western society's concern with age; and it is clear that despite the higher profile of older women, they remain the least likely group to be offered counselling and therapy. Moreover, much of what is written does not address the issue of ageing from the perspective of black women nor address life cycle issues for ethnic minority women.

In addition, though there may be phases in our lives, we are often not aware of them until we have passed through them. We do not experience our lives in ten-year chunks.

> I feel I've been a bit like an onion, opening out in layers. One of those layers was my father and I feel that's been peeled back quite a lot. Then there was my mother and my brother, worrying about them, what was going to happen to my brother and my relationship with my mother. I feel I've peeled that back and what is left is me. *Theresa*

> There's layers and layers of the other person's experience and perceptions that have to be accounted for. And then, of course, my own in reverse. It's a harmful activity both ways. Not only

is it people I need to learn to let go of but old ideas of myself, of them, of the world . . . *Janet*

This stage model fails to stress cultural contexts, and is really a statement about white, middle-class women's lives. Not surprisingly, this does not describe the reality of life for the vast majority of us. Even if our lives could be described according to this model, how often was this pattern made out of choice? How much control do we exert over our lives?

Life is a process which means it moves on. It is punctuated by certain events. These events can be commas, full stops or the beginning of a new paragraph in our lives. Some we choose to place. Other punctuation marks are provided for us. Our previous experience affects the way we adapt our scripts.

About then another stage of my life was about to begin. I met a man a lot younger than myself. He seemed very genuine but I trusted no one. He wasn't going to hurt me. I had enough hurt to last a lifetime. So at the beginning I used him also. I was seeing him but I was also seeing someone else at the same time. I finally dropped the other man when I started to realise we had something going for us. It started to get serious and I panicked. I thought I am leaving myself wide open, so I told him all about myself. He knew a little but – only as much as I wanted him to. When he started to talk of marriage, although by now I had started to depend on him, I explained all the pitfalls – all the reasons why he shouldn't marry me. You see, by now my past had convinced me that there was something wrong with me. I wasn't fit to be loved. There was something in me that caused people to reject me. I told him he would be better with someone younger who could give him children which I couldn't. I told him about my psychiatric history; that I wasn't much use to anyone. I knew afterwards that I was trying to get him to reject me. This was the treatment I was used to. He convinced me that he loved me because I was me. My past didn't matter. If I was sick he would take care of me and so we were married which should be a happy ending to an unhappy tale. *Chris*

Certain events in our lives have very powerful effects on our future development. For instance, the study by George Brown and Tirril Harris showed that women who had lost their mothers in childhood were more vulnerable to depression when further stress occurred later in their lives. Our ability to deal with trauma is affected by the resources we have available to us.[7] These resources are not only financial, social or physical, but also psychological. At different stages in our lives we are more or less equipped to deal with major life events.

This chapter touches on significant events in women's lives that can play a part in depressing us. The chosen emphasis is on the depressing effect of these events.

Loss

Frequently loss is seen as the root cause of depression. We can experience feelings of loss over our health, after a relationship breaks up or we lose our job. Moving on, as we all must in living, necessarily involves giving up something. There are times when what we value is taken rather than willingly given up.

Death

Death is the most obvious loss, in that it is the irreversible absence of someone. We all know about it. It will happen to all of us – to some sooner than others. Privileged lifestyles not surprisingly prolong life.

Because of death's inevitability, we have been forced to cope with it. We have developed mourning rituals which help us through the experience. We can be depressed after someone dies. Our friends and relatives frequently respond to our needs by taking care of us.

Problems can arise when death is unexpected; friends or family think we have mourned enough; we can't talk about the person any more; we feel enormously guilty for the death. These issues highlight how little control we have in these situations. The rituals, helpful as they may be, often take over in an unhelpful way.

Talked today of my grandma's death . . . more sadness . . . remembering her lying on the couch, having fallen over from sitting up . . . looking death in the eyes . . . her eyes were still open . . . I did wonder what she thought, what she felt as she died and I had this horribe slow motion picture of her falling sideways on to the sofa . . . dying as she fell or was she dead before she fell? I loved her and I didn't want her to die. They came [the ambulance men] and I remember being angry at how they picked her up . . . like a piece of old furniture . . . no dignity . . . with her arms and legs flopping and I begged them to carry her properly. We went out to the ambulance and I rode in it – sitting with my gran on the stretcher. I remember the siren wasn't on . . . it felt like we went slowly . . . At the hospital a doctor came out and put his best sad face on to tell me she had 'passed away' . . . I remember her things being handed to me . . . her valuables. I left carrying them. I wondered what happened next, not having attended a death before. Soon, others took over, but for a long time I was alone with my granny. No one ever answered my questions, but then I never asked them aloud.

Marie, December 1980

Frequently, when someone dies, we feel we have lost something of ourselves. It can be difficult to try and carry on living. 'When my mother died, I felt like part of me died . . . the caring gentle part . . . I am frightened it is gone forever.' (*Dorothy*).

Being depressed is the obvious and expected reaction to a death. Often time and space are not given to the bereaved to talk about all of their feelings. Sometimes we don't feel sad when someone dies. It could be a feeling of relief or one of anger. These feelings often seem unacceptable.[8]

The pain of my father's death never goes but it gets better. He died of a heart attack and I used to get terrible psychosomatic pains, like I was going to have a heart attack – pains up my arms and across my chest. I cried every day, absolutely every day for ages. I don't cry every day now and there are some days that I don't think at all about my father – but when I do, I'm sad. And it's anger, not just sadness. It's anger with him and anger with the world. Why me – it's not fair. I felt that very much at the beginning. *Theresa*

We are all aware of death. Our understanding of it changes as we grow on. All cultures have rituals to mark death. These rituals often help us to mourn the loss of someone significant in our lives.

Yet other losses, often equally significant, do not have cultural recognition in the form of ritual.

Disability

We frequently take our health for granted. Our ability to see, to hear, to walk dramatically affect how we perceive the world and how the world perceives those it labels 'disabled'. Chronic illnesses, often unseen, can sap our strength both physically and emotionally. The search for a cure can become very important but for the 'incurable' there is no hope.

> I am now registered 'disabled' and cannot do anything stressful like housework, ironing, cleaning windows. I can only walk about 150 yards without getting chest pains and extreme breathlessness. All this happened over two years ago but for six to twelve months I was almost a complete invalid and was feeling very sorry for myself. Why me? Haven't I suffered enough? I was suicidal. I wanted to get it over quickly in my own way. But with help I think I have come to terms with it. I know it will kill me eventually. *Chris*

> I think the main reason why I became so depressed was having to slow down so much after I had a stroke. I had always been a very active person. I liked to run around. Now I can't do a lot of things that I used to do. I hate that. I also hate having to ask for help. *Gaynor*

Ill-health or the inability to use all of our senses is not a choice we would make for ourselves. Trying to feel in control is extremely difficult especially if the medical profession intervenes with a prolonged treatment package and a potential cure as the final outcome. It can seem as if the illness or disability takes over your life. Being deprived of choice, losing control and living in a society that is frightened of illness and prejudiced against the disabled are factors that could contribute to feeling depressed.[9]

Children

The birth of a child is seen as a joyous occasion. This rose-coloured haze is so overpowering that it is impossible for the

85

feelings of loss many women feel with the birth of a child, to be expressed. Not all women may experience birth as a loss but for those who do, there is little space and acceptance of those feelings. As more is written, postnatal depression, as it is called, becomes more visible and women do not suffer in silence and isolation.[10]

The sadness some women experience when becoming mothers often involves the loss of independence and freedom; for some it can be the 'apparent' loss of sexual attractiveness, body shape or the pleasure and attention received while pregnant. Some women do not experience having children as a loss but a fulfilling and richly rewarding experience. For most it is a mixture of both.

Motherhood is an issue that affects all women whether we choose to produce children, if we can make that choice, or not. The ability to reproduce is often taken for granted and frequently women do not exercise choice in conceiving. When conception is not a possibility for gynaecological reasons, or difficult because we do not sleep with men, we are forced to think about our commitment to children and our desire to parent in a different way. We may have to give up some of our previous expectations of ourselves as parents and experiences this as a loss.[11]

'I know that despite my love for Mary and her desire for a child it is something I can never give her – it will be something we cannot create between us' (*Marie*).

Planned parenting does not mean we escape possible depression. Often the best made plans go wrong; you fail to conceive; you miscarry; you make choices about how you want to have the child 'delivered' and find you have little control over that process. You make plans around sharing childcare and find them difficult to put into practice.

There is a lot of praise and encouragement for women to want to have children. We are taught from a young age to see ourselves as future mothers. It is perfectly acceptable for young girls to want to be 'mummies' when they grow up. The same is not true for the little boys who want to be *just* 'daddies'.

If getting pregnant is difficult, then the medical profession is there to help us fulfil what is seen as our natural destiny. Women can and do undergo operations, horome therapy, bedrest, miscarriages to produce children. These practices receive the support of society, friends, family and, not least, the medical profession, the notable exception being when lesbian or single

86

women wish to use artificial insemination. A lesbian's desire to have or keep children is not seen as natural nor is it supported by society. Recently, both in the United States and the UK, it has become possible for parents of the same sex to be recognized in law. In the US, this is possible in some states through adoption while, in England, it is possible for a Residence Order to be obtained after the non-biological parent has lived with the child for three years continuously.[12]

It is ironic that in our desire to conceive we are taken seriously. (Except if we are lesbians.) All the support and back-up that was so much in evidence prior to the birth will suddenly vanish afterwards. Women are left literally holding the baby. Surely *this* is maternal deprivation!

Breaking up

Relationships give us security and stability. We have many different kinds of relationships with other people in our lives that vary in intensity and duration. When our intimate relationships, often with lovers but also with close friends, come under stress and/or break up, we often feel depressed regardless of who 'ended it'.

> My friend has decided to live with her male lover and instead of being joyful about it, I am filled with gloom. The feeling that I have lost her to him. *Marie*

> It didn't matter that she ended it. What was so difficult was believing it was ended, that we would never be the same again. Other women pointed out it was over but I couldn't see it. I had several great bouts of crying but would always bounce back. It wasn't 'til I left that I became angry and sad. Moving out, packing everything up, arriving somewhere new – I just sat for hours like being in a state of shock then gradually I cried and cried and shouted. *Mary*

We will experience feeling of loss, emptiness and loneliness. These feelings are specially difficult to get over if the relationship was not recognised by others as being very important (as in close friendships), or invisible, as lesbian relationships are sometimes. If we get involved with someone else immediately we may not allow ourselves, or have time, to feel some of the sad feelings that turn up at the end of an important relationship.

I felt like a part of me had died – half of me had died. It was really weird, so I decided to go out and buy sombre clothes. I've got to show that I am sorry about it. No one else will know but I'll know. I went around with a glum face and sombre clothes . . . I felt I had to wear them for a long time. I felt really low and I couldn't get it out of my mind. I kept crying and gradually it got less and luckily I had someone to talk to . . . I suppose it is like a death in some ways. *Elizabeth*

There is no way to mark the end of a relationship other than divorce, which is the 'official' recognition of the dissolution of a 'legitimate' relationship. For women who are not married, there is no formal process of disengagement. This may be a blessing in disguise as divorce is a legal procedure disconnected from the emotional experience of separation.

In the situation of the break-up of the marriage, which has been so traumatic for me, I feel confused because for some period of time I couldn't see what I could do. In a way I felt I had to take this because 'the man' had decided. One of my greatest depressive things at the moment is a sense of impotence: that whatever I say, whatever I do, I still am not able to influence that particular man in what he has decided will happen. And I feel outraged by that. *Caroline*

Parents may make decisions about their lives together in which children have no say. Recently there has been more recognition of the need for a child to mourn the loss of her family as she has known it, in order to adjust herself to the necessary reorganisation that will follow. This is equally true for children accommodated under the Children Act. This new piece of legislation does give children access to their own legal representation and should make it possible for them to ensure they can keep in contact with different members of their family if they are no longer living with them full time.

When my parents separated, it felt as if my whole family splintered into tiny fragments . . . isolated individuals alone with their own hurt and pain. We weren't a family any more but a collection of indviduals living in the same house. *Marie*

Our culture marks out as deserving of ritual, birth, marriage and death. The first two supposedly have no place for sadness. The natural feelings of loss that women experience at these times are denied expression and the tears on these occasions are seen as evidence of joy.

Depression can stem from a loss of someone we are close to because of death, or their absence; the loss of an important relationship with a lover or friend; the loss of a job with the money and friends it has provided; the loss of our good health or physical capabilities; or a symbolic loss such as part of ourselves.

Growing on does involve loss. Not only is it important that we move on but that we allow ourselves to feel and experience a whole range of emotional states. We can carry our experience with us in the form of memories. They are our relics of the past. History keeps them for us. It is important that we keep records, notes or rememberance of our lives, so we can pass our knowledge on. We know that it has been men who have made history and men who have the most access to the tools needed to record history. It is necessary that we mark our own histories, pass on our own pasts. We often forget what is or has been important to us because we are told to 'grow out of it', or that it is silly, childish or immature to feel a certain way. But we do remember and in doing so we keep our experience intact and add to our fullness as individuals.

It's strange that so many things so many years back when you put them on paper and read them out . . . it's still so much alive in your mind. The feelings never go . . . you can experience the same feelings all over again because you remember . . . so vividly how you felt. *Chris*

Violence

Violence has also become part of our everyday life. It is portrayed and glorified in television, the press and in music to name but a few sources. Contrary to the original belief that violent scenes in our 'entertainment' provided a 'safe' outlet for our own aggressive feelings, recent research has shown that the depiction of violence in fact normalises it and thereby makes it seem more socially acceptable.[13]

Sexual and physical violence against women has a massive and potent effect. The impact of one attack sends waves throughout our lives. Our frustration and anger against these types of violence has had far-reaching effect. Yet it still carries on depressing and oppressing all women collectively.

Childhood Sexual Abuse

Sexual abuse is part of every little girl's childhood. A recent research study into the prevalence of sexual abuse amongst young women found that one per cent of those interviewed had been sexually abused by a parent or parent figure while up to 47 per cent reported an unwanted sexual experience before the age of eighteen.[14] It most frequently occurs in subtle guises, like being passed around to relatives to hold, having to kiss people you don't like, being asked to lift your dress and show your knickers at school. These examples in and of themselves do not constitute abuse but they cumulatively have an effect. These experiences teach us that we have no control or choice over certain aspects of our lives. We learn that women must basically 'grin and bear it' when it comes to expressing ourselves sexually. We are not encouraged to be initiators. Men are both the 'voyeurs' and the 'exhibitionists' of sexual experiences.

If the violence and/or the proximity of the abuser to ourselves is increased, the effect is much move devastating. Children are trusting, especially of adults they know and love. Being abused by your father, grandfather, uncle or brother will affect how you feel about yourself. The full extent of your hurt may not be evident until you are much older.

The difficulty we often have in dealing with this experience is first and foremost the denial of it. Sometimes we deny it to ourselves. There is no doubt it is denied by society. Many years after, we may feel the effects of early sexual abuse reliving the terror and confusion in our dreams or our madness.

Because sexual abuse happens so often and throughout our lifetime it is difficult to recognise it as a critical point. It isn't a point. It is a process – a very depressing and potentially deadly one – which erodes our sense of self, fragile almost from the start.

For many women, the sexual abuse in their lives remains a secret. 'Psychiatric treatment' may be offered or even sought with little reorganisation of the long term impact and effects of childhood sexual abuse. However, acknowledgement of the need for services for both children as well as adults who experienced sexual abuse in their childhoods is much greater than it was ten years ago. There are now many specific services, help lines and books written to help overcome the effects of early childhood sexual abuse.[15]

Rape

Rape is much more easily defined as a critical point in our lives. It affects all women as we all live wth the threat of rape. For some of us it becomes a reality.

Like childhood sexual abuse, rape deprives us of choice and control. It is an act of sexual violence by men meant to humiliate, degrade and put down women. It serves as a means of male control. It keeps us off the streets and on our guard in certain situations by the mythology generated around it. We all grow up with the idea of the 'bogey man'. He lies in wait for us under our beds, in the dark of night.

Depression is not an unusual response to rape. The experience can be seen as a punishment for something we have done, a confirmation of our own worthlessness, a stripping away of our power. We often feel we are to blame for rape, that in some way we brought it on ourselves; we asked for it. This may be comforting in some strange way. If we believe we are raped because of the clothes we wear, then to avoid rape, we don't wear 'those kind of clothes'. It is much more frightening to recognise that we are raped because we are women; something we cannot stop or avoid. We cannot predict where, when, or by whom, because we can be raped anywhere, anytime, by any man.

Living on my own frightens me still. I think it would anybody, if the Queen ain't safe, who is? That's what went through my mind . . . if he can get into her bedroom he can get into mine.[16]
Janice

Sexual violence is often accompanied by physical violence. The threat of it is implicit. The right of men to beat their wives and

91

children has historically been protected, or condoned by law. This is because the law assumes that women and children are the property of men, who can therefore do as they please with their possessions. Although the state will now intervene on behalf of children being physically (and sexually, if this is recognised) abused, rape within marriage has only recently been recognised as a crime. This makes it possible for a woman to prosecute her husband but it is still very difficult to prove legally. The same is true for 'date rape' where prosecutions will now be brought but securing convictions remains extremely difficult.

Domestic Violence

Despite the police making a concerted effort to intervene in domestic violence it is still difficult for women to come forward and ask for help in dealing with it. The law technically does provide protection, but because of the economic repercussions in leaving a violent partner, legal reforms have not made an appreciable difference. There is a real need for more refuges and counselling services for both the man who is violent and the women and children he attacks. Research has shown that a battered woman's chances of being killed by her partner rises more than thirty fold *after* she leaves him.[17] It is also difficult to measure the extent of violence within the home because it is such a private crime. There is an enormous pressure on women to maintain the facade of domestic bliss.

> Trying in your mind for the sake of appearances to pretend that everything is fine and trying to clean the house, love the kids, act like normal (?) respectable people, whilst being rushed to hospital in between the pretence.[18]

Intermittent or continuous physical violence, often coupled with sexual and mental cruelty, destroys your perception of yourself as a potent capable person. The fact that one person (a male) violates the other (a female) maintains the power imbalances that are present in numerous other forms throughout society. In some ways, male partners beating and abusing their female partners are conforming to gender stereotypes in an extreme fashion.[19]

It is interesting to note that society has provided a register for children at risk of physical and sexual abuse but not one for women. It is often only when violence is directed at the children that women feel able to leave or seek help.

Research suggests that domestic violence is widespread. Statistics are very sobering. Domestic violence is estimated to occur in 25 per cent of all households.[20] Furthermore, the links between domestic violence and longer term mental health problems is much clearer. Criminal statistics collected by the Home Office do not give breakdowns of crimes of physical violence committed by men against women. Terms like 'manslaughter' and 'murder' conceal the number of attacks on, and murders of, women by men. The statistics on rape indicate that women are, contrary to the myths, more likely to be raped by someone they know in some capacity within their own or the rapist's home.[22]

It is crucial that we recognise the damage physical and sexual violence does to women. If you know no other relationship but an abusive one, it can take a lifetime to recognise and escape from it. The lack of alternatives and support make it very difficult even for the most courageous of us.

> If I'd had a bit more support when I needed it after leaving my husband perhaps I would have been all right. Instead, I came back from work to find the kids not being looked after. So, in the end I went back to him. Truly I was desperate . . . where else could I go? I'm still paying for it now. *Lyn*

> I do think it a fallacy. It used to be more so years ago, that you've got to stick it out for the children. I think if I did it over again now I'd have left. There are facilities available now that weren't then – homes for battered women – there was nowhere you could go then . . .[23] *Chris*

Racism

The violence of racism frequently goes unnoticed or is minimised but racism is often coupled with direct physical assaults on people.

> I experienced a racist attack from a group of white young men, who started spitting, kicking me and calling me 'black bitch,

bastard, Paki' – the usual sort of abuse. I felt down for days afterwards. *Gita*

It can cause depression and serves to remind black people and those from other ethnic minority communities that they and their culture are not valued or respected by the wider dominant group.

There were things that made me feel less of a human being. I couldn't get any products for my hair or my skin. I had to go along way if I needed my hair cut because there weren't any African Caribbean hairdressers. There was none of the food I was used to. All of these things made me feel unwanted. *Ayesha*

Moving away from friends, family and community that have insulated you from the brutal impact of racism, can leave you very vulnerable and even unprepared for the hatred that many people still feel towards people who are visibly different.

A time that was very depressing for me was when I left the city I had grown up in and went off naively to another part of England . . . It was only as my father was driving me there that I suddenly thought about the fact that there wouldn't be many black people there . . . It was very difficult. I had an experience where a white woman called me a 'black bitch' at the bus stop . . . That was the first time I thought about being in a minority and feeling really unsafe. I thought 'My family aren't here . . . What if I was the victim of a racist attack? I could be killed and no one would know about it.' *Ayesha*

When I first went to another town to start my professional training, I really believed that I could leave behind all the pressure from my family about what girls do and don't do; leave behind all the racism and horrible, horrible feelings when people show that they hate your guts because of the colour of your skin. At first I was actually glad there were so few black people there. I thought no one would bother about one or two. It turned out to be the most painful years of my life and the most isolating . . . *Gita*

Homophobia

Like racism, homophobia is often accompanied by direct physical violence. However the possibility of benefiting from heterosexual privilege by virtue of not 'looking like a lesbian' may serve to reduce some of the risks. This invisibility though may contribute to depression because underpinning the lack of visibility is a hostile attitude.

> The total lack of recognition that lesbian couples get, together with the overt hostility expressed publicly (especially recently over issues relating to children) contributes to my depression. Invisibility – even when you think you are being visible. *Marie*

This theme of invisibility was echoed in Ayesha's interview where she said: 'The whole structure made you feel visible but invisible at the same time.' Compare this comment to that made by Marie:

> The invisibility is also coupled with a startling visibility where we are conspicious by our difference – two women and a child in what seems a sea of mummies and daddies and children. All of this takes energy to deal with and sometimes I get tired.

Frequently we live in hope that things will change, that the abuse will stop somehow.

> I had a client who refused to see me because I was Indian. He actually came to the appointment and hurled a load of very personal abuse at me. The team I was working with did not give me very much support. I realised that I had believed that being a professional and dressing a certain way would make me immune to racism. *Gita*

Isolated and often made to feel responsible for the violence done to us by others, we think we are going crazy. This world that we live in does not seem as safe. It can become a terrible place to be. We experience a sense of helplessness because violence controls us. Its unpredictability makes it more frightening. These experiences can be surrounded by silence. We frequently don't feel able to tell anyone what happened. When we do, we are not only confronted by disbelief but also a lack of understanding and adequate protection.

Violence, in any form, penetrates to our very souls. It profoundly affects our sense of self and our estimation of our own worth. Society has undeniably allowed and encouraged men to use violence against each other as well as against women. Women however are expected to suffer in a silence which can be fatal.

Medical Violence

Oddly enough, our interactions with the medical profession often combine these depressing elements: loss and violence. The psychological aspects of disease now receive more attention, at least in theory. It is now recognised that women may need to mourn the loss of their wombs, or breast, for instance, following surgery. The meaning of these parts of our bodies is very important. Depression may be a necessary stage to go through in the healing process. Audre Lorde talks about this.[24]

> During my following hospitalisation, my mastectomy and its aftermath, I passed through many stages of pain, despair, fury, sadness and growth. I moved through these stages, sometimes feeling as if I had no choice, other times recognising that I could choose oblivion – or a passivity that is very close to oblivion – but did not want to. As I slowly began to feel more equal in processing and examining the different parts of this experience, I also began to feel that in the process of losing a breast I had become a more whole person.

Surgical removal is not only a loss but can seem violent. With advances in plastic surgery, doctors could reconstruct your face following a car accident. Yet removing a breast is still a physically mutilating experience. Needless removal of wombs and cutting vaginas to 'aid' birth are examples of medical misogyny and one frequently experienced by women as violent.

but I still remember
knife serrated
grapefruit knife   curved into my flesh
bruised are blue, purple red and I moved slowly,
    clumsily for a fortnight

difficult to reach for my baby
difficult to sit to feed her . . .

Caroline Halliday[25]

It is difficult to get angry when treatment is ostensibly for our own good. We are expected to feel grateful for the 'cure', or the experience. Our 'consent' to these experiences is often not informed. More often than not we submit through lack of information or even misinformation about the treatment itself and little nor no discussion about the available alternatives. 'Doctor knows best', is still the pervading ethos of the medical establishment[26] and despite the Patients' Charter it can still be difficult to get access to the treatment of your choice. This is true of home-births, and you can still be struck off your GP's list for wanting one.[27] There have also been recent scandals around specifically women's health issues, such as cervical smears and screenings for breast cancer where individual women have had their lives placed at risk through inappropriate treatment or diagnosis. On the whole, the services being offered to women remain patchy.

These issues are equally relevant to the psychiatric specialities. The 'mentally ill' are deemed not able to even give 'informed consent' to treatment. Psychiatric interventions have a history of violence attached to them from straitjackets, padded cells, to ECT.

With loss and violence, control is taken from us. There is no element of choice in the situations described earlier in this chapter. However, medical treatment often does precisely the same thing – offers no choice and takes control. If we trust the person we are working with, then the relinquishing of control can be experienced differently. There are numerous studies which indicate conclusively that if women are more actively involved whilst having medical treatment, their recovery and experience is better than those women who are the passive recipients.[30]

Psychotherapy can often inadvertently take responsibility away from us. The word therapist divided, becomes the rapist; a reminder that information and intimate experiences can be forced out rather than voluntarily shared. This can be done even with the best intentions of trying to help. Doctors (and anyone working in a professional capacity) have power over another person. There needs to be an increasing awareness around how

97

this power needs to be an increasing awareness around how this power imbalance affects the person seeking help or advice. The issue of control and who has it is fundamental in the understanding of depression.

Support and self-help groups have been set up to help each other through debilitating and depressing encounters with the medical profession. Unfortunately this violation can also occur within a psychotherapeutic context where mental health practitioners sexually exploit the vulnerability of their clients.[29] Sometimes we need space to talk about the feelings of loss and violence we experience when we put ourselves into the hands of the experts. It is ironic in a world so clearly anti-woman, that we absorb those feelings to such an extent that in depression we can act them out in various forms of self-abuse and mutilation.

> I didn't like to blame anybody for anything, so if they hurt me I hurt myself instead . . . I couldn't hurt them so I hurt myself . . .
> *Elizabeth*

7
Contradictions, Conflicts and Collapse

There are times when we feel depressed and an immediate stress is not apparent. This type of depression can be the result of unresolved conflict or a delayed reaction to previous stress in our lives. Conflict is the clashing of opposing points of view. Sometimes we can agree to differ, other times we need to reach a working solution. In order to do this, the conflict has first to be recognised and then decisions made about whether to work it out and, if so, how.

For me the real struggle has been about holding on to myself as a black African Caribbean woman and a black African Caribbean British woman. Holding on to those two things feels difficult. I have been going through a struggle about whether I am becoming more 'white', or managing to hold on to my blackness when involved in a certain milieu . . . struggling to hang on to who I am as an individual. *Ayesha*

Women are supposed to be indecisive. Yet we make numerous decisions throughout every day. Advertising of household products and foods is aimed at homemakers; recognising that it is women who will decide what brand of this or that will be bought. We are able to make decisions on behalf of others far more easily than on our own behalf. Perhaps that happens *not* because we don't know what we want for ourselves but because of the frustration of not getting, for many reasons, what we *do* want.

I was always picked last for teams and that depressed me . . . There's nothing worse than you'd like to be picked first once and you're always picked last and you know that if they have you on their side you're going to let the side down . . . it's terrible! *Elizabeth*

At the age of about seventeen or eighteen I was becoming aware that I wanted to reach out for all sorts of things. I wanted to travel, I wanted to be different, I wanted to break away, and I didn't know how. And that engendered a sense of helplessness and hopelessness. I don't recall blaming anyone else for not being able to do what I wanted to do. It was a very unspecified, general sense of frustration. *Caroline*

My dream then was to have a baby, something of my own to love and be loved in return. My first baby died during birth of a broken neck. Once again the feelings of despair, the hopelessness that my life would never change. I think that was the time I truly felt I was being punished. *Chris*

Frequently we feel we are being punished simply for wanting something for ourselves. Fighting for what we need to survive can seem more righteous than fighting for what we want.

I suppose I have a hard time reconciling my needs and wants. My stingy self rules my indulgent self as I am afraid of being caught short . . . It seems I always want more than I need and I feel bad about that. Why can't I be happy with what I *do* have? *Marie*

Sometimes we don't realise the contradictions and conflicts within ourselves. They often become clear when we have to make a particularly important decision. There seems to be a part of us that wants to do one thing and another part of us that wants to do another incompatible thing.

I feel that I should keep him because he's my son and yet, on the other hand, I feel that I don't want him because he's causing so much turmoil in our life – not all the time, but sometimes I just want him to go but if he went I just know I'd want him back. It's sort of . . . I'm in the middle . . . I always seem to put myself in that position. *Lyn*

I can't have both. I have to put off the secure place to live, and

100

live a fairly nomadic life which feels unsettled in a way. My depression is sometimes to do with living with that. Knowing that on the one hand I'd love to be really settled with a studio and be comfortable and know that it was always going to be there, but on the other hand knowing that next year I might get rid of all my stuff, sell everything and go off travelling. *Sue.*

Trying to juggle contradictory points of view within ourselves takes a lot of energy. We can *choose* to avoid confronting the issue. Sometimes this can be a positive step and is an effective way of reducing tension. If it is an important life issue the lack of resolution, or the temporary solution, will need to be re-negotiated. Like the proverbial bad penny, these issues don't seem to go away.

When black clients come in, you wonder whether they still see you as a black person, or as someone who is black visibly but white inside. You can start doing quite crass things to try and prove to them that you are still in touch with your blackness. At the same time you have to deal with a lot of projections from white colleagues, who see you as having all the answers and projections from the black community who see you as potentially someone who has sold out and joined the oppressors . . . *Ayesha*

I had this increasing sense of suspicion that I had to put away my Indian-ness to become a professional and that's when I started to get depressed. *Gita*

Having to hide or conceal aspects of ourselves may become a necessary survival strategy but it carries a price. We may find we are not able to get the support we need from other people within our community because they view this 'hiding' as a form of collusion and may be very critical of our actions.

Living with internal contradictions and conflict isn't easy. It is difficult to give voice to both sides of the argument to help yourself reach a solution or a compromise. Having an internal dialogue leaves a lot of unanswered questions, is prone to getting stuck and often does not provide the additional information that may help you to sort things out. It may at least highlight what the conflict is for you. This is often when we turn to friends.

Is there a proper mix of old and new? How far do you go to make a point when you maintain a 'liberated' stance? I suppose it depends on how liberated you are – might be one answer. But that stinks of circularity or rather dead ends. Who wants to be liberated and alone? *Marie, 20 February 1976*

It is difficult however, if part of our dilemma involves something that is seen as unacceptable. For example, trying to discuss our sexuality is certainly easier now than it was, *if* we want to talk of men. You have to be more careful in choosing who you talk to about your sexual feelings for women. Ideally, we would like to talk with someone we feel will be able to accept our conflicting or contradictory feelings and help us work out for ourselves what we want.

Contradiction can, sometimes, be more easily overlooked. It can be more subtle than conflict and we can be totally unaware of it. You can be giving contradictory messages, when verbally you are saying one thing and physically you are saying something else.

I feel isolated here – as though no one touches the real me – the me that likes to curl up at night and go to sleep – who likes to snuggle, cuddle, feel close, so unlike me who laughs and is gay all day – who keeps people away by her endless chatter.

Marie, 3 May 1977

It may be important to remind ourselves that conflict and contradiction do not reside solely in our heads.

Sometimes you can feel dissatisfied with a situation but feel unable to change it. Friends can be supportive at first and then withdraw their support over time because they feel they are being used, not to help you change the situation but, to help you *stay* in the situation. This is a difficult dilemma for us all. How can we be supportive to an individual woman while not supporting the situation she is in, especially if we feel it is hurtful to her?

Feeling stuck can be frustrating, but it can also be reassuring. This is conveyed in sayings like 'the devil you know is better than the one you don't.' It does take courage to make conscious decisions to change situations, or resolve ambivalent feelings. It is possible. This doesn't mean there isn't room for contradictions in our lives. They are going to be inevitable and perhaps even desirable. The alternatives women are faced with are often either/or choices. We either put up with things the way they are or we get out altogether. This type of approach, which often helps to crystalise the issues we are confronting, fails to include the whole range of 'in between' solutions. Contradiction and conflict must be an inevitable part of growing on. There may also be times when some issues have to be shelved. Having put them there does not mean they can never be taken off the shelf. For example, you may be thinking of leaving home but after discussing it and figuring it all out, you just can't afford it so you decide not to move out, just yet. You may save up some money or you may meet a friend who could share with you. At that point you could start thinking about it again.

Usually the contradictions we live with are not so obvious.

I think that coming to terms with, and accepting, being alone, living your life alone which gives you more choice, is very hard. One of the things I love about living is sharing experiences with people I'm close to. And that recognition and the acceptance that I shall have to spend most of my life not sharing a lot of the important things with someone I love and am close to is difficult. I've had to come to terms with it before and I found myself saying that I wasn't going to come to terms with it. I was going to have a lover and a friend. *Sue*

Frequently, they involve the issues raised in earlier chapters.

From my father it was a feeling that the only thing that would be acceptable in life was to be an academic success – the emotional personal growth side of life didn't come into it at all. And from my mother, realising that I was more 'intelligent', academic and strong than her, but having to fall in with her view of the world. I felt that I didn't acknowledge the conflict with my mother because I was too busy fighting my father, which was an obvious conflict – the academic thing – it was tangible in a way that the one with my mother wasn't. *Theresa*

Women's lives are filled with contradictions. It is hardly surprising that we have not resolved all of them. Somehow we have to find a comfortable balance between our feelings and our thoughts; a comfortable balance that meets our need for closeness and our need for separateness.

103

I am afraid of being hurt, of being laughed at, being made the fool . . . I feel I don't think the right things, don't read the right things, don't listen to the right kind of music . . . so I rush and listen, read and think. I feel unprepared to speak about anything because I haven't decided what I think or like. I feel very inadequate. I want my ideas to be my own, to have thought them out myself. I have been thinking and put my feelings to one side – now *they* are trying to catch up.

Marie, 28 May 1978

Perhaps contradictions reside individually, and conflict is what happens when our own contradictions meet someone else's? Conflict between two people makes it easier to see the two opposing points of view. Sometimes in the heat of an argument, we can find ourselves arguing a point of view that is much more extreme than our own position. Strong feelings often push people to adopt stance they might not otherwise hold. This polarisation can stop any resolution from being made.

Women are not taught how to deal with conflict. We tend to be the peacemakers and often purposely try and defuse conflicts.

I thought my mum was a perfect mum. She always got round and the did the job, she didn't mind hard work, I thought that's what men like, that's what I'll be like and that's what I was like to an extent, anything for a quiet life . . . well, providing it's not too much against what I want! But then I'd speak up, she wouldn't. *Janice*

The rationale for this tactic is 'the quiet life'.

In reality, perhaps women give up struggling because we so often lose. We ask, is it worth the effort? We think it is easier if we do it ourselves. Maybe in the short term, but in time we come to either resent putting our own feelings to one side or we don't feel ourselves anymore.

One of the strongest conflicts I have is when I get this immense desire to express the pain and outrage I feel about it, which wells up in quite an overwhelming way and what happens is that a part of me says 'No, you can't do that. You've got to keep a stiff upper lip, you mustn't give in to that, you mustn't

104

feel distressed.' But, a very strong part of me is saying: 'You've every right to feel outraged and you must express it.' *Caroline*

It is important too, that we make decisions about where to draw the line. As women, we're not taught *how* to draw the line let alone *where*. We need to be clear about what we want, first in our own minds, and then, be able to put those thoughts into words and, if need be, beck those words up with action. Even then there is no guarantee of success.

What I need to do is to sit down and work out for myself what I want, because at the moment, I'm not even acknowledging to myself what I want, never mind to anyone else.

Lucy, September 1975

We also need to be aware of being drawn into other people's conflicts. There are times when it is best to try and avoid the disagreement, although we frequently have no choice about this as we are the focus for anger. This is especially true of violence in the home. This does not mean you don't try to sort it out for yourself. Sometimes open confrontation is not the best way.

I got to the stage where I couldn't face up to my husband, I just didn't want to know. I walked away once during an argument. I think I'd do it again if it ever happened. I'd walk away. I just can't stand arguments. *Lyn*

We may need to remind ourselves why we made the original decision to leave. Once out of a depressing environment we can forget what prompted us to get out and give it up.

Sometimes of a weekend when I'm here, I think to myself, I'd be doing so and so now . . . then I think afterwards . . . just think what you'd be doing . . . cooking, washing, cleaning and I think, oooh, I'd rather be here, in my place, cleaning out the guinea pigs and eating a bag of sweets. *Janice*

We disagree with each other in the hope of finding agreement. Sometimes we can forget that and seem to be fighting for no apparent reason. Frequently, there can be no agreement and this represents a breakdown in the relationship. Irreconcilable differences are considered legitimate grounds for divorce.

> I find it very hard now with my dad. You know, I gave him so
> many chances as a child. Give him one more chance he might
> change.
> I don't think I'll ever get over what happened. It doesn't stop
> with me but there are my children to think of . . . they'll never
> stay in that house so long as he's under the roof. People don't
> understand that . . . but I know what he's like. He'll never
> change. Spots on a leopard don't change . . . neither will he.
>
> *Janice*

We can also find ourselves in conflict with an institution or
some other abstract construction like an ideal. Although we may
feel furious with the person behind the glass in the dole office (and
perhaps rightly so), it can also be a fury we feel for what they
represent. Fighting with bureaucracy is terribly demoralising,
often coupled with little chance of success. The whole set-up is
precisely that – a set-up, so that there is a maximum distance
between you and the man (usually) at the top. As long as you
conform, institutions can seem amazingly benign, but step out
of line (the line again) and you can wonder what hit you! Now
you know, it's probably an institution – hospital, school,
government . . .

There are many institutions that remain invisible. They
become visible when you try to do something that makes
complete sense to you but the reaction you receive seems out of
proportion to what you are doing. In the past this may be seen as
going against convention. Yet a construction like 'convention'
hides the massive and complex system that maintains, advocates
and reinforces conformity. Feminists have renamed many
'conventions' as institutions. For example, racism is institutionalised. The fact that legislation exists to prevent it happening is an
indicator of its accepted pervasiveness. For black women, rules
are made to include them which indicate they are often not even
considered to be part of the system.

Loving another woman could mean losing your job or your
children. This reaction is not merely a punishment for being
unconventional but also a reaction that indicates you are a threat
to an institution, in this case, heterosexuality.

Conflict in relation to ideals is tinged with sadness. It usually

106

means we must continually strive to realise our ideals, or relinquish something we cherish. We will constantly need to balance reality with our dreams. But ideals, like institutions, seem to materialise from nowhere. We need to feel able to set our own ideals.

I get depressed about the fact that nowadays in our society, people's relationships don't last very well. Not just lesbian relationships but heterosexual relationships also. If they have children they sometimes stay together a bit longer. I know why it is – I can rationalise it – but that conflicts with all the romantic stuff you were taught as a child. *Sue*

If a conflict is hidden or difficult to resolve, our justifiable angry feelings have no place to go. We can turn them inwards. If we do try to stand up for ourselves, we may experience constant defeat, especially when we confront those more powerful than ourselves. For women, as second-class citizens, this means just about everybody! The notable exception being that in our society children are seen as less powerful than adults. At times, women can have power over children. At other times they, too, are treated like children.

If we do not act for ourselves, we can find that we have to react to others and are constantly being caught off-guard.

I feel full of self-doubt again, and my neck is stiff. I hate the feeling that I don't really know what is going on – that I'm not in control. I'm afraid of responsibility – feel like I'm going with what everyone else wants, but I can't see anything else to do.
Lucy, September 1975

We can see our energy being directed into matters that are deemed trivial, fights that don't resolve anything or battles we have no hope of winning. In the end we may be confronted with our own powerlessness.

One of the strongest senses I have about depression at this stage is that it doesn't matter how much I fight and how much I try to acknowledge my own worth, I can still feel negated by the action of others. *Caroline*

Longstanding and unresolved conflict can contribute to depression. If you have been feeling down you are much less able to cope with conflict of any kind. However, it is difficult to know which comes first, depression or conflict. Perhaps that is not an important question. Suffice it to say they know each other well.

When you're depressed you don't want to be a fighter. I know I didn't, I wanted to give up. *Janice*

When you're depressed you can't fight what anyone says about you. You think it's all true and you're never right. *Elizabeth*

It is hard to struggle when we don't know what we are struggling for. How can we be assertive when we have so many other people's feelings to consider? When we don't think we are worth it? The voice that asks, 'What about me, my feelings, my needs?' is only a whisper.

How can we trust ourselves when we don't know our own thoughts or feelings? Without discussion, it can take a long time before some conflicts come to light. That light is only one of recognition; we then need to struggle for a resolution. Being in control of our lives and making conscious choices isn't necessarily any easier. It demands a responsibility for ourselves. Filled with conceptions that work directly against us feeling confident in our decisions, we do hesitate or get stuck.

Accumulated stress makes us more vulnerable to depression. This can be due to fatigue. The tiredness we feel can seem odd given the struggles are often not visible.

I have spent many hours wondering why I became depressed. It was obviously to some extent a build-up of traumatic experiences. I didn't have one moment when I became depressed. But looking back now I can see that the build-up was the pressure of all the things I was trying to cope with. *Margaret*

Many women struggle because they have no choice. There are very real pressing financial problems especially for single-parent families. It is very draining to be using all your energy just to keep up, never mind get on top of things.

When I am depressed I have this recurring dream about a big

dark hole. It keeps getting wider or smaller. I have to keep eating these slops at the bottom – things I don't want to eat. And there are all these people laughing at me. There's this wall I have to climb up and sometimes I would be in the clouds free from all of it – but sometimes I wouldn't be – I'd be very near the top or right down the bottom, drowning in the fluid at the bottom, choking on it. *Elizabeth*

Depression can arise when past feelings are reactivated by present circumstances. If we cannot recognise the connection between the past and present situations, the depression can seem incongruous.

In spite of the love and care I was getting, my mind was in torment. I missed my children so much. I was being treated by the army doctors for depression. Again, that word depression. How can that word describe what I was going through? I would remember my childhood and how my mind was scarred by feeling that nobody cared about me. I would worry that my children were experiencing the same feelings. *Chris*

There can be very obvious similarities between and past and present, which make it easier for us to spot them. For example, if you have been raped or sexually abused as a child, it is possible you will find other sexual relationships difficult. Your depression may signal some unfinished business. It is also important that we try to feel in control of our past experiences not the other way round as it often feels – our past experiences controlling us. No doubt they do affect the present. But it need not be only negatively. They can give us courage and strength. We can learn from them and from those of other women when they are shared. Growing up and leaving experiences behind is, or can be, a flight from facing the pain of some of the experiences. Yet, they can come back to haunt us. It seems unspoken thoughts or feelings collect in our minds, waiting to be let out or failing that, to escape. They can brew up like storms and break when we least expect them. Frequently, this is because we are not guarding against these feelings. It can also be when we have lost control in another way like being very angry, and these old feelings have an opportunity to escape. It is not so unusual to start being furious and then find yourself crying in despair, leaving the original anger behind.

It would be nice if we could 'get over things' once and for all, but we don't. It may be different aspects we deal with each time. It is important that we feel safe enough to express our hurt feelings. A lot of the time, to do so, would have impeded our survival. It can be some time later that we *feel* what has happened.

> All the time I was at home I could hide it . . . there were different things to do . . . lots of people to hide it from. I hid it untik I left home and then I just couldn't control it any more. Being on your own you could just sit and stew all the time. There was nothing to occupy yourself unless you forced yourself . . . the whole bloody thing just exploded out of proportion. *Janice*

Often when the immediate crisis has passed and we do have time to think about what has happened, the overriding feeling we have is guilt. It is appropriate for guilt to come into a discussion on collapse. It is truly a crippling emotion. Guilt seems to motivate us to do things. This idea must be challenged. Guilt is about taking responsibility but in a totally negative way. It is about blaming. The more we do out of guilt the *more* guilty we become because our actions can only confirm our guilt, not remove it.

> I just felt I have to help out. It made me feel good. Maybe I felt guilty and doing these things would hide my guilt. I used to get blamed for most of the things that happened and trying to do things that we were good was a way of trying to get them to think better of me. It's amazing how I still feel compelled to do these things. I see it now as trying to give my mother an easier life. I don't believe things were my fault any more. I want to make up for what I didn't have by giving to mum and my younger sisters. *Janice*

It is important for us to distinguish between remorse and guilt. The former is a more constructive feeling which helps us move on. It leaves us positively responsible and able to redress the situation.

If you feel sorry for the way you treated someone, sorrow helps you to treat them differently next time . . . it's good to have a conscience but when your conscience goes all out of proportion, that, I think, is depression. It gets out of hand. You criticise yourself over everything. That's not conscience, that's going *too* far! *Elizabeth*

Delayed reactions seem odd because they occur some time after the seeming run of bad luck or the crisis. We can be so busy caring for others that we forgot or don't have time to care for ourselves. It is difficult to get the support or space we need when the reason seems so far in the past. 'The woman who always copes' can find it difficult not only to get the support she needs but also to use it when its offered.

I could never cry about anything. After being attacked in an alleyway, I still had to go to school the next day just to show them that I was tough. I never gave in. I cried on my own at home. I could never cry out openly if anybody was there. *Janice*

Loneliness bothers me because I think it is a weakness in me as an individual that I cannot exist independently on my own. And, of course, I cannot tolerate weakness in anyone, most of all in myself. If I admit my loneliness, it is still up to me to remedy it.

Marie, September 1975

There is an incipient type of depression that seems to creep up on you gradually. It can be hidden from most people you know until the sad feelings seem to take over completely. The 'smiling depression' hides our feelings of worthlessness and despair for a time.

At one time I didn't really feel that anybody loved me – not even my parents . . . I just couldn't feel that anyone could love such a horrible, useless failure of person as me. Now that is the real depths of depression. *Elizabeth*

We can feel even if people show they care that we are not deserving of that care. We can hide certain emotions that do not fit in with the popular images of women. We can feel that there are parts of ourselves that are so awful that others would be terrified, shocked or disgusted to see them.

111

You are a little girl inside who is frightened of most things but who acts brave. You don't want anyone to know though, because then they might not like you. *Marie, 28 May 1978*

Woke up feeling really scared of waking up. I am frightened – scared – of being alone. Realising how little I can fully be myself with people. Feeling that I will be put down, disliked, not wanted, if I show the full strength of my feelings.

Lucy, September 1975

We smile politely even when we don't want to smile. It is very painful to think that someone who loves you cannot even see beneath a polite smile. We can feel that what we receive is for this false front we put on to please and if we were our real selves we would not be liked. As we do not value ourselves it is difficult to see what others value in us.

At other times, people may make it very clear what they value in us and make it exceedingly difficult for us to express emotions that do not conform to their picture of us.

He would say, 'You're a strong girl, you can cope' and I used to think, 'I am a strong girl, I can cope', when all the time I was crying out, 'I don't want to be strong' . . . I didn't . . . I wanted to break down and cry. I wanted to say to my mother, 'I can't cope really'. *Janice*

We can also feel depressed after achieving something we thought we have always wanted. The blueprint that serves as a model to us all does not necessarily offer the rewards some of us may have expected from it. When our actual experience of something doesn't measure up to our expectation of it, we can become more than disappointed. Depression is more likely to occur if the experience is one in which you have invested a lot of personal energy.

I'm not prepared to just sit back and say, 'I see, that's what's happened – I have to accept it.' An enormous amount of energy even now – and it's nearly two and a half years since my husband left – an enormous amount of energy is meshed into a feeling of despair that something quite earth-shattering to me can occur and yet I have absolutely no choice, as I perceive it,

112

than to go with the rest of the world which says: 'Ah well, these things happen. Time will heal. You'll get used to it.' And things of that kind. *Caroline*

If what we have worked towards is not as we expected, or it is not as fulfilling as we might like it to be, we can feel very guilty about the feelings of disappointment or dissatisfaction that we have. This guilt can make us work harder to hide what we think are unreasonable feelings. Sometimes we can achieve the goals we have set for ourselves and having reached them, think, 'Is this it?' It can be very puzzling to feel depressed despite having the things you thought you always wanted. There isn't a complaints department for ideals that don't measure up.

They say the best days of your life are your schooldays. They were the unhappiest days of my life. My school work suffered for it. I couldn't take any 'O' levels because I couldn't cope with the work. Going home of a nightime – with a big family – there was too much for me to do. No time for studying. There was no quiet space in the house to study because I have younger sisters. *Janice*

Sometimes we can realise that we have been fooling ourselves all along that things are different now. We think we ought not to feel as we did with a change in our life circumstances. We bring with us a history of experiences that shapes our present perception of our lives. Crises can make us re-evaluate our life situations and strengthen our resolve to stick out for what we want.

However, after more breakdowns and with a psychiatrist's advice, I filed for divorce. I was very confused and upset at that time and didn't know if I could face life alone. I sorted my mind out a bit and then realised that I had always been alone . . . as a child, an adolescent and, strangely enough, as a married woman. *Chris*

Criticial points can help identify a process that could otherwise go unnoticed.

I'm a giver. I always seem to meet men who are takers. I've

never met one who is both. I can do both but I've never met anyone who can do both with me.

If I can't find somebody (I know I'll never find the perfect match – nobody will) that can give as well as take, then – I've got my flat, I'm happy and I don't care ... if I can't have some of the things in life I want ... I've gone through a lot – I want something; if I can't have a few rewards then I'll make my own rewards. *Janice*

A bout of depression in a way makes it possible for us to get the comfort we need. We get space to ourselves because we are unable to give to anyone else. Depression can be a way of getting a balance. The care we need from others is more forthcoming when the precipitant for the depression is obvious – like a traumatic event. The contradictions and conflicts described in this chapter are not so easily identifiable. Fatigue, lack of recognition or the guilt we experience for having doubts or negative feelings can lead to collapse. Yet, what could be a bout of depression often becomes a way of life.

8
A Way of Life

Often without realising it, a sameness or predictability creeps into our lives. We develop routines or patterns that make living seem easier. Routines do save our energy and ideally allow us to be more creative in other aspects of our lives. We may not question those patterns unless a crisis occurs which forces us to reconsider our 'ways'. A crisis point makes it possible for us to change. We can find new patterns of behaviour or we may return to patterns of behaviour that have been successful in the past.

Sameness is in some ways reassuring and comforting. Anything new takes a while to get used to. In our lives there is a natural and expected resistance to change. This chapter is about examining why women find it difficult to change once depressed. It is important to remember that change does not happen in isolation. If we change, others might change too; our new actions will encourage different reactions. Unfortunately, not all of them will be positive, but knowing this, we can anticipate and not be daunted. Initially, disapproving reactions are confirmation that you have indeed changed!

Change is related to the issue of control which we discussed earlier. If we are being, or feel, controlled, we often lose sight of our power to make choices for ourselves. Depression is very controlling and seems to have a momentum all its own. Yet we must realise where that momentum originates. Experiencing depression as an illness that comes from nowhere, denies the very real factors that influence and affect all of us. Yet, we are often encouraged to do just that . . . to see ourselves as ill, sick and suffering passively from depression. This potentially fatal 'illness' can become, ironically, a 'way of life'.

Of the roles available to us as women, the languishing melancholic has a long history. It is romanticised in books and films. In the past, it was even fashionable for women to be

virtually invalid! Yet for those of us whose daily lives are filled with despair, this 'role' has no glamour. For those women who live with disability, there is no romance in that reality.

An Epidemic?

Women, in our thousands, are depressed to such an extent that many of us are on daily dosages of drugs to cope with our lives.[1] Research indicates that women receive more prescriptions than men in all classes of drugs, especially psychotropic drugs. Women also use them for longer. You are more likely to be prescribed tablets if you are retired, unemployed, at home or a middle-aged woman. It is also interesting that women who have paid work or other activities that take them out of the house are less likely to use psychotropic drugs.

In a survey done in Winnipeg, Canada, 20 per cent of women reported using drugs in the two weeks prior to the study.[2] The findings that women are more likely to be depressed and prescribed psychotropic drugs, are more than just interesting facts. There is no mention of an epidemic of depression sweeping the country. We must ask why?

116

Women can be depressed and manage to carry on with the daily routine of their lives. Things like housework are boring and require little concentration.[3] No comments are made about how nicely the house is tidied; the clothes are ironed; the meal cooked . . . Because our own needs frequently come at the bottom of the list, it can be easy to stop caring for ourselves. You may not eat properly or not bother to cook for yourself. You may feel you haven't had a night's sleep in ages, especially if you have young children.

We can quite easily slip into depressing lifestyles. If our eating and sleeping habits are very poor, we will soon begin to feel tired and run down all of the time. We forget what it feels like to be on top of things. It becomes as if 'I've been down so long, it looks like up to me' and worst of all, we get used to feeling that way. We even start to think it's normal and natural for women to feel like this all of the time.

Depression is incorporated into the fabric of women's lives. It is considered perfectly normal for a woman to feel depressed once a month with her period, to be blue after having a baby, or at the silently whispered 'change'. Men do not have these equivalents because they are all related to our hormones. This connection to our biology paves the way for the 'natural predisposition' explanation of depression. But the naturalness of our depressed state doesn't stop at the mercy of our hormones. It is considered perfectly 'natural' for women to feel depressed when the children go to school, leave home or when a relationship finishes.

Equally expected is the depression for being 'past it', 'on the shelf' and on the way to assumed lonely spinsterhood. Here the facts contradict 'nature', for the single woman remains the healthiest psychologically. While 'marriage' acts as a protective factor for men, it has a detrimental effect on women's mental health.[4] Emile Durkheim noted that the highest rate of suicide in women was among childless wives. He believed that children offered women more protection than men because they gave them more happiness.[5] However, it is thought that between ten and thirty per cent of women experience depression following the birth of their child.[6] Additionally, George Brown and Tirril Harris postulate that children, far from making women happy, just prevented them from killing themselves.[7]

Once in a depressing situation (and it rarely is the situation, but ourself, that is perceived as depressing), it is very difficult to change especially when we are feeling bad about ourselves. How we are contained in these depressing situations, which will differ for each of us, is very complex.

Firstly, we think it is natural to feel the way we do. If we talk about our feelings to our friends, who are probably in a similar situation, we may discover we all feel the same. This can sometimes confirm our feelings that it *is* natural to feel this way as everyone else does. It can also be a tremendous relief to realise it isn't just you who feels that way. This confirmation could make you more accepting of a situation, rather than motivate you to change it.

If you are the only one who expresses dissatisfaction, you may stop talking about it because it sets you apart from your friends. It can make you think: 'There must be something wrong with me that I'm not enjoying what everybody else does.' You can then start feeling alienated from your friends.

Breaking Down

In order to get recognition for our depressed feelings, the situation will have to deteriorate badly. We don't eat, get out of bed, get dressed, or bother about our appearance. For those who live alone, these things may never be recognised. The news of, in particular, older people being found dead in their flats after many days or weeks, is a tragic reminder of isolation.

In relationships or families, recognition often only comes when we do not do what we usually do. This can be making the meals, doing the laundry, taking care of the kids, having sex . . . Once the work women do routinely grinds to a halt, those around must find ways of managing that work. This 'breakdown' rarely gets more care for the woman herself. It merely provides a break, usually brief, from that work. Sometimes the work is saved for her, put to one side so it will be there when she is 'feeling up to it'. For some women it isn't worth being ill because there is too much to do when they get better.

I knew I needed to see somebody . . . nobody believed me . . . they sort of thought, 'Oh, she needs to see somebody as much as I do' . . . but I think I knew in the back of my mind that I was at the point where I needed something or someone to help me. If I didn't get it soon I would go mad, or I would have a nervous

118

breakdown right in the middle of the street . . . I would break down and cry. *Janice*

If you decide you are not coping or do not feel right, the first place you may go to is your GP, frequently male.[8] In the time alloted, you barely have time to articulate feelings or symptoms that are vague and distressing. If you go often enough, complaining of vague discomforts, nervousness, insomnia . . . sooner or later a course of anti-depressants or a tranquilliser will be prescribed. It will seem like your efforts have been rewarded. There *is* something wrong with you and this is the cure. Little pills three times a day.

Unfortunately, nothing could be further from the truth. Some women will improve with tablets. A large portion of their improvement will be due to the 'placebo effect'. This means the expectation of feeling better is responsible for the change, not the actual tablets themselves. For the vast majority, the tablets will only mask feelings and further complicate the problem with drug addiction. The real problem can remain undiscussed.

The first time I was given anti-depressants was *after* the first time I tried to commit suicide. I had been feeling very depressed for a long time but nobody took any notice . . . *Chris*

The 'help-seeking behaviour' that women display is tolerated by the medical profession to a certain extent, after which we become 'managed'. If we go to our doctors with some idea about what is wrong, we are often discouraged from doing so. We are not only discouraged from diagnosing our problems but also from finding out about them. In our interactions with the medical profession, all too often women are not taken seriously.[9] Very real legitimate illnesses are labelled 'hysterical' and equally, real feelings of frustration, despair and depression are met with either a prescription of valium or a pull-yourself-together approach. Sometimes the GP will refer you on to a psychiatrist (also usually male). All too often, psychiatry's cure is no different than your GP's – pills!

I thought at long last help, but then I thought to myself, people will think I'm mad . . . you know, regular help, but I didn't care. It may sound silly but I felt proud because somebody had

119

noticed. I got the notice I needed and it was the right kind of notice, and the right kind of help. *Janice*

The effects of poverty, racism and sexism impact on women's physical and mental well being. Black women are more likely to be misdiagnosed and offered medication and ECT than their white counterparts,[10] and their specific needs are often not addressed. Multiple discrimination and disadvantage are likely to decrease the likelihood of the state sector providing a relevant and sensitive mental health service.[11] Many women who have felt that their needs have not been met have turned to alternative therapies, self-help groups and counsellors they have found for themselves rather than use state provisions.

Pills and alcohol can help make life seem easier. With them there is an absence of feeling. The ensuing numbness is a relief of sorts. Yet often it is not relief women are looking for but a release. Sometimes the only way out seems to be suicide.

The doctors never used the word despair; perhaps if they used this word it would prove that they were able to understand better what is going on inside me. At my worst, utter and total despair . . . the word incorporates many of the feelings, the frustrations, the feelings of inadequacy, the inability to cope, the confusion one feels, the lack of interest in anything or anyone around you. In my case all these feelings built up 'til there seems no point in going on living. The result many, many times is attempted suicide. *Chris*

An overdose is a powerful way of making others take notice of the real intensity of our feelings. But it is done with the highest possible price tag attached – our lives – and often the people around us do not understand our self-harming messages. Overdosing, cutting, drinking, and other forms of self-injurious behaviour can seem like the only way of managing the pain we feel. For the people around you, it is painful to watch the slow self-destruction.

Tyler struggled the majority of her life with depression among other things. It didn't seem to matter what we, her friends, did – nothing seemed to make anything better. She withdrew from us and I certainly withdrew from her. I began mourning her

120

long before she actually died. In the last few years, it was hard to keep conversations going. All we seemed to talk about was how bad she felt, how hopeless her life was and how many drugs she was taking (all prescribed I might add). There would be odd moments when she would ask how I was and I would be caught off balance. She was, at her best, wonderfully funny and sensitive. She possessed a great deal of insight and was very helpful when it came to other people's problems. But her own just piled up on top of her, weighing her down with unbearable pain and distress. I suppose in the end I felt like she felt in relation to her own family – impotent, frustrated, unable to change their views, angry at the futility and the waste. But I could withdraw. She just couldn't cut herself off. She started killing herself when she was very young, twelve or thirteen, cutting away at herself as if this act would free her from her real nightmare. Finally last year, her body just gave out.

I think she struggled with being visible in her family. Her pain at home was always made invisible as was her death. Some explanation will have been thought up which bears little resemblance to the truth. Yet she was never invisible to me and I miss her. *Marie*

Hospitalisation

Being hospitalised, although it provides some respite from daily chores, means the label 'psychiatric' will be well and truly fixed round our necks. All our future behaviour will be construed around this knowledge; that we 'have trouble with our nerves'. As psychiatric patients, whether in-patients or out-patients, women are more vulnerable.[12] Additionally, the issue of female in-patients' safety has not been critically addressed. Many women who spend time as in-patients report being very frightened and experience direct sexual harassment from some of the male in-patients. Women can easily become 'victimised', 'infantalised' (being made into permanent children), or institutionalised. These processes are related to our everyday experiences as women in that they are situations where control is not negotiable. It is not surprising that some of us find ourselves playing, or perhaps even choose to play out these roles more permanently. Finally we have found something we do well! Our careers as mental patients are lived out in stunning silence.

Middle-class women are more likely to escape hospitalisation, as well as the labelling process. When hospitalised, women with the privileges based on class, white skin and education, will be treated differently. Psychiatric patients are accorded little respect or dignity. Psychiatry is among the least valued medical speciality, along with mental handicap and the care of the elderly. This only reflects the attitudes of the dominant culture.

Within the therapeutic context of hospital and treatment, women are open to all sorts of abuse. We can be (and no doubt are) sexually abused by doctors, therapists, male nurses and male patients. Our vulnerabilities can be exploited all the more while under their care. Our right to recourse is even more diminished. Who would believe a mental patient? Just as rape, sexual abuse of children, sexual harassment at work have been brought out in the open, it is of equal importance that the sexual abuse of women by their psychiatric caretakers be spoken about.

Research in America[13] in 1973 indicated that 10 per cent of psychiatrists admitted to sexual activities with their patients; 5 per cent including sexual intercourse. In the same study, 50 per cent of the psychiatrists acknowledged that they had non-erotic (?) physical behaviour such as hugging, kissing and touching with their patients. These were all *voluntary* disclosures by the psychiatrists.

Not surprisingly similar findings have been made in Britain.[14] This has prompted the British Psychological Society to develop clear policies on ethical issues relating to sexual harassment and worker–client relationships.[15] There are also special ethical issues to consider when working within closed community groups where the likelihood of a therapist from the same closed group, knowing and/or coming into contact socially with their client is much higher.[16] The Prevention of Professional Abuse Network (POPAN) exists to support women who have been sexually abused by their therapists. The implications of this research are very disturbing. The woman who is depressed and desperately needing care and affection is an easy target for sexual exploitation. The abuse of trust this represents is not only unethical, it is also damaging.[17]

A Way of Life?

We may ask why it is that we do not change, what is it that keeps us from changing? There is the silence. This silence is maintained by the isolation of women especially if we are depressed.

> Although women ourselves have not been responsible for the building of walls between us, for the intense privatisation of our experiences of pain, we can exercise a choice about whether to allow these walls to continue to separate us, or whether to use our combined strength to bring them down. This obviously applies to lots of barriers – those of race, class, sexuality and so on – as well as to those related to mental illness. I have never really thought of it in this way before, but I really do feel separated off, behind some sort of enclosure, from most of the women I know.[18]

This wall around us not only stops more painful feelings coming in, but also discourages support, should it be there.

We accept depression as our fault. We experience self-blame. In fact, self-blame is considered a symptom of the depression. When we have taken in what we have been told by others (i.e. it is your fault), this is twisted around and said to have come from us in the first place, as a symptom of our 'illness'. Having accepted the blame for depression, we are then denied the responsibility to deal with it. 'Experts' take over as we are deemed clearly not able to deal with what we have brought on ourselves. We are not given information that may help us understand our feelings. We are prepared from an early age to expect depression to be a part of our lives, if only periodically (so to speak!).

When, and if, we pluck up the courage to seek help, we are often not taken seriously. Sometimes we even feel guilty about feeling depressed!

> I think feeling guilty when I was depressed was one thing that kept it in the dark so long . . . I didn't think I had the right to feel depressed. *Janice*

Payoffs

For some individual women and couples, there may be benefits from a woman's depression. It is an incredible indictment of women's lives, that we may get more reward for being 'sick' than we do otherwise. In some relationships one person must occupy the depressed position. In heterosexual couplings it is often the woman. This pattern is called the 'Doll's House Marriage'. The name is taken from Ibsen's play where he describes one such marriage. In this kind of relationship only one person can be well. If the 'up' position is not shared equally between two people, over time, the balance of power does shift in favour of the 'stronger' partner.

Your friends may take more notice of you when you are depressed than when you are well. (Unfortunately, the reverse is more likely to be true. So we often feel we have to keep our depressed feelings hidden lest our friends abandon us.) It is believed that people can stay depressed because they enjoy being taken care of and discover that being depressed has more benefits than disadvantages.

In the 'helping' professions this is often termed 'secondary gain'. Most frequently, it is viewed from the position of the person identified as the patient, without recognising that others may get payoffs too and undoubtedly do. For example, it may make your partner feel stronger when you are weepy and dependent on her or him. Many relationships operate within fixed roles. Most function with one person in the 'down position' (usually a woman in heterosexual relationships). One person's strength is often at the expense of the others. The gains someone else can get from your depression can encourage them to maintain the relationship as it is, for their own personal reasons.[19]

There are obvious benefits for drug companies when the 'treatment of choice' is the prescription of tablets. Lots of money is put into advertising, trying to influence the prescribing practices of doctors. Most advertisement for tranquillisers and anti-depressants make their message and audience very clear. They usually picture a woman slumped over a chair or at the kitchen sink! . . . the 'before drugs' pose. The 'after drugs' pose is of her smiling happily with her family.[20]

Despite growing bad press, psychotropic drugs do remain fashionable and project powerful images that they will make things better. For example, the most recent wonder drug, Prozac, which has received both good and bad press, was said to be taken by the Princess of Wales. This almost confirms that it must indeed be magical!

The benefits to society of having chemical straitjackets available through the local family doctor means that a powerful social control mechanism is regularly being employed. Complainers, usually women, are being silenced.

> Valium helps to ease the pain away, (you give me)
> Valium, help me cope another day, (you give me)
> Valium when it's all too much to bear, but
> It won't pay the bills, it won't cure my ills, it'll teach me not
> to care.[21]

The power of our complaints is being diluted not only by chemicals but also by the insidious labelling procedure gong on in every GP's surgery and psychiatric clinic. Formally it is known as diagnosis. The 'manipulative patient' joins ranks with the 'over-anxious mother', 'castrating bitch' and 'nagging wife', to name but a few of the caricatures of female psycho-pathology. All of these labels are essentially women hating. Manipulative men are seen as being positively assertive and masterful. Over-anxious fathers, castrating dogs and nagging husbands exist but certainly are not commonly used epithets.

The oppression in every aspect of women's lives is real and in turn, creates real distress and unhappiness. We are not encouraged to understand the problems in our lives as the manifestation of male dominance. Instead, we are encouraged to believe that our problems are of our own making. Our complaints about our circumstances are not considered to be justified but taken as admission of our own incompetence. 'Everyone else is happy, what's wrong with me?' Eventually no one needs to say it to us, because we say it to ourselves.

Our justifiable need for recognition and caring can become so distorted that we will take on destructive and demeaning roles to get these needs fulfilled. Our economic dependence, usually on men (and some of us are only a male partner away from financial hardship) and the lack of real alternatives for women, means we often feel obliged to do things for our keep, despite the psychological cost. If we are economically dependent on the State, we are kept on the edge of poverty and then expected to feel grateful for 'free' money.

For many of us, it is not one bout of depression but a continuous battle. Sometimes every time we pull ourselves up out of one, something happens and we find ourselves back down again.

It still gets me down every time I think I can see a light ahead of me, some hope even if it's only for a couple of years, there's some hope there and something keeps cropping up and setting me back down. I think the only thing I've ever searched for is peace of mind but I don't think I'm ever going to get it.

> Where have I been?
> To hell and back.
> Why did I have to suffer?
> What did I lack?
> Now that I'm accustomed
> To taking the blows,
> Where am I going?
> God only knows.
>
> *Chris*

Depressing lifestyles are often not a choice but a fact of life. Poverty affects women disproportionately to men with many women being only a male partner away from the poverty line. It creates depressing living situations, which at their worst can lead to homelessness. Many young women leave their homes to escape from sexual abuse and live on the streets where they are extremely vulnerable to the sex industry which will exploit their situation further. Homelessness brings a host of practical problems about meeting basic needs for shelter, food and good medical care. Looking after yourself on the streets is survival at its bleakest. Many of the homeless have mental health problems that would be dramatically improved by dealing with the depressing conditions in which they live.

Trying to create new alternatives for ourselves requires inner vision, courage and strength. It also means we need to locate the depressing factors in our lives rather than believing them to come solely from ourselves. It is difficult to disentangle what *is* our responsibility. We need to learn what is reasonable and practical to expect both from ourselves and others. We are not taught how to negotiate freely to get our needs met.

Responsibility for ourselves is removed at a young age. We are not told to 'stand tall like a man' but 'to sit pretty like a woman', and for many of us there we sit, with the frozen face of smiling depression, coping on the outside while dying on the inside.

126

PART TWO

9
Coping with Depression
Should I Do Anything?

'I feel down today but if I don't think about it too much I'll feel better tomorrow.' Sometimes this works. Distracting oneself, getting on with things, or trying to concentrate on something other than awful feelings can allow the mood to pass; whereas concentrating on being depressed may sometimes seem to feed it and allow it to become worse.

> Depression is something that has to be fought hard with all the energy at your disposal. What you have to do is nip depression in the bud before it takes hold of you and tries to destroy you.
>
> *Elizabeth*

But often this is easier said than done. If you try to ignore or push away the bad feelings they seem to fight back harder. Or they go away for a while and then hit you later.

Before you can decide whether to do anything about depression it is essential to recognise that you are feeling depressed. This may sound obvious but it is often hard to do. We can keep ourselves busy with activities to avoid facing unhappiness. This may be because we are afraid the bad feelings will overwhelm us if we allow them to exist. Or it may be that we believe we have no right to feel bad because there is no immediately apparent reason for it. We desperately try to make things all right by doing all sorts of things for other people.

> For years I was depressed most of the time but I don't think I acknowledged it because I didn't think I would be able to cope with my life if I did. I worked furiously and put my energy into activities. From time to time I cracked with physical

exhaustion and I'd cry a lot then and realise I was actually very unhappy. *Theresa*

The first step is always to admit to yourself that you are feeling awful. Only then can you begin to work out what you might do about it. To take this step requires some faith that others will be there to support you if you cannot cope. This is an enormous risk for many of us. Unfortunately such support is not always available. In the following chapters we shall be discussing ways to look for help outside your immediate circle of friends and family, as well as ways to build up the support we need from each other. In this chapter we shall talk about ways of coping with the different aspects of depression. We shall make suggestions about some of the ways that we can help ourselves and our friends. There is no one answer for all women at all times. We need to get to know ourselves and our moods over time and try different ways of coping, so that we can discover what works best for each one of us.

Ways of Helping Yourself

Your Needs are Important

The first difficulty in helping ourselves with depression is that when we are depressed we feel worthless. We feel that we are no good and that we do not deserve anything good to happen to us. Feeling that we do not deserve anything makes it difficult to even start to help ourselves or to look for help. It can be like trying to pull yourself up by your own boot straps.

You have to break out of this vicious circle somehow. To be able to say 'my needs are important' may be incredibly difficult when you are depressed. But this is what you have to do. Sometimes the first step may happen through a friend noticing that you are unhappy. 'You don't seem to be yourself – what's wrong?' Even if you deny this at the time you may think about it later. At some point you have to be brave enough to say to yourself, 'If I'm feeling bad, there must be something wrong that matters a lot to me, even if other people don't recognise it!'

So the first step is to acknowledge that *you* as a person are important. You do not deserve to be depressed. You deserve to feel better. You deserve to get some help if you need it. You have

probably given a great deal to other people in your life and now is
a time when you need something for yourself.

Give Yourself Time

Once you are prepared to admit to feeling depressed your first
impulse may be to look for a quick way out of it. In our culture we
expect instant cures or panaceas. We panic at the idea of taking
time. With depression we need to give ourselves time to deal with
it. Feeling depressed is a sign that something is not right in your
life. It is going to take time to find out what is wrong before you
can begin to think how to put it right.

   You need to give yourself time to look at your feelings. At first your depression may seem to be an enormous cloud of heaviness and misery hanging over you, or a deep hole swallowing you up or dragging you down. It may seem impossible to put any words to it. If you can face it, you will find that you are experiencing a mixture of feelings. You may be feeling sadness, anger, guilt, anxiety, inadequacy or loneliness. Any combination of feelings can be mixed up to produce this heavy cloud and it is only gradually that you can disentangle them.

You have a right to feel pain, happiness, sadness or whatever emotions you feel. Face your feelings head on and admit them. After a time they will become easier to bear . . . *Elizabeth*

This process of finding out what you are feeling may be possible to do on your own, although more often you will need to do it through talking to a friend. Sometimes you may need time on your own to start with. You need to have time and privacy when no one else is going to demand your attention. You may need to shut yourself in a room, roll yourself up in a duvet or blanket, or you may want to go for a walk. You may be able to write in a diary or use drawing or painting to express your feelings. For many of us it is too frightening to face unhappy feelings on our own. It feels too lonely. We need to be with someone who will listen and not be critical.

I'm one of these people who can't store things in my brain . . . I need to talk it in my mind before I can write things down. If I couldn't talk to myself I couldn't get my thoughts together . . . I just can't think thoughts, I have to talk them through. *Elizabeth*

Whether you start off by yourself or with a friend you do need to give yourself this time that is specially for you. This can be a very difficult thing to do in most of our lives where we are busy with jobs, looking after children or organising families. But depression gets worse if we are not prepared to stop and care about ourselves. Start saying 'no' to other people's demands for a change. Try to say: 'I can't do that—I need some time for myself.'

I have learned that depression must be talked about. The dreams, thoughts and experiences you have are crippling and if you keep them to yourself they go on crippling you . . . It's terribly difficult to talk sometimes because you're afraid what you're going to say will offend or shock – but you *must* find a way to come out with it. *Margaret*

Talking to someone else is the most important way of trying to help yourself. Even if you are the kind of person who prefers to keep worries to yourself, at some stage you are going to need to talk. There is no substitute for being able to share some of the muddle that is inside you and to feel that you are not rejected for it. If you do not share what you are feeling with anyone you will feel more and more alone and cut off. Being isolated makes depression worse and can lead to total despair. Being able to talk with someone may not solve your problems but can at least reduce the burden of loneliness. At best it may help you realise more clearly what is wrong.

At that stage I had no way of releasing the conflict that was going on inside me. I had nobody I could talk to, nobody to give me reassurance and most important of all nobody could say 'Chris, I know what you are going through' or those very important words 'I understand'. *Chris*

The times when we most need to talk are the times when it is most difficult to ask. When you are depressed it is very hard to ask someone to listen. You may feel that no one will want to know you if you are not able to be cheerful and entertaining. 'Why should they want to listen to all my problems?' The point is that when you are depressed you need to talk it out in order to survive. Your need is very important. You need to find someone who will listen, preferably someone who understands the need to talk. You need to keep trying to talk until someone does listen. Do not be put off by other people's busyness. If one person has not got time, try someone else.

Who is the best person to talk to? It is easier if there is someone you are close to, with whom you are used to talking about worries or problems. A lover, close friend, sister or mother may be the person with whom you feel best able to communicate. Women often find it easier to talk to another woman rather than a man, because in our culture, men tend to be less in touch with their feelings and less able to listen to someone else's feelings. However, this is not always true. It may be that for you, the best person to start talking to is a close male friend, brother, father or husband.

But often we feel inhibited about showing our depression to those we are close to, particularly if we have not done so before. You may feel that your problems involve your family too closely and you need to talk initially to someone who is outside your immediate circle. If you suspect that your depression may be due to a situation at home then you will probably want to talk to someone who is outside that situation to begin with.

You may have to talk to someone you know less well because no one close to you is available. Since depression often springs in part from loneliness it is quite likely that we do not feel in touch with our friends at the times we are most depressed. At the worst times we may feel as if we have no friends, although this probably is not really true. It is usually possible to tell whether someone is a sensitive or caring person without having known them very well or very long. If you can manage to start talking to *someone* then you may find more courage to talk to those people who are most important to you. The essential thing is to find someone who can listen without trying to tell you what to do or to solve your problems for you.

> My friends were helpful by just being there. They were supportive and they were prepared to let me rabbit on and on and on. It must have been painful to them, but they put up with it because they were friends. Just being able to talk about it, whatever it was at the time – that's what helped me get through my depression. *Sally*

How can I start talking? It may feel difficult to put anything into words or to know where to start. You can start by talking about how awful you feel. It can be a great relief to fully admit this to someone else, particularly if you have been covering it up for a long time. After that you may want to try to understand why you are depressed. A good way to start may be to try to remember when you first felt depressed. You may then find a clue as to what is causing it.

> I remember the first time I felt depressed it was when I was hanging out the washing one day just before my eldest daughter went away to college. I suddenly thought 'I'm not going to have anyone to talk to when she goes.' I realised that I hadn't been able to talk to my husband for years and that I did not have any friends I could talk to either. *Penny*

It is best not to worry about what to talk about. If you can get started you will probably find you have a lot to say. If it all comes out in a jumble you can sort out which are the most important bits gradually. You do not have to 'get it right'.

Let Yourself Cry

One of the inhibitions which can stop us from talking is the fear of crying in front of someone else. As soon as you start to talk, tears may well up and you may feel you should fight them.

> I hate to lose control. I need to be in control of me all the time. When I cry sometimes I don't feel in control. That frustrates me. When I cry with you I get angry with me because I feel I'm losing control and I'm letting you see. I don't want people seeing me to do that. *Lynn*

If you feel the need to cry it is much better to let yourself. Most women can cry on their own but it is more difficult to let yourself cry with someone else. You may feel more vulnerable and exposed but the sense of comfort and relief will be greater.

> Crying releases tension . . . say I'm not feeling very well and I sit and try to cry, I eventually think of something that makes me cry. That doesn't relieve the tension. But if I'm talking to someone and they say something and I start to cry, then it does give me relief. *Lyn*

To cry on someone's shoulder, even just a few tears, can relieve the isolation of never showing anyone how bad you feel. If you let your feelings show, you will be better able to put things into words, whereas if you hold back it will be much harder to talk.

Sometimes it would be better if I could go into it, rather than switching off. If I have a good cry or a good upset, then I'm relieved of a lot of tension. *Sue*

Crying is often considered to be a sign of weakness, but in reality you will probably feel stronger when you have had a good cry. Stopping yourself from crying is much more painful than letting yourself cry. After a good cry, whether on your own or with someone else there, you will probably be better able to think or talk about why you are depressed.

Do not Punish Yourself

'I should be able to snap out of this.' I shouldn't be depressed – I'm just selfish.' These are ways in which we can definitely make our depression worse. We can persecute and punish ourselves for being depressed. We believe that we have no right to be depressed or that it is a sign of our own terrible failure. As a result we get more and more angry and critical towards ourselves. This reinforces all our feelings of worthlessness and hopelessness. It makes it harder to care about ourselves or be nice to ourselves.

To be depressed made me feel guilty. I used to think, 'I've been feeling like this for so long – why am I depressed? – is it because I want people to love me or notice me?' I wasn't sure if I was genuinely depressed or just seeking attention. I didn't think I had any right to be depressed. I felt guilty most of the time and I think that feeling guilty when I was depressed was one thing that kept it in the dark so long. *Janice*

This is also why other people saying such things as 'cheer up' or 'pull yourself together' can be so unhelpful.

When I was depressed I berated myself for being so in-adequate. It did not help when a person came along and said 'Cheer up dear – it's not that bad', because I was already saying this to myself. Someone trying to help me seemed to highlight my inadequacy, my inability to cope, a side of myself which I didn't want anyone to see. *Sally*

136

In order to help yourself you need to try to believe that there is a good reason why you are depressed even if you do not yet know what it is. You need to be patient and try to be good to yourself, even if only in small ways.

Now when I get depressed I can usually find some reasons for it and I can say to myself, 'It's okay to feel like that'; I can allow it. Then there is a healing process. Gradually a scab forms over the wound and I can begin to make more positive moves. *Sally*

Allow Yourself to be Angry

Some of my best times have been when I've let my feelings take over and I have become angry. The anger has helped. The resentment has helped. Anger made me start to *feel* again, which is what I was desperately groping for. *Margaret*

Women are not expected to be angry. We are expected to accept things. We discussed in Chapter 4 the images of women which inhibit us from getting angry. If you are depressed, allowing yourself to feel anger can be very strengthening. You may be scared that your anger will be destructive. It may be very frightening to be angry if you are not used to it.[1]

I find it very hard to deal with my own feelings of self-destructiveness. These are the most terrifying feelings. If I'm depressed with a mixture of destructiveness, I'm afraid of saying to friends 'I'm feeling destructive', because I'm afraid I might act out those feelings and be really cutting. Now I tell myself 'It's okay to have those feelings without acting them out.' *Betsy*

Anger can be channelled in ways that are not violent or harmful to others. Our anger is a way of asserting that we do not deserve to go on being depressed. If others are treating us badly, our anger is a way of showing that we feel we have the right to be treated better.

If you could actually get angry with the people you meant to be angry with even if it's in replay – you can replay it to a wall or something, or play it to another person if you can. If you feel

137

like being angry, be angry, because it's healthier to get it out in the open and actually feel what you do feel . . . If you try and pretend that you don't feel what you do feel then the feelings sort of lurk around. It's like an ugly liquid inside of you – a big sort of sore – a big boil, and all the anger that you felt for everybody – if you haven't had a chance to get rid of it – it's mighty big. *Elizabeth*

If we have been hurt by people or events, instead of allowing ourselves to be angry we may have blamed ourselves. We may have felt that we must have done something wrong to deserve this hurt. 'I feel as if I am being punished for something and I keep trying to work out what I have done wrong.' (*Penny*). We may have done nothing wrong. There may be no answer to the question 'Why did this happen to me?' When we have been hurt by people who matter to us or when life has not worked out the way we wanted it to, coming to terms with what has happened is a very painful process.

If you can allow yourself to get angry it reduces the feelings of guilt and self-blame. You may need to get angry with people you are close to. You may need to write an angry letter to someone who has hurt you in the past. You may need to release your anger by hitting pillows or kicking the wall.

The anger comes out in many different ways. I started to get angry with the person who said 'pull yourself together'. I realised I was right to feel angry because it was a stupid thing to say. I stopped blaming myself so much. *Margaret*

However it comes out, our anger is a sign of our vitality. Once we start to feel it our anger can give us the energy to take action. We may feel ready to ask for what we want from other people or to start doing new things for ourselves.[2]

Anxiety and Tension

Depression is a frightening experience. It can feel never-ending. We may fear that we shall never be able to cope again. Often anxiety and tension goes with feeling depressed. We cannot always disentangle the different feelings.

138

They are kind of labels that help professionals compartmentalise people in terms of drugs, but I actually feel that they mould into one – depression, anxiety and fear. *Theresa*

The most difficult thing was waking up at 6:00 am with panic attacks, which were about fear of isolation, loneliness and loss. *Sue, December 1994*

Sometimes we may get depressed because we feel anxious. For example, looking after a new baby for the first time can provoke a great deal of anxiety about being a mother: fears about not being good enough, or about not loving the baby enough. We may feel afraid that life will never be 'normal' again, and worried that we are not going to cope. This fear of not coping leads to feelings of guilt, which can lead to depression. Any situation in which we feel anxious but think that we shouldn't can make us depressed. If we are already depressed, anxiety about not coping with situations which we would normally take in our stride can make us feel worse.

One of the worst fears we may have when we are depressed is the fear of going mad. 'Sometimes I think "Is everything that's happening to me really true or am I crazy?";, or "Have I got a persecution complex?"' (*Chris*). You may not know what you mean by 'going mad' but the fear is usually of losing control of yourself. If you are not able to relax, it may be because of this fear of losing control. The tension seems to be the only thing that holds you together and without it you believe that you will fall apart. This fear of disintegration or cracking up may lead you to withdraw from other people. You may feel you need to protect yourself from any contact with other people's feelings.

I want to be completely alone. I just want to curl up in a little ball or jump in a big deep hole and not come out till it's safe. *Marion*

The tension caused by trying to keep yourself together creates an increase of pressure which can make everything seem worse. Paradoxically this pressure of trying to cope is more likely to make you fall apart than if you allow some of the awful feelings to surface. Being able to relax will probably mean allowing yourself to feel more depressed and not being able to cope with everyday

139

activities so well for a while. You will need support and understanding from other people.

Anxiety can feel as if it is going to overwhelm or destroy us. It is good to know some ways of coping with it and some ways of reducing physical tension. Try to recognise and accept the physical signs of anxiety. If you notice your heart beating faster, feel yourself sweating, your head getting lighter or sensations of dizziness or faintness, remember that these are the natural physical symptoms of anxiety. If you fight these symptoms or worry about them you will get more anxious. The symptoms will then escalate and you will feel panic. Even though you may feel as though you are about to die, try to tell yourself, 'I'm just feeling very anxious – I'm not having a heart attack.' If you can allow the anxiety to be there and not fight it then it will gradually lessen.

The fear of having a panic attack can stop us from going out. It feels safer to stay at home. You may think 'At least if I panic at home no one will see me, but if I panicked outside, I wouldn't know what to do.' Or it may feel as if when you are outside you lose your boundaries. At home you feel contained. Not feeling able to go out is often called 'agoraphobia'. There are ways of getting help and helping yourself with agoraphobia which we cannot describe in detail here. Many women have found self-help books, networks, groups and phone lines useful.[3]

Agoraphobia is often a sign that something is wrong in your life or that something is bothering you. You may be in conflict about how independent or dependent you want to be. You may be feeling angry with someone and feel unable to express it. You may be in the process of adjusting to a new way of life and increased responsibility after having a child. Or you may be trying to adjust to your children needing you less. As women we have to cope with enormous changes in our lives and it is not surprising if there are times when we feel anxious and vulnerable.

Other phobic symptoms such as worries about being ill or fears about travelling can, like agoraphobia, be a mask for depression. It can be too frightening to face how bad we feel about fundamental problems in our lives. Instead we channel the bad feelings into a specific fear. However uncomfortable it makes us, this specific problem protects us from facing depression. Another way in which we can channel our bad feelings is through obsessive behaviour. This includes a need to keep washing and cleaning, having to check things more than necessary and being obsessed by a specific worrying thought. We cannot discuss these in detail here but they have been shown to be connected very often with depression.[4]

It may be very difficult to see any connection between these things and other problems in your life. If you do start to make connections you may have to face the awful feelings of depression. At first it may seem as if things are getting worse. Usually the use of phobic or obsessive behaviour to mask depression is not a conscious choice that you are in control of. So the 'snap out of it' approach will not work, even if you do recognise the connections.

If you feel very tense most of the time it may be worthwhile to practise some form of relaxation. Relaxation is something which should come naturally but with many of us does not. We need a certain level of tension in order to get things done but we do not know how to let this tension go when it is time to rest. You may need to start by setting aside some time for relaxation. This is usually the most difficult bit. You may be so used to being busy that it feels wrong to 'do nothing'. You can always think of something else that needs doing. As soon as you sit down you may start to feel restless or bored because you are not used to it. This is why you may need to learn specific ways of relaxing. Watching television or listening to music may be enough. If it is not, then try learning some relaxation exercises. There are some good books available for learning relaxation on your own.[5] But it may feel easier to join a relaxation or yoga class, where you have the support of other women. These are often available at women's centres, health centres, or adult education colleges. Swimming, walking or any form of physical exercise can be good for relaxation.

Another way of learning to relax is through massage. Massage for women is now widely available (although not usually on the NHS) and you could join a class in which you would learn to give and receive masage. Aromatherapy massage is also very popular. Here, essential oils made from plants are used to increase the therapeutic effect of the massage.[6]

Relaxation time is valuable because it is something we can give to ourselves. It is a simple way of starting to care for our own needs. However, if we are in a situation which is causing us to be anxious and tense then no amount of relaxation will take away this tension. If we are not yet ready to change our situation or other people are preventing us we may have to live with tension and anxiety until we are ready or able to change. Tension is not in itself a bad thing. It can provide us with the motivation to want to change.

Feeling Suicidal

> I really want to die. I know it seems selfish when I've got kids to look after but I just don't feel like carrying on. *Janet*

> I felt so terrible, I didn't know how to stop the pain. I took all the tablets because it was the only thing I could think of doing.
> *Alison*

Suicide is the extreme end of a continuum of self-destruction. When we are depressed we hurt ourselves in many different ways. We may cut ourselves, starve ourselves, over-eat and make ourselves sick, use alcohol or drugs to abuse our bodies. Sometimes we do this to try to dull the emotional pain we are in. Sometimes we are already feeling cut off or numbed. We want to make ourselves feel something or anything. Feeling pain can be better than feeling nothing. Finding a physical way to hurt ourselves can be a way of making the emotional pain visible.

Most often trying to commit suicide or having thoughts about suicide does not mean you really want to die.

> Today I thought my feminism is poisoning my mind. Then I corrected myself. It is this world and the way it is now that poisons me. Now I see what has caused me pain in the past. I know what it is and it is huge and very hideous. Sometimes it frightens me and I feel like killing myself, but I wait and my fear passes. *Marie, March 1981*

The statistics show that women make far more attempts at suicide than men but far fewer successful suicides.[7] Thinking about suicide means that you find your present state of mind unbearable and death looks like the only way out. If someone could offer you another solution you would want to take it. Feeling suicidal means you are at the lowest point in your depression. You feel completely uncared for. You may believe that you are a

142

horrible person and that the world would be better off without you.

I felt a failure. I couldn't sleep. I thought I had no friends. I didn't know why I was living. I thought I was so awful and useless. I didn't know why I had been put on the earth . . . I just couldn't stand life any longer. *Elizabeth*

I have felt very deeply suicidal. I was really in a bad way. I was going to jump out of the window. I felt totally hopeless and despondent and that life couldn't go on and I didn't care about myself. I felt so much self-hate at that moment. *Betsy*

Sometimes trying to kill ourselves feels like the only way to show other people how bad we feel. We are angry at others' lack of concern and feel that we have had enough of trying. We want to give up.

Another dream I had just before I attempted suicide: I dreamt I was in a mad house and I couldn't get out. I was in this walled cage. I kept banging on the walls and shouting and I couldn't make anyone hear me. *Elizabeth*

It may be frightening when you first realise you are thinking about death. Such thoughts may appear to come out of the blue.

For years my depression was under control although it sometimes felt unbearable. I used to get mad urges to jump off moving trains. It's amazing some of the things I used to think of doing. One minute I was all right and the next minute all of a sudden I was thinking of jumping off the train. *Janice*

Having such thoughts does not mean you are going to do it. It means that you are feeling extremely depressed and desperately looking for a way out of your depression. Or it may mean that although most of you wants to carry on, part of you wants to give up.

Sometimes we toy with the idea of killing ourselves for years. It is like an escape route we keep secretly in the background.

There were several times I nearly tried. I made excuses

143

sometimes – like the knife wasn't sharp enough. I did take a knife to bed with me once to kill myself and I fell asleep. I woke up and thought, 'What am I doing with a knife in my hand?' Thinking about suicide did enable me to have a good cry and then a good sleep, which made me feel better. *Janice*

Talking about death is taboo in our society. The idea of choosing to die is even more unacceptable. Wanting to die is therefore the most difficult aspect of depression to talk about. Once again guilt makes it worse. We can feel so guilty at having thought about killing ourselves that we feel even less that we have a right to live, let alone ask for help.

If you are thinking about killing yourself and are afraid that you may do it, you must tell someone. If you do not have friends whom you feel able to tell, then you can ring the Samaritans. Many women feel able to use them as a lifeline, both because you can talk to someone anonymously and because you know they are used to people talking about suicide. If you can manage to tell someone else then it will probably be a great relief to talk about it. The suicidal thoughts will lose some of their power when you are able to share them.

It will make a difference whom you choose to talk to about suicide because knowing that you want to die is a difficult thing for someone else to cope with. If you choose to tell your doctor, she or he will probably urge you to take some anti-depressant medication. We shall be discussing the advantages and dis-advantages of using medication in the next chapter, but it can help you through a very bad patch.

If you choose to talk to someone close to you about fears of killing yourself then you must realise that their behaviour towards you may change, if they take you seriously. They may start watching you more closely, or getting very anxious if they do not know where you are. This can feel very uncomfortable because it seems that they do not trust you. You want someone to take your feelings seriously but not to watch over your behaviour. But if they do genuinely care about you, it is natural that they will feel responsible and will want to check up on whether you are all right or encourage you to get some more help.

If you are the person in whom someone feeling suicidal confides, you will have your own feelings of anxiety to cope with. It may help to remember that ultimately you cannot stop anyone else killing themselves if they really want to. What you can do is to give them the opportunity for their feelings of despair to be listened to and understood. The possibility of suicide needs to be discussable rather than being something unthinkable or worthy of punishment. If someone is encouraged to talk about it they are less likely to do it, although this cannot be guaranteed.

Feeling suicidal usually involves ambivalence. This means that part of yourself wants to give up and put an end to your life; while another part of you still feels some hope of things getting better or some desire to survive and go on struggling. If you can fully acknowledge that part of you that wants to give up, then the more positive side may be able to come through.

> The doctor I was seeing did prescribe me tablets to slow me down. My mind was overworking and I never got a rest. I thought 'If they slow me down then they'll stop me.' I got as far as putting every one in my mouth. I left them there for a while. Then I thought, 'No way will I give the world the satisfaction!' And I spat them all out. It left a foul taste in my mouth and it was numb – but that was better than being numb all over.
>
> *Janice*

Feeling suicidal can be a turning point. If you can somehow survive and come through this low point, you may be able to make a real choice to carry on living. You may become more open to change: to living your life on a new basis. You may allow new people into your life, or discover new ideas about what you want for yourself.

Can Depression be Positive?

> Ten years on from the intense distress and deep depression that was triggered by my marriage breakup, I view depression as a vital learning experience. That does not mean that it is ever okay to say to a depressed person, 'You will grow through the pain'. What it does mean is that my ability to ride out the periods of anxiety, and low spirits is greater than before. I am stronger as a result of having been so vulnerable. I know that feelings can pass, that I can admit to having them, that strong

people can feel hurt and cry and that I don't have to be strong all the time. *Caroline*

When we have emerged from a long period of depression we can sometimes see in retrospect that it served a purpose. Depression may be a means of withdrawal from the outside world. We may need a period of withdrawal when recovering from loss or trauma, trying to resolve conflict, or needing time to digest our experience. It may feel like time to heal our wounds, time to think things out or a time of waiting.

The need for withdrawal or periods of less outside activity is not well recognised in our culture. There is an emphasis on external achievement; on having something to show for ourselves. We are not encouraged to allow ourselves to just *be*. We are expected always to be *doing* something.

We may fight against a need for time to slow down and work things out. We think we should have everything worked out already. This contributes to the self-punishing aspect of depression which is painful and damaging. For women it can be particularly difficult to withdraw emotionally from other people. We are expected to be available to care for others most of the time, in our families and in our jobs. We also feel frightened of withdrawal. We feel afraid that if we stop giving we will lose our connections with other people.

If we need to be on our own for a time, we do not know how to find the privacy. We do not know where to go when we need a safe place to which we can retreat to nurse our wounds or think things over. Such places do not seem to be available in our society. This is why women sometimes find themselves on a psychiatric ward when they simply need rest and comfort.

There is a lack of respect in our culture for our natural rhythms and cycles. In her book *Female Cycles*, Paula Weideger[8] has drawn attention to the depth of the cultural taboo surrounding the subjects of menstruation and menopause. To be menstruating is still considered to be unclean. Because of the distaste for this aspect of ourselves, we know little about the way our cycles really work.

Today is grey, cold and rain pours down, tapping on the skylights. I can feel blood trickling out of my body. This always makes me sad now. Something leaving me, my life's blood. It is sadness; the emptiness inside and my womb cries bloody tears. I feel the need to be creative in other ways as if to compensate for the inability to produce. *Marie, February 1979*

Penelope Shuttle and Peter Redgrove wrote their book *The Wise Wound*,[9] after Penelope Shuttle had suffered very bad premenstrual depressions. They explore the possibility that the menstrual cycle may not be a women's curse but rather an unexplored resource. So many women suffer from pre-menstrual tension or depression but we have little understanding of the meaning of the personality changes which we experience throughout our cycles. It might be that we have a need to slow down and rest more for certain days of the month or that we feel more sexual or more creative at certain times.

The point is that there is a *rhythm*, however one may divide it up in one's own personal experience. If mental experiences reflect, as they often seem to, bodily ones, then there are many possibilities of experience if one opens oneself to this rhythm. One is often asked or encouraged to detach oneself from them, by regarding them as an inconvenience or an illness. Detachment from the changes does of course ensure that they remain merely bodily ones, and may even force them to express themselves in the body language of illness. Harmony with them, so far as is possible, can lead to a different form of independence – understanding of one's nature rather than repression of it.[10]

Perhaps we can apply this idea to other forms of depression. Depression may be part of the ebb and flow of our lives on a larger scale as well as on the smaller scale of our monthly cycles. It can be a necessary phase in the process of 'growing on' which we discussed in Chapter 7.

After the birth of my child, I got depressed for several months in a way that I hadn't expected, even though I knew about 'post-natal depression' in theory. It seems to me that looking after a small baby can re-evoke all the hang ups that you thought you had left behind. For me there was a tremendous need to 'get it right' and a lot of anxiety about not being able to do so. At the same time I was resentful at losing my freedom to do what I wanted when I wanted to do it, and felt a longing to be looked after myself. All of this gradually passed and I started to feel more 'normal; again, but it has made me think about cycles of depression and how it can come back at times of change, even when the change is a welcome one; and how you sometimes have to work through things again in a different way. *Lucie, November 1994*

We know that depression can become so severe that it takes the form of an illness. We shall describe some of the medical treatments available in the next chapter. However, it is interesting to speculate about whether it might be possible to deal with depression differently if we were more in touch with our physical and emotional rhythms. Perhaps depression would have to be medicalised less often and we could deal with it more as a difficult but normal part of life.

Without feeling sad you can never realise what feeling happy is. Depression can change your character. It can make you bitter, sharp and unkind to people but it can help you to understand people much better . . . I can feel their pain. *Elizabeth*

10
Looking for Help –
Medical Approaches

Sometimes you cannot help yourself, even with the support of friends. Depression may feel so bad or have been going on for so long that you have to look for help elsewhere. In this chapter we discuss the forms of medical treatment which are available.

> I went to my doctor because I had to, and because at that time I didn't know who else to turn to. I felt that if I didn't get help from somewhere I would go mad. I was coping – but only just. I felt I was getting to breaking-point. My husband and my friends were trying to be supportive but they didn't understand what was happening to me any more than I did. *Sandra*

In this book we have been looking at depression as an experience, rather than as an illness, relating this experience to our lives as women. However, we also have to acknowledge that, at its most extreme, depression does take on the form of an illness. We may become completely unable to carry on our lives. We may have great difficulty in eating and sleeping. Our bodies feel sluggish and heavy, or they may seem full of aches and pains. The numbness in our emotions is mirrored by a numbness in our physical sensations. We can actually lose our perception of colour in the world. At worst our bodies seem to be at a complete standstill.

> Depression creates physical feelings which I never expected. I thought depression was a mental thing but suddenly I felt like a sack of potatoes. I really felt as if my body was disintegrating. I found myself looking at my body and saying 'These are not my arms, because the arms I knew could cope.' And of course as I

became debilitated I naturally got other ailments that perhaps I wouldn't have got otherwise. *Margaret*

The Medical Model

The 'medical model' looks at depression as being like a physical illness with certain definite symptoms which can be cured by drugs. We are critical of this model both in theory and in the way it is applied.

Kate Millett in her book, *The Loony Bin Trip*, vividly describes the devastating effects of a crude application of the medical model, and how medical treatment can be used in ways which are punitive and terrifying.[1] Since her experiences in the early 1980s, the way in which the medical model is usually applied has changed to some extent. Many psychiatrists are now interested in taking account of the social conditions of their patients' lives, and most psychiatrists work in collaboration with multi-disciplinary teams in which a variety of approaches are used. As a result, the medical approach is less likely to be applied crudely or on its own. However, we feel that the basic criticisms still apply, particularly as the dominance of this model can prevent enough resources being used to develop other ways of helping people.

Fundamentally the medical model still assumes that women are passive sufferers of an illness which can only be alleviated by an expert. It does not encourage women to think that they can understand the problems in their lives and find ways to take more control. It does encourage women to remain helpless victims of fate, needing the doctor to intervene from time to time.

The medical approach to depression implies that it is something which should be got rid of as soon as possible. Drugs are prescribed to 'cure' us of bad feelings. The terminology used accentuates certain ideas of abnormality. For example, to have a psychiatric 'disorder' implies that the normal healthy mind is always an ordered one. It suggests that if you are depressed something is 'out of order' inside you. And yet to feel confused, or even chaotic, may be a state of mind which is not at all abnormal. It may be a creative state: one which is uncomfortable but which enables new ideas of who you are and what you want to emerge.

In their training, doctors learn about people as bodies. They are interested in whether these bodies are functioning properly or not. It is often very difficult for doctors to deal with emotional pain because they have learned not to respond to many of their own emotions. They have to find a way not to be overwhelmed by their awareness of illness, suffering and death. The result can be that they are not able to listen to someone else's distress and accept it. Their first impulse is to find a way to alleviate it, rather than to understand what the person is trying to tell them. Since we first wrote this book there have been some changes in attitudes within the medical profession. Some doctors are more aware now of the importance of listening to the patient. But this still cannot be relied upon, particularly as doctors do not usually have much time available for listening.

We have written the next sections as a guide to the way doctors and psychiatrists usually treat depression. We hope that it will help women use the medical system when they need to, while avoiding its worst dangers. If we can try to gather more information about the forms of help available, there is greater possibility of making choices for ourselves, rather than feeling we have to accept whatever is offered without question.

The issue of whether depression is 'really' an illness is a difficult one and can itself cause conflict for women who are depressed. We can recognise that the way depressed women are medically treated is part of a system which works to prevent us from changing our lives. On the other hand it may be helpful at times to allow yourself 'to be ill'. It may be a way of showing that you can't always cope. It may be the only way that you can get others, as well as yourself, to recognise the seriousness of what you are experiencing.

I tend to keep away from people if I feel a bit low or shaky or panicky. I try to keep away from people 'cause they won't understand. If I fell over and broke my leg – that's fine. You go to hospital and get your leg done but if I went up to somebody and said 'I feel terrible. I feel I'm going to pass out', then they'd look at me as if I was a nutcase. *Lyn*

I suspect that many women like myself, have found it easier to see and describe themselves as ill in order to make sense of what's happening, both to themselves and to other people; and also because it has an easily defined role that goes with it that entitles you to privileges and concern, and excuses you from normal responsibilities. In a way it is so much easier to be 'ill' as you feel less guilty for 'letting things go!' *Ruth Elizabeth*

Our minds and bodies are less separable than we often imagine. Inevitably our physical and mental states will reflect each other. Some people are more likely to notice emotional or mental changes. Sometimes it may be helpful to do something to alleviate the physical aspects of depression before or at the same time as trying to deal with the emotions involved.

However, we feel that there are other gentler ways for women to look after their bodies, than the strong drugs which doctors prescribe so readily. On the simplest level, women often need real physical rest; not only sleep but a chance to wind down and feel less pressured by the many demands on them.

When we originally wrote this book, we said we would like to see more exploration of the use of 'alternative' or, as they are often now called, 'complimentary' medicines, some of which we describe later in the chapter. Since then, these medicines have become more widely available and known about. There are even some GP practices where homeopathic medicines are prescribed, or where acupuncture is practised. The practitioners of these medicines usually believe in looking at a person's whole lifestyle when treating them. They give advice about improving diet, sleeping patterns and so on. The remedies they prescribe do not involve strong chemicals which produce side effects in the body, as do the conventional medical treatments.

Types of Depression

Before describing the various medical approaches to treatment, we need to explain the distinctions which doctors make between different types of depression. These distinctions are necessary in order to apply 'a medical model'. Doctors work on the assumption that they need to diagnose the nature of the illness before they can prescribe the correct treatment. In fact there has been great controversy within psychiatry as to the classification of different types of depressive illness. This controversy has not been resolved. Among doctors the question remains as to whether the various forms of depression are best understood as being one illness which shows itself in different ways or as being different illnesses. The distinction most often used is between neurotic or reactive depression and psychotic or endogenous depression.

Psychotic or Endogenous Depression These are forms of depression which are more severe than neurotic depression. The diagnosis of endogenous depression is often given when there is no obvious external stress to account for the person having become depressed. The cause of endogenous or psychotic depression is considered to be a disturbance in certain biochemical processes connected with nerve cells in the brain. This produces the physical effects of depression. The symptoms of physical retardation, loss of energy and appetite coupled with feelings of inferiority, guilt and hopelessness can be very extreme. The depressed person may even have delusions or hallucinations connected with her feelings of guilt, wickedness and the need for punishment. It is argued that endogeneously depressed people are not helped by talking, because of the difficulty in relating to another human being at all.

Neurotic or Reactive Depression These forms of depression are thought to be caused by stressful life events. Reactive depression is diagnosed when there is some obvious recent traumatic experience to which the person seems to be reacting. The symptoms are similar to endogenous depression but a person who is neurotically depressed is more able to relate to other people and may become cheerful after talking to someone else.

This distinction does not work very well in practice. If depression is diagnosed as endogenous because there is no obvious trauma or stress which may have caused it, it may be simply that no one, including the depressed person, has discovered what the stress is. There may be internal conflicts, frustrations or fears or a delayed reaction to something that occurred in the past. We discussed these possibilities in Chapter 7. There may be problems in her relationships which are not obvious on the surface. In reactive depression which has occurred in response to a loss or trauma, there may be also be a physical or biochemical process going on which corresponds to the emotional state.

Clinical Depression A phrase often used to distinguish depression as an illness from depression as a mood. Someone is said to be clinically depressed if they show the characteristic physical symptoms of insomnia, worthlessness and hopelessness.

In practice there is a continuum along the spectrum from reactive to endogenous depression in terms of the depth of depression and the degree to which a person's physical, emotional and mental functioning are disturbed.

Manic-depressive Psychosis   This is sometimes referred to as bipolar disorder, as opposed to unipolar depression. It describes a form of psychotic depression in which a person suffers from mood swings or cycles, alternating between episodes of mania which involve euphoria, excitement and non-stop talking and activity and episodes of depression which involve intense feelings of worthlessness, self-reproach and withdrawal. Usually there are periods of stability in between these mood swings.

Manic depression is much less common than 'ordinary' depression and unlike other types of depression is thought to occur equally in men and women, although there is some evidence that women are given this diagnosis more often than men.[2] Our analysis of depression is this book applies mainly to neurotic depression rather than to manic-depressive psychosis. However, the precipitating factors in women's lives which we have described may well also apply to manic depression, even though this phenomenon probably involves some hereditary predisposition.

Agitated depression   This term is applied to someone who is depressed but also feels a lot of anxiety, with symptoms such as restlessness, tension and panic attacks. Often post-natal depression is like this and is also sometimes called *atypical depression*.

Involutional melancholia   This is a label which is seldom used now, but which was formerly used to describe a type of agitated depression occurring for the first time in mid-life or later. It was considered to occur often in women at the menopause. This category has been excluded from more recent versions of psychiatric classification, because there is a lack of evidence that there is a particular type of depression occuring at this stage in life that is any different from 'ordinary' clinical depression. There is also a lack of evidence that clinical depression occurs more often during menopause than at other times.[3] Rather than there being a clear association between hormonal changes during menopause and depression, there seem to be clearer connections between depression and the social problems for women who, in middle life, are trying to find new roles for themselves after their children have grown up.[4]

On the other hand, Gail Sheehy has argued in her book, *The Silent Passage*, that even if there is no increase in clinical depression, very many women do in fact experience mood changes, irritability, and feelings of malaise, and that this is related to low oestrogen levels.[5] There may therefore be a tendency for doctors not to take emotional difficulties at mid-life seriously enough. Germaine Greer has also argued that women may often be blamed for having emotional problems at menopause, particularly if they are told that they are 'bad copers' and that it may be more helpful to see emotional changes as being related to a physical process, especially when that process is understood to have a beginning, a middle and an end.[6]

The use of these diagnostic labels can vary, according to current medical fashion. For instance the term 'puerperal psychosis' was at one time used to cover all severe mental disorders occurring after childbirth, while now it is more common to give a specific diagonsis such as schizophrenia or manic depression. 'Post natal depression' is now the usual label given to most of the less severe reactions after childbirth.[7] Certain diagnostic labels may be more commonly used by one psychiatrist than another.

Sometimes it has been necessary to apply a medical-sounding label in order to get a condition of distress taken seriously. For example, many women now prefer to talk about post-natal 'unhappiness' rather than post-natal 'depression'. However, psychologists doing research in this area have found that they had to use the label 'post-natal depression', with its connotation of being a medically recognised syndrome, in order for their work to be taken seriously enough to be granted sufficient funding.[8] It is therefore less important to worry about the diagnostic label you are given, as it may well sound more awful than it is. It is more important to find out what sort of treatment a doctor is intending to give you and what she or he hopes to achieve by it.

Tablets

For many years, if a woman went to her doctor for help, she or he was most likely to prescribe medication. Now there is a much greater awareness of the danger of addiction to tranquillisers such as Valium and Ativan, and many doctors are quite cautious about prescribing them. They are more likely to prescribe anti-depressants which are thought to be less addictive.

Some women strongly prefer not to take drugs. Certainly there are dangers. The side-effects may be unpleasant. There is a danger of staying on them too long so that it becomes difficult to stop taking them. Some women find that drugs seem to numb or suppress their feelings so that although they feel less unhappy they also feel less alive. There is a danger that by taking drugs to make ourselves feel better we are less likely to deal with what is wrong in our lives.

Medication can be used oppressively, as we have already discussed in Chapter 8. We may feel that a doctor gives us tablets just to keep us quiet. Relatives or friends may say 'Why don't you get something from the doctor to make you feel better?' This may seem to mean that they don't really want to know what is upsetting us.

However, drugs can be very helpful to some women at certain times. Perhaps it is not so much a question of whether tablets are a good or bad thing in themselves but more a question of working out how we can best use them.

After my father died I went to the Student Health Centre and I was put on anti-depressants. It was very badly handled in terms of how I felt – how they dealt with my grief – well they didn't deal with it at all. But I actually felt that those drugs helped me. They lifted my mood and made it easier to cope. I did also have a lot of emotional support through talking to a social worker. But if anyone else was going through a similar experience I wouldn't hesitate to say try an anti-depressant. *Theresa*

Tablets enabled me to live normally at a time when I found the tiniest normal detail of life too much to cope with. In particular they helped me to sleep, which made all the difference to my ability to cope with the day. I knew they weren't a miracle cure for all my problems, but they did make it possible for me to survive an acute crisis and gradually to come to terms with those problems. I realised that in a sense my peace of mind was artificial, but I also knew that it was better than disintegrating altogether. I used anti-depressants exactly as a crutch is used by someone with a broken ankle – as a temporary aid, preferring to be able to get around somehow, rather than not to walk at all. *Diana*

I've come across a lot of condemnation not only of medication but of those who take it. This has only exacerbated the guilt and conflict I already feel about taking anti-depressants. But I have often owed my continued functioning to those tablets and on more than one occasion agreeing to take them has kept me out of hospital. I have often been far too badly depressed to do *anything*, and then I feel medication is the only way to get you active enough to start talking and wanting to *do* something.

Ruth Elizabeth

If you do take tablets it is important to feel that they are being supervised properly by a doctor. You should have the chance to discuss your reactions to the medication and when and how to stop taking it. There is a danger in accepting repeat prescriptions without visiting the doctor because this can lead to carrying on taking the tablets for a long time without questioning whether you should still be on them. If you have been taking tablets for a very long time then you may need to discuss with your doctor how to come off them gradually, if you want to. It can be frightening to stop all your medication suddenly when you are used to taking it, so it is usually better to cut down bit by bit.

I think people should go on anti-depressants for a really short time. They should be monitored carefully to check that they are getting the right amount of tablet, that it's not giving them unpleasant side-effects and that they are only on them for a limited amount of time – the amount of time it takes to lift their mood sufficiently so they can talk about things, do things, become part of the world again. I stayed on them for about three months and I took the decision to wean myself off.

Theresa

I think they drug you far too much . . . I don't know if it's because you're less trouble when you are drugged highly, but if you're on an awful lot of drugs, how can they tell just how bad you really are? You could be getting worse . . . I weaned myself off drugs. I think because despite what they said *I knew* they were addictive and that I was becoming addicted. *Chris*

Often doctors do not seem willing to discuss the type of medication they prescribe or to tell you about side-effects. If possible, we need to assert our right to be given this kind of information. When actually feeling depressed it is especially difficult to be assertive. It may be much easier to take the tablets without any questions. There may be some immediate comfort in being given something which *may* help. But in the long run it is important that we feel we have some choice about what we are taking into our bodies, at the same time as we are trying to regain control over other areas of our life.

In Appendix 2 of this book there is a detailed list of most of the drugs which may be prescribed, together with their usual side-effects. It is important to understand the distinction between anti-depressants and tranquillisers, and to know which type of drug you have been prescribed. Basically, anti-depressants are intended to lift your mood ('uppers'), while tranquillisers are intended to calm you down if you are anxious ('downers'). However, some anti-depressants also have a slight sedative effect. So they may be intended to calm you down at the same time as making you less depressed.

Some new drugs become fashionable. For example, Prozac, a new type of anti-depressant first put on the market in 1987, enjoyed a boom of popularity as the 'wonder drug' of the nineties. Claimed to be as effective as the older anti-depressants but with fewer side-effects, it has also been prescribed in the USA to improve performance in people who are not clinically depressed. People who take it apparently become more out-going, confident and resilient. However, it has already become clear that Prozac does still have side-effects, and it would seem important to weigh up the advantages and disadvantages of taking it, as much as with any other drug.

When you take anti-depressants (such as Trypitzol, Anafranil, Bolvidon, Prothiaden, and Merital), they usually take up to two or three weeks to take effect fully. This is because it takes time for them to build up to an adequate level in the blood stream. There is therefore no point in taking anti-depressants occasionally. You have to take them regularly as prescribed or not at all. On the other hand when you take tranquillisers (such as Valium,

Librium and Ativan), they have an immediate effect. You can therefore use them to ease anxiety by taking them from time to time when you feel you need to.

Some doctors do prescribe tranquillisers for depression. So if you are taking Valium or Ativan and feel that you are more depressed than anxious, it may be that the drugs are not doing you much good. You might want to consider stopping or changing your medication.

Many women who have been taking tranquillisers over long periods are realising that they are addicted to them. Doctors now acknowledge that there is a 'withdrawal syndrome' when people stop taking these drugs. This means that when you stop taking them you may experience certain physical symptoms, such as sweating, shaking, insomnia and palpitations. These effects are not necessarily connected with the original anxiety or other problem for which you were prescribed the drug in the first place. The organisation 'Release' has available a very good pamphlet *Trouble with Tranquillisers*[9] which gives information and advice about how to cut down a little.[10]

> The secret is to wean yourself off gradually, and to work out a timescale in this that suits you. The problem with doing it too fast is that you may panic, go back to your original dose and give up. Whereas if you go more slowly, you can still call a halt at any particular level, and stay at this level until you feel you can start reducing again – which may be months. But you will already have gained some confidence and control by having cut down a little.[4]

This method can also be used to wean yourself off anti-depressants. In order to start cutting down, it may be helpful to break your tablets in half, or to have your prescription changed by your doctor to one for tablets with a smaller amount in them; for example, to change from taking 10 mg tablets to taking 5 mg tablets. This would give you more flexibility about how much you cut down at a time.

If your depression is not with you all the time but seems to occur specifically before or during your menstrual period, then it would probably be better to try taking some milder remedy, such as Vitamin B6 or Evening Primrose Oil, rather than taking drugs which may have a heavier effect than you need. There are several recent books about pre-menstrual syndrome which may be helpful.[11]

Out-patient Psychiatric Treatment

If your GP does not feel that she or he can help you enough, she may refer you to a psychiatrist. This does not necessarily mean you will be taken into hospital. At your first appointment you will be interviewed by the psychiatrist and the most likely outcome will be a prescription for drugs and a further appointment in a few weeks time.

It is commonly assumed that a psychiatrist will be a psychoanalyst or someone who 'sees into your mind'. In fact most psychiatrists are not trained as psychoanalysts or psychotherapists (although some are – see Appendix 1), and work mainly through a medical approach. Usually when you go to a psychiatrist, it will simply be for a short chat and another prescription. As with in-patient treatment, there may be some benefit but only if you feel some trust in your doctor.

> The consultant I am under at out-patients is a very patient, understanding person. I see her every few weeks for a 20 minute chat. I enjoy talking to her. She is a quiet and unassuming person but so on the ball. Her questions are always very relevant. *Patricia*

Many women are rightly very wary of seeing a psychiatrist, partly because they will be expected to talk about their intimate lives with a stranger. For women who are lesbians, single mothers or whose lifestyle is in any other way different from what is considered to be 'normal', this can be especially difficult. Undoubtedly the same prejudices exist in psychiatry as in the rest of society.

> You could go to them and say 'I've got this problem', and they could ask you about your personal life. It might come out later that you are a lesbian. I feel that that's irrelvant. The sexuality of a person should not be taken into consideration, because

they don't actually take it into consideration that you're heterosexual. Heterosexuality is never felt to be the problem.

Sue

Black women may also be wary of discussing their problems with white psychiatrists or any other white health professionals, due to uncertainty as to whether their concerns and issues, particularly if related to racism, will be understood. Different belief systems and cultural assumptions, if not acknowledged and respected, can be a major barrier to feeling that your distress is understood.

I think the biggest problem with our mental health services is this attitude that our clients should fit into our service. People say, 'Here is our service. Why aren't black people using it?' rather than asking what are the reasons why black people might not be using it; what are the obstacles that might be in the way; and how can we be creative about changing our service to meet their needs. There's still an arrogance about finding that black people don't actually use our services very much. *Gita*

Some studies have looked at the low uptake of statutory services by minority ethnic groups and identified barriers such as problems with communication, lack of knowledge of the services and lack of confidentialty and trust.[12]

The danger for any woman seeing a psychiatrist is that you are likely to feel particularly vulnerable to someone else's criticism, judgements and advice about your life, when you are depressed. A psychiatrist, particularly if male, will not necessarily understand your situation, especially the dilemmas you have as a woman. There is no reason to believe that he or she has a right to judge you, but you can easily end up feeling worse through being misunderstood by someone from whom you were desperately needing some help.

If you do feel you need a psychiatrist, ideally it would be best to consult first with other women locally who might know which psychiatrists in the area are likely to be most understanding and sympathetic towards women. You are likely to be able to get this sort of information from a local women's centre, women's therapy centre, or from a local branch of MIND. In many places there are now local mental health users' forums, which may be able to give you advice and support, and in a few places, there are women's mental health forums. You can find out about these from your local community health council or local branch of MIND.

The way that mental health services are organised is changing in most areas, so that seeing a psychiatrist is no longer necessarily the first port of call. In some places, there are now community health teams, which deal with all mental health referrals. This would mean that if your GP refers you, you might be seen initially by some other member of the team, rather than by a psychiatrist. This could be a psychiatric nurse, a social worker, clinical psychologist or occupational therapist. You would only see the psychiatrist if it was thought to be necessary. In many places there are now walk-in services or open-access clinics operating at certain times, where you can go for help without necessarily having been referred by your GP or having made a definite appointment.

Hospitalisation

There has been a gradual closure of large psychiatric hospitals in the UK over the last few years, due to the government's policy of implementing 'Care in the Community'. As a result, many people who lived for years in psychiatric wards with little privacy or sense of their own identity are now able to live in ordinary houses in the community with suitable support. These changes are still in process and being implemented more effectively in some places than others.

However there has been little change in the provision of 'places of refuge' for people in acute distress. For people who are extremely depressed and need somewhere to go temporarily to be looked after, there is usually no real alternative to an acute psychiatric ward. These are now more often located within general hospitals rather than in separate psychiatric institutions, thus reducing the stigma to some extent. But they are still very medical in orientation, which is not necessarily what someone who is looking for a refuge from the stresses of their life needs.

We would like to be able to recommend alternatives to hospital

162

such as crisis centres, mental health refuges or therapeutic communities, but there are very few of these available. In the UK money has simply not been made available within the NHS or within Social Services to develop these sort of alternatives.

Ideally try to avoid hospital by staying with trusted friends. However, even in the most supportive environment, there may come times when it is impossible for you to be looked after by friends alone. If you contact your GP, local psychiatrist or local mental health team, because you are so depressed that you are suicidal, or so withdrawn that you cannot get on with life at all, you may be offered treatment in hospital. If you are manic, that is you are running around non-stop doing and saying 'crazy' things, or if you are making active suicide attempts, then it is possible that you will be forced into hospital. In the United Kingdom this is called 'sectioning' because it involves certain specific sections of the Mental Health Act. (See Appendix 1 for details of these sections).

I just became ill and didn't realise how ill I was. I apparently didn't sleep and I was very high and my husband didn't know what to do. I went to the doctor who gave me tablets but I still didn't sleep. So I went back to the doctor and he admitted me to hospital. Then I became depressed. *Patricia*

A stay in a psychiatric ward at worst can be a threatening and undermining experience. At best it can give you a breathing space; a chance to think and talk things out away from the pressures of your everyday life.

When I was in hospital I could escape into a sort of vacuum. I was left alone to float. I needed that period when I was allowed to float. It seemed to make it worse when people came to see me and took me out. I would panic because of the gap between the way I was and their normal life. Gradually this improved – the difference between how I felt and how the rest of the world was carrying on became less and less until I became completely part of the stream of things again. *Patricia*

If you are treated in hospital, a lot will depend on whether you feel you can trust the doctor who is looking after you.

After I'd been in hospital for two or three days, I was allocated to a doctor. He used to spend long periods talking to me and drawing me out. In the beginning I wasn't at all confident and I didn't talk to him a great deal. But as I got to know him and the drugs started working, I did talk to him and I found it very helpful. I had a lot of faith in him which was important. I felt I could trust him. *Patricia*

In many psychiatric wards the doctors are too busy or too medically minded to spend time talking with patients. The relationship between doctor and patient is often an authoritarian one and, as we have discussed in Chapter 8, this can reinforce feelings of helplessness and make a woman feel more like a child or a victim. You may find that you can talk more easily to other staff such as nurses or occupational therapists. In some hospitals individual therapy or group therapy with a psychologist or social worker may be offered but more often the main treatments are drugs and ECT. Psychiatric wards do vary a great deal as to how they are run.

In one hospital – I've been there for as much as six or seven weeks at one time and hardly anyone speaks to you. I've been through the early stages where you sit crying all day – nobody ever comes up to you and say 'Why are you crying? Do you want to talk about it?' They totally ignore you . . . I've then gone on to the second phase where you're sitting in a corner very withdrawn. You don't want to mix with any groups. You want to be left entirely alone. So you watch a lot and notice other people in the first stages crying a lot. Nobody goes near them either. The only time you get to talk is about once a week when the consultant (psychiatrist) holds court and there's usually about ten to twelve people in the room.

But in the other hospital, the nurses were there all the time and if you were upset you'd never get any of this 'do stop that nonsense'. You could cry on their shoulder and then when you'd spent yourself a bit, they'd try and get you to talk . . . You spent an awful lot of your time talking which I found very helpful. *Chris*

The wards are often run on a basis where control and compliance are considered more important than individual needs. If you are extremely depressed, it may not be difficult to accept being told what to do but as you get better you will probably find it increasingly difficult. The desire not to comply is probably a healthy sign that you are feeling more alive but may not always be recognised as such by doctors and nurses.

When you're an in-patient you already feel you're on a lower level than anybody else and then to be treated like an idiot on top of that makes it even worse. They play music and you stand in a line and shake your hands about like a child. They give you a paintbrush like they do in kindergarten and say 'Paint me a little picture!' I think, when you're going through all that, it's the last thing you need. It degrades you even more than you already feel. *Chris*

If you are a voluntary patient, you have the right to refuse any treatment that is offered to you. If you feel that hospital is not helping you or even making you worse, you also have a right to leave at any time. However, there is usually some pressure put on you to stay until the doctors feel you are ready to go home. As there is usually a shortage of beds in hospital, they are not likely to keep you longer than necessary. The maximum time for 'reactive depression' is usually about three or four weeks and for 'endogenous depression' two or three months. If you want to discharge yourself it will be easier if you have friends or relatives to support you.

In fact you may have the opposite problem. Due to general financial constraints within the NHS, there is tremendous pressure on beds in psychiatric wards in most places. This means that you may not be 'allowed' to stay as long as you might want to. You may be discharged to go home while you are still feeling fragile and not ready to cope, because your bed is needed for someone else.

If you feel that you are being discharged before you are ready, you should discuss this with your doctor or whoever is in charge of your treatment. If you are not satisfied, you could complain, through the hospital or NHS Trust complaints procedure (see Appendix 1).

If you are under a 'section', then you have the right to appeal against it. The hospital itself should tell you how to do this. It is probably better to wait a few weeks until you are feeling a little bit

165

stronger before you start this procedure and again you will need support. If you do not have support from outside the hospital, then sometimes the social worker is the best person to talk to about getting help as they are usually more aware than the doctors of the social pressures which may have forced you into becoming a psychiatric patient. If you or your friends or relatives can, contact a local community law centre or women's centre. They also may be able to help or advise you.

When you have left hospital, the stigma of having been a psychiatric patient is very difficult to cope with. People generally are frightened of the idea of psychiatric hospitals, thinking of them as 'looney-bins' or 'nut-houses'. This can mean that if you mention having been in a psychiatric ward, people will understand you in terms of a stereotype, rather than as the person you are.

Another reaction I have often met is a kind of morbid fascination. I am asked questions about padded cells and suicide attempts, what mental patients are like, whether I've ever tried to hang myself and so on. I'm sure you can imagine how that makes me feel.[13]

There can also be real problems in applying for jobs. While some employers are more enlightened, many are not. Where possible it may be better to tell a 'white lie' and play the whole thing down, or not to mention it unless specifically asked. Feeling you have to hide something is inevitably a strain.

It must be five or six years since I was last in hospital and I still find it hard to believe that I'm fit to be let loose in the community! – a feeling that's reinforced when I apply for a job, or discuss my past with someone for the first time. *Ruth Elizabeth*

The worst aspect of a stigma is that it affects the way you view yourself and you have to fight very hard to counteract this. Just as we can take in ideas about what women are like, so we can take in ideas about the 'psychiatric patient', particularly as they fit in so well with the ideas we already have about women being helpless. If you have been in a psychiatric ward, you may come to believe that you are untrustable, unstable and unable to cope with stress.

Only gradually, with support from people who care about you, can you start to believe in yourself as a full person again.

Electroconvulsive Therapy (ECT) This is sometimes called 'electric shock therapy' or 'electrical treatment'. This treatment is usually only given on an in-patient basis and if you are hospitalised you may well be offered it. During ECT, electricity is passed through the brain to produce a convulsion. For reasons that no one as yet understands, this often seems to have an immediate effect in lifting someone's mood. Putting it in common sense terms, it may be that a shock to the system gets it going again.

Nowadays ECT is given under a quick-acting general anaesthetic together with a complete muscle relaxant so that you actually are asleep and do not feel anything. It may seem like a magic cure. However, one of the main problems with ECT is the immediate side-effect of loss of memory. It is a controversial issue within psychiatry as to whether there is any permanent damage to memory or whether this memory loss is completely recovered over time. One recent research study[14] showed that one week after the end of a course of ECT memory was disrupted even for events which occurred many years previously. After seven months, distant memory had recovered completely but the patients' ability to recall the events of the day of their admission to hospital (two to thirty-six days prior to starting ECT) was still impaired and to some extent their memory of public events that had taken place two to three years before had not recovered fully either. Some studies[15] have shown that there are fewer complaints of permanent ill-effects if the ECT is given unilaterally, that is to one side of the brain only, than if it is given bilaterally, to both sides of the brain. However, many hospitals still give ECT bilaterally because other studies have shown that it is more effective that way.

Women who have had ECT usually do describe some loss of memory from a subjective point of view.

I had it in the days when they didn't give you an injection first. I had it five days a week for three weeks non-stop. I had a two-week break and I relapsed so I had it for another two weeks, five days a week. That's why I've got such a poor memory now. It deadened part of my brain I suppose. There are little gaps in my life I still can't remember. I used to say

'Why couldn't you pick out the bits I don't want to remember?'
All of those things stayed with me! *Chris*

Another major problem with ECT is that its effects are short-lived. Some research studies have shown that ECT can be effective in lifting depression in the short term but there is no evidence that these effects last in the long term.[16] There is evidence that women are 2–3 times more likely to receive ECT treatment than men.[17] The danger for women is that ECT is used to provide an immediate effect that makes them feel better but which does not last. The result can be that every few years or even every few months they need more ECT. This enables people to ignore whatever other problems are contributing to women's depression.

In November 1981 a report on ECT was published by the Royal College of Psychiatrists which criticised the way in which ECT is carried out. It exposed the use of obsolete equipment and the administration of treatment by underqualified staff. It did not however criticise the use of ECT itself. Ginny Cook commented on this in *Spare Rib* of March 1982:

> It is in psychiatrists' interests to reveal suffering caused by the so-called *abuses* of psychiatry so that they may divert attention from the suffering caused by its *use*. As in most areas of the NHS, deterioration of services has been deplored, while little assessment has been made of the effectiveness of those same services in individual patients. The psychiatric system is seen to be quantitively inadequate rather than qualitatively inappropriate.[18]

In most places ECT is no longer used routinely to treat depression and is much less common than it was 10 years ago. However, it is still seen as an appropriate treatment, if depression is very severe and the person has not responded to drug treatment.

Many of us feel a revulsion at the whole idea of allowing our bodies or those of other women to be subjected to electric shocks. It may well be important to you to retain your memory while trying to work out why you became so depressed. You may prefer to let your depression lift gradually with or without the help of drugs, rather than look for the immediate 'cure' which doctors favour.

If for those or other reasons you do not wish to have ECT, no doctor can force you to do so, since a consent form has to be signed. If someone tries to persuade you into it, you should stick to your own point of view. Only under extreme circumstances, such as continuous suicide attemts or a state of depression in which a person cannot move or eat or speak, can ECT be enforced without consent from relatives.

Staying Out of Hospital

If you have been hospitalised for depression, it is most probably an experience you do not wish to repeat. It may be important to think about ways to prevent it happening again. It may not be enough just to hope that it will not happen or to believe you can prevent it by your will power alone.

When you are feeling less depressed, this may be a better time to think about seeing a psychotherapist or joining a self-help therapy group. If you are at the stage where you are building up an active life again, then you are more likely to have the strength to use therapy as a way of exploring the deeper reasons why you get depressed. We discuss the possibilities offered by various forms of therapy in the next chapter.

If you have managed to find a doctor, whether GP or a psychiatrist, whom you trust to talk to, then it may be helpful to continue seeing her or him occasionally. The same would apply to a psychologist or social worker whom you feel you can talk to. To keep in touch with someone, who knows what has happened before, can enable you to feel that there is someone there whom you can tell, if you do start to feel much worse again, before it gets to the point where hospital is needed.

On the other hand, if a doctor is discouraging about your own efforts to get better, do not be put off. Doctors can be very wrong.

I was still under Dr X at the time. I told Dr X I was tapering off the drugs I was on and was going to find a job. He remarked 'If I was going to do either of those things I would be back in hospital in less than a month.' But within a week I started work and within three weeks I was taking no drugs whatsoever.
Chris

Sometimes it may be helpful to stay on a very low dose of

drugs, until you feel more confident about your stability.

> I still take a low dose of an anti-depressant at night. I have been
> on different drugs, but this one seems to have no side effects. I
> wake up bright and breezy. But it helps me to sleep. *Patricia*

Having had a 'breakdown' is such a shattering experience that it
does take a long time to build up your confidence again. You
should try to be patient with yourself and allow yourself plenty of
time.

Perhaps the most important thing you can do is to start
building up a network of friends with whom you can share some
of your feelings.

> I have avoided antidepressants and tranquillisers, even though
> I think they might have been appropriate, through taking time
> to process my feelings. I've used and listened to four close
> friends, to try to keep in touch with reality – to keep my feet on
> the ground. It was like using other people's experience as an
> anchor. *Sue, December 1994*

Becoming isolated is one of the most common reasons why
depression gets worse. If you have not just one but several people
whom you can talk to when you start to feel down, this could
make all the difference. We discuss support networks further in
Chapter 12.

Complementary Medicines

These used to be called 'alternative' medicines, because they are
different in certain ways from our currently accepted western
system of medicine. However, many practitioners now prefer to
talk about 'complimentary' medicines to imply that they are not
necessarily intended to replace conventional medical approaches.
Most of the complementary medicines assume a unity of body
and mind. Disease is not defined as either physical or mental, as it
is in our conventional medicine, but as being a dysfunction of the
whole person in relation to her environment. Whereas western
medicine works on the idea that something external, a chemical,
can cure a disease in the body, the complementary medicines are

based on a belief in the body's natural capacity for healing itself. Their methods aim to promote this natural healing potential.

Because these methods aim to treat body and mind together, they have an obvious potential for helping with depression which involves both physical and mental components. The remedies are usually worked out very carefully for each individual, taking into account her particular history, personality and lifestyle. One advantage with these methods is that there are normally no side-effects and at worst they will do no harm to your body.

Until recently these medicines were very seldom available on the National Health Service. Now there are a few places where GPs have employed alternative practioners, such as acupuncturists or healers to work in their practices, or where an NHS hospital has a department in which complementary approaches are available. Many practitioners are very interested in the idea of working in conjunction with conventional medicine, and feel they have something to offer in areas where conventional approaches have little to offer. So we hope that this trend will continue. However we are not aware of any examples of complementary medicine being made available within a mental health unit or centre.

If you can afford to pay, there are now natural therapy centres in most areas, where you can consult a range of practitioners. Because there are so many people offering these types of medicine or therapy, it can be difficult to know how to choose a practitioner whose skills you can rely on. It is important to ask about someone's training and qualifications. Most types of medicine have a central organisation, from which you can obtain lists of practitioners who have done accredited training courses.[19]

We cannot describe here all the complimentary medicines that are available, but we shall mention briefly four that are fairly well established. These would be worth trying if you are looking for a physical method of treatment that is an alternative to taking drugs.

Acupuncture

This is the traditional Chinese system of medicine. It is a preventative system aiming to keep the body in a balanced state and based on the Chinese philosophy of Yin and Yang. This philosophy holds that everything in the universe, material or

171

immaterial, is a manifestation of 'chi', loosely translated as 'energy'. In its densest form, chi is matter, the substance of all things, including the human body. At its most refined it is mental or spiritual energy. Hence all illnesses, whether physical or mental, are seen as imblances of chi. This means that acupuncture often succeeds in curing diseases which orthodox western medicine would label 'psychosomatic' and can be most effective in clearing up physical symptoms associated with depression or stress, such as lethargy, lack of energy, allergy, headaches, lack of sexual desire, insomnia, palpitations, eating disorders and so on.

Treatment involves inserting very fine needles a few milli-metres into the skin at certain special points. These acupuncture points are grouped along lines known as 'meridians' which are thought to control the different organs of the body. The needles stimulate these meridians so as to re-establish a balanced energy flow. The needles are very fine and sharp and do not usually cause any pain more than that of a pin prick.[20] This is how one woman practitioner of acupuncture has described her work.

Acupuncturists normally take a lengthy case history to ascertain the origin of the condition. This diagnostic session is often a treatment in itself, because the person is encouraged to talk, while the practitioner listens and observes as sensitively and impartially as possible. If there is good rapport, a sympathetic ear is sometimes all that is necessary to initiate the process of cure.

The needles by themselves can do much to calm agitated energy or to raise it in cases of physical or mental depletion. There are specific treatments which in some case can re-establish balance almost miraculously in people who are seriously disturbed.

However, in many cases a rearrangement of lifestyle is necessary if the treatment is to be effective. I always try and help people understand the background to their condition, if they don't already understand it, and they often come up with their own solutions. The combination of needle treatment and encouragement provides a valuable support while they re-arrange their lives.

I am aware of how important sympathy and warmth are, but it is more important in my view to help the person to stand on her own feet. Making the decision to come for acupuncture can

172

be the first step in getting well – but she has to decide for herself or it won't work.[21]

There are also systems of massage, such as Shiatsu and Acupressure, which apply pressure to the same or similar points as acupuncture, with the shared aim of encouraging a balanced flow of energy around the body.[22]

Homeopathy

This is a fairly well-established system of medicine which is available on the NHS in some places. Many GPS are qualified to practice homeopathy and will prescribe some homeopathic remedies. However to practice it properly needs more time per patient than the NHS allows. The system is based on giving very dilute doses of substances which actually produce in a healthy person the symptoms which the patient is experiencing. These substances are cheap, taste-free and never produce side-effects. The idea is that they will stimulate or 'remind' the body to use its own method of fighting illness.[23]

Herbal medicine

This is an ancient system of medicine practised throughout the world, which uses plants to prevent and cure illness. Herbalists usually give advice on diet and lifestyle as well as prescribing herbal medicines. The aim of these remedies is to return the body's balance to normal and enable self-healing processes to operate. One particular system of herbal remedies called the Bach Flower remedies was developed specifically to affect emotional states rather than physical ones. It has been claimed to be effective in treating some 'mental illness', such as depression.[24]

Aromatherapy

Aromatherapy uses essential oils, which are very concentrated liquids, distilled from certain relevant parts of plants. These oils which work partly through our sense of smell, can be used in a variety of ways, such as for inhaling, as a massage oil when mixed with vegetable oils, or to create an aromatic bath by adding a few drops to the water. Certain essences are claimed to have the power to lift depression or to calm turbulent emotions. These oils can be used for self-help, as described in various books on the subject[25], but for any serious problem with depression it would be preferable to go to a qualified practitioner.

Other complimentary medicines or methods of healing, which may help with at least some of the symptoms of depression, include the Alexander technique (specially good for learning to release tension), Radionics, Biofeedback, Reflexology and Colour Therapy. It may also be helpful to try eastern methods of exercise and movement such as Yoga or T'ai Chi.[26]

Although trying a different approach from that authorised by conventional medicine may seem risky, in fact the risks in terms of side-effects are probably much less than with the type of medication normally prescribed for depression. The main risk will be wasting your time and money. These methods are not magic cures and they do take time to act. It is therefore best to choose one that makes some sense to you and then stick to it – rather than changing around from one to another.

Women have traditionally acted as healers in most cultures. In our western society we are now gradually re-learning some of these traditional methods and finding out how to use them for ourselves. It may be possible to contact women practising these medicines through local women's centres or health groups.

11
Looking for Help –
Psychological Approaches

In using a psychological approach we are able to look at depression as a state of mind and body which can result from a variety of life events and emotional dilemmas. Rather than understanding it as an illness that happens to someone out of the blue, we try to discover how a person becomes depressed through certain experiences and their reactions to these experiences.

Psychological approaches to treatment are usually called 'psychotherapies'. In a broad sense of the word, psychotherapy covers any form of treatment which uses mainly talking rather than medication. There are many sorts of therapy that have been developed, aiming to help people with emotional problems and we cannot describe them all here. What we hope to do in this chapter is to give you some guidelines about what to expect when looking for help from a therapist and how to find one who is right for you. We shall also describe feminist approaches to therapy and self-help groups.

As with medicine, psychology and psychotherapy have been used to keep women in their place. They have been used to encourage women to adjust to their existing social roles, rather than to question them. In both theory and application psychology has reflected the prejudices and gender bias of society as a whole.

There's nothing that socially sanctions being a lesbian. Even psychiatrists and psychologists still sometimes see it as being a deviation from the norm. So there's no trust, in the lesbian community, of psychologists or of therapy because of their history of behavioural treatments, of aversion therapy and all that stuff. We have learnt to survive on our own. *Sue*

Women from ethnic minorities have expressed similar sentiments, and some clinical psychologists who are themselves black or of mixed race have discussed the biases inherent in psychotherapy as it is usually practised.

For those black women who are offered therapy or counselling, the techniques and goals chosen therein are often wildly inappropriate. The colour divide is obvious. Most psychology books do not have any idea of the wider social and political context. Distress is seen as being located within the individual, never without, and so the impact of racism and poverty on black women is ignored. *Anuradha Sayal*[1]

My criticism of white psychotherapy is that it is used within an institutional system which is Eurocentric, which dominates society in many ways, and which tends to offer merely regulatory, adaptational ways of getting people ticking over again. It does not make any headway towards providing an understanding of why black women feel as they do.

Sue Holland.[2]

As psychologists ourselves, together with many other women who work in the area of psychology and therapy, we are now trying to use psychology in ways which can help women to increase the power and control they have over their lives and to be able to make their own choices. In doing this we aim to demystify the process of therapy and enable women to have more information about techniques so that they can find their own ways of helping themselves. This book is a contribution to that aim.

Why Go to a Therapist?

I didn't want to be given a prescription for more tablets. I wanted someone to listen and try to understand me. *Janet*

Perhaps the most common reasons for wanting therapy are these: the need for attention and the desire both to understand and to be understood. There may be a variety of reasons why you feel that you need to talk to someone outside your immediate circle of

176

friends and relatives in order to get that attention and under-standing.

I found that my sister and my daughter could not really cope with me when I was upset. Although they were sympathetic they wanted to stop me crying. I needed to talk to someone who could allow me to be miserable without trying to cheer me up. *Vera*

I needed to talk about my husband a lot and I don't think I could have done that with someone who already knew us both as a couple. *Pauline*

Some women feel very suspicious of the idea of therapy, or feel unconvinced that talking will change anything.

Why should I talk to an outsider about my problems? The whole idea of someone listening to me because it is their job seems strange. *Penny*

These doubts are to some extent justified. Perhaps if we lived in more cohesive communities we would not need professional 'carers'. Talking on its own does not change a situation. Therapy is certainly sometimes used as a way of carrying on talking about a problem without making any real changes. However if it works well, therapy can provide a space where someone will help you in exploring for yourself the reasons why you get depressed. Although the understanding gained does not automatically lead to changes, it can be a step along the way.

I recognise that I do need time for introspection. Therapy provided me with a formal structure within which I could have that time. It was good to know that every week on the same day I would have that hour when someone else would give me their full attention. This enabled me to show my feelings more easily, especially my feelings of weakness which I had been very afraid to acknowledge. It has been an enormous leap forward for me to feel that now I don't mind bursting into tears or getting very angry. *Sally*

Sometimes we feel our greatest need is to be accepted and we

177

are afraid that peole who know us will be critical.

It was a very positive thing for me – going into therapy – even though many of my friends didn't like it. I couldn't talk to friends at that time. First of all I felt totally rejected by my lover and I felt some sense of shame about that. There's a certain stage of depression where you do worry a lot about what other people might think. I couldn't talk to my friends because I was afraid they would judge me. When you're very depressed and vulnerable you can't cope with judgements. You take them in and feel that you are an awful person. *Betsy*

Psychotherapy should not be forced on anyone. It can only help if you yourself feel thcre is some point to it. If you wish to get help through a psychological approach, you need to be open to the idea that there may be ways in which your own feelings, attitudes or behaviour at least contribute to your depression and that there is a possibility of trying to change these. You are most likely to benefit from therapy if you actively want to understand yourself better rather than hoping that someone else will be able to take your depression away.

Therapy was a painful process. The most important thing I learned was how to feel perfectly myself without having to feel I'm perfect. I actually got recognition in therapy for my weakness and that it was okay to feel evil and hateful and angry and in a rage. That all those things are okay because I'm a human person with feelings. What therapy also did was to help me differentiate between what I was feeling and why I felt it. As a result I developed a stronger sense of self and a clearer knowledge of what I want and need. *Betsy*

When I first went to therapy I used to spend just about every session crying and I was crying about my father, I think. So first of all I didn't feel better – I just felt 'Oh no – I'm going to cry for ever.' But I haven't. I don't cry so much now. I always had strong feelings but I didn't know where to take them. I don't think I had a problem getting in touch with my feelings. They overwhelmed me more and that's what my depression was about. There wasn't any space for *me*. I didn't *give* myself any space. Therapy is giving me space. I feel that since I've been

178

in therapy, I don't think so much about the past and the future. I think more about now and enjoying now. *Theresa*

It is important to be clear about the limits of what therapy can do. It cannot solve or take away all our problems or provide answers by itself. Jean Baker Miller, who is herself a practising psychotherapist, sums this up at the end of her book:

> It is only because women themselves have begun to change their situation that we can now perceive new ways of understanding women ... In my own work in therapeutic situations, for instance, many women now seek to explore their own needs and to evaluate themselves in their own terms – and it seems as if there is a point in doing it. This may seem simple; it was not always so. In the past women tended to begin by asking what was wrong with them that they could not fit into men's needs and plans. This difference bespeaks a tremendous change. It is a kind of change that therapy cannot make. It precedes therapy, but its impact on therapy is enormous.[3]

Types of Therapy

Counselling

This type of therapy is very simple but extremely powerful if practised well. The aim of a counsellor is to listen and try to understand what you are feeling and what you are trying to say. She will then feed back to you what she has heard in a way which shows that she has understood, without giving judgements or advice. This is perhaps the best type of therapy for getting you through a crisis, when what you really need is emotional support rather than trying to understand yourself in more depth.

Counselling is the least intrusive therapy, in the sense that you, as 'client', should have maximum control over what is discussed. Carl Rogers originated 'client-centred therapy', sometimes called Rogerian counselling, which, as the name suggests, is based on the idea that the client should be in control. There are certain basic principles of counselling: warmth, empathy, positive regard and concern, which have been shown to be most effective in helping people to talk about their problems.[4]

Counselling has developed enormously as a discipline in the

last ten years. There are now numerous training courses in most parts of the country. Prospective counsellors may be taught a variety of psychotherapeutic models, such as psychodynamic, person-centred and cognitive behavioural, which can provide a basis for their counselling practice. Counsellors with sufficient training and experience can become accredited by the British Association of Counselling (BAC) which also specifies professional guidelines and a code of ethics for its members. If you are looking for a counsellor, you can get a list of local accredited counsellors from the BAC.[5]

Feminist centres of various sorts use counselling as a central part of their practice. Rape Crisis Centres, which exist in most big cities, provide counselling for women who have been raped, sexually assaulted or abused. Counselling can be done anonymously on the telephone as well as face-to-face on a prearranged basis. There are also some feminist centres which specialise in providing counselling for women with HIV/AIDS, women with eating problems such as anorexia or bulimia, and women survivors of sexual abuse (see Appendix 3 for contacts).

In some places local mental health centres have a walk-in counselling service, which means that at certain times in the week you can ask to talk to someone without having a prearranged appointment. You should be able to find out about the availability of these services from a health centre or doctor's surgery. Also, many GP practices and health centres now have a counsellor or clinical psychologist working in the practice at certain times in the week. A local women's centre or local branch of MIND would be likely to have names of women counsellors, and in many parts of the country, there are groups of women counsellors, working privately, who have organised themselves to form referral networks.

Co-counselling is a system of therapy where two people can act as counsellors for each other, dividing the time equally between them and taking turns to be client or counsellor. There are co-counselling groups, in which you can learn techniques of counselling, and networks for finding a co-counsellor in most areas. (See Appendix 3 for names of organisations and contacts.)

Co-counselling indulges the child in me – in a constructive way. It is like giving my 'little girl' free rein and not having to be sensible and grown-up. *Lucy*

Behaviour Therapy

As its name suggests, behaviour therapy focuses on what we do in our lives and makes suggestions for changing this in rather specific ways. A behavioural approach views depression as being due to a lack of enough rewards or 'reinforcement' for our actions. Behaviour therapy would help you look at how you can structure your life differently in order to make it more likely that you will feel rewarded for what you do. The therapist would encourage you to set goals of your own and help you structure the stages towards achieving such goals, with ways of rewarding yourself as you go along. Behaviour therapists can also teach you methods of relaxation and ways of coping with anxiety.

This approach has something to offer, particularly if you are not very interested in exploring your 'inner' self. The danger might be that you could learn to cope better but avoid facing some more fundamental reason for your depression.

Cognitive Therapy

This is a form of therapy developed by Aaron Beck, rather specifically to help people who are depressed. The theory is that depression is caused by certain thoughts, attitudes and ways of viewing the world. A cognitive therapist will help you to identify the pessimistic and self-derogatory thoughts which lead to your depression and will teach you to substitute more positive thoughts. This is obviously not as simple as it sounds and has to be worked at as a process over a period of time. We have already discussed it critically in Chapter 1.

Cognitive Behavioural Therapy

This approach, as its name suggests, uses a combination of cognitive and behavioural approaches, as described above. It is very widely practised within the NHS, mainly by clinical psychologists, but increasingly by other professionals as well, including nurse behaviour therapists and counsellors. When used flexibly by an experienced practitioner, it can be very helpful in encouraging you to look at things in a different way, and to try out different ways of tackling your problems, with the support of the therapist. When used in an empowering way, the emphasis would be on enabling you to set your own goals, rather than having an agenda imposed on you by the therapist.

Analytic (or Psychodynamic) Psychotherapy

This developed from the theories of Sigmund Freud, Carl Jung and Melanie Klein about the unconscious processes of the mind. Feminists have criticised Freud's theories about women's sexuality and the way in which Freudian psychotherapy has been used to make women adjust to a traditional role. These criticisms are well justified. However, some feminists now believe that we can use the methods of analytic psychotherapy to help us unravel the ways in which our female identity is formed on an unconscious level. What we think we *should* feel about ourselves does not always coincide with what we actually *do* feel about ourselves. Analytic psychotherapy can provide a way of exploring these contradictions in some depth.

A book which gives a simple introduction to analytic psychotherapy, as it is practised now, is *Introducton to Psychotherapy* by Dennis Brown and Jonathan Pedder.[6] A book which describes how a psychonalytic approach has been developed by feminists specifically for women is *Understanding Women* by Luise Eichenbaum and Susie Orbach.[7]

What the various schools of analytic psychotherapy have in common is their emphasis on exploring a person's inner world of fantasy and discovering how this interacts with their experiences in the outer world. There is also an emphasis on acknowledging conflicts between different desires or different parts of the self. Much of this exploration takes place directly through the relationship with the therapist. Within this relationship primitive feelings and fantasies connected with early experiences as a child may be re-enacted. Problems in relationships can be not only talked about but also looked at as they occur in the context of the therapy relationship.

This can be a deep and intense process and is not to be embarked on lightly. It would not necessarily help in getting you through an immediate crisis. It would be more likely to be of use if you want to try to understand a recurring tendency to get depressed which you feel has been with you for a long time. Analytic therapy often involves seeing a therapist over a period of several years and sometimes more than once a week. There have been some attempts to develop briefer methods of analytic psychotherapy, focusing on specific problems rather than analysing the whole personality.

Brief Psychotherapy
There is now an increasing interest within psychology and psychotherapy departments within the NHS in developing methods of brief psychotherapy. This can mean anything from about 6 to 30 sessions of psychotherapy, over a period of time lasting between two months and one year. Often the approach used is a psychodynamic one, as mentioned above, but there are other models, such as Cognitive Analytic Therapy, which has recently become popular within the NHS in certain places in England.[8] These methods are being developed because of the pressure to become more cost-effective, due to limited NHS resources, and similar pressures are being felt in the USA from insurance companies.

However brief psychotherapy can have advantages for the client. It can feel good to have a clear idea of how long the therapy is going to last, and this can increase your motivation to work hard to understand yourself better and make changes within that time. Obviously, the disadvantage can be that if you start to explore yourself within a time-limited contract and then feel that you have got in touch with aspects of yourself or deeper issues which are going to take much longer to work out, it can feel tantalising or even very painful to have to end at the agreed time. Your only alternative at that point may be to start again with a private psychotherapist if you can afford it.

A recent research project, looking at the effectiveness of psychotherapy, has shown that either 8 or 16 sessions of psychotherapy can be beneficial to a high proportion of people with emotional difficulties. The results of this project also suggested that booster sessions, at intervals after the therapy has finished, can be helpful to people in maintaining any positive changes, and that different themes may emerge at different times in a person's life.[9] It may be helpful to think of psychotherapy, not as something which you only undergo once in order to 'cure' yourself of depression for good, but rather as something which may be helpful in limited 'doses' at different times in your life.

Group Therapy
This is usually psychoanalytic in orientation. Its main advantage over individual therapy is that you have the opportunity to communicate with more than one other person about your problems. It can feel very supportive to do this with other people

who also know what it is like to be depressed even if their problems are not the same as yours. You have the opportunity to explore your feelings towards different people in the group within a safe context. Its main disadvantage is that you do not get as much individual attention from the therapist as you might desire. Group therapy is quite commonly offered within the NHS for the obvious reason that there are not enough individual therapists to go round. As with individual analytic therapy it might not be a good idea to start this form of therapy at a time when you are at the worst stage of depression. You would probably need a period of individual counselling or other supportive therapy first.

Encounter Groups

These are similar to group therapy in that a number of people arrange to meet and share feelings and problems on a regular basis, usually with a leader or therapist. The term 'encounter' has actually been applied to a range of techniques developed within the humanistic 'growth movement'.[10] The emphasis is on confrontation between people and direct expression of feelings, often in non-verbal ways using touch, movement and sound. Encounter groups sometimes use exercises suggested by the leader to get things started and generally more structure may be provided than in analytic group therapy.

Male encounter group leaders often have a great deal of 'charisma' and have been known to abuse their power by persuading female group members to sleep with them. So you need to be cautious and preferably choose a group with a female leader or one that you know something about from other people. Although this issue is particularly pertinent in relation to 'growth movement' therapies, it is also worth bearing in mind when considering other types of therapy.

Marital and Couple Therapy

This could be what you need if your depression seems to be connected with problems in your relationship. Marital or couple therapy will not necessarily help you stay together. The outcome is always uncertain and helping you to separate from a partner might be more important than patching things up. On the other hand, if communication between you is bad, it may be that bringing things out in the open will improve your relationship.

Relate is a voluntary organisation, which changed its name a few years ago from The Marriage Guidance Council, to emphasise that people can come to them for help with relationships, whether or not they are married.[11] You can refer yourself to them for help.

Although Relate or similar organisations would in principle offer a service to a lesbian couple who were having relationship difficulties, most lesbian couples would not feel comfortable with the idea of going to a predominantly heterosexual organisation. As a lesbian you would probably do better to go to a specialised agency which has some experience in working with same sex couples: for example, the Institute of Family Therapy in London, which has a special project for same sex couples, or The Pink Practice (see Appendix 3 for details).

There are also Mediation Services that exist if you and your partner decide to split and need help to do it in a constructive way. This can be especially helpful if you have children, as you and your partner will always be parents to your children even when you are living apart. The trained mediators will facilitate discussions regarding access and custody that try to avoid acrimonious court battles. (See *National Family Mediation and Conciliation Services* in Appendix 3.)

Family Therapy
This is an approach which is becoming more popular. It views the individual's problems as being related to family structures and communication patterns. The family therapist works with the whole family and tries to enable them to use their own resources to develop better ways of communicating and dealing with problems. As we have discussed elsewhere in this book, many women who are mothers bear the whole burden of giving emotional support in a family. They are often not able to get what they need for themselves and can get depressed as a result. A family approach to therapy would enable this problem to be brought out into the open and recognised by all members of the family.

Family therapy most often uses a systemic approach. This means that a person's position in the various social systems within which she operates is seen as important. It is based on the assumption that family members can, with help, find solutions to their problems or difficulties by making changes in their relationships. No one member of a family is seen as the problem.

I think it's one of the very few psychological models that actually demands of the therapist to take context into account. I don't just mean the context within the family, but all the issues of the wider context. For black women, this context will be about issues of racism.

Particularly for cultures where the family is still seen as the pivot of society, I think it makes therapy more palatable if the therapist can see you as part of the world you have grown up in, with your family members or your partner, rather than imposing a different way of viewing yourself. It enables you to work within your own world view of what self is. *Gita*

Other Therapies

These include Gestalt therapy, Reichian therapy, Transactional Analysis, Psychosynthesis and more. *In Our Own Hands* by Lucy Goodison and Sheila Ernst[12] provides good descriptions of the basis of most of these, together with a feminist critique. It is also possible to find books about therapies in local libraries and there are a few guides to therapy from the consumers' point of view which can be useful.[13]

Feminist Approaches to Therapy

We decided not to call this section 'feminist therapy' because we do not feel that a clearly separate or different form of therapy has as yet been developed. The idea of 'feminist therapy' sounds like a contradiction and may be confusing. Feminism is a political stance which draws attention to the external factors which limit women's lives. On the other hand, doing therapy involves helping people to see the ways they themselves are responsible for their problems and is supposed to be politically neutral.

This is in some ways a false dichotomy. The notion that therapy is politically neutral has been challenged. It is clear that it has often been used to adjust people to their situations; thereby upholding the political status quo.[14] Feminism is not only concerned with external material reality but also with how certain ideas about women get inside our own heads.

The idea of 'feminist therapy' has grown out of the philosophy of 'consciousness raising'. Consciousness-raising groups are small informal groups of women who meet regularly to talk about their lives. These groups began in the Women's Liberation Movement of the late 1960s, as a way by which women could explore together, not only the personal aspects of their problems, but also the wider political issues. Women became able to make a connection between their own feelings of discontent and those of other women. They began to distinguish which aspects of their problems were due to personal factors and which were due to prejudice and restrictions placed on women in general. Feminist approaches to therapy were originally developed by women who had themselves grown through this experience of 'consciousness raising'.

'Feminist therapy' is not a single approach to therapy but covers a variety of ways in which therapists who are also feminists have tried to incorporate an awareness of the oppression of women into their work[15]. Moira Walker has written about feminist counselling, saying that it is not a technique that could be learnt in a workshop, but a perspective that 'allows fluidity, acknowledges interconnectedness, and encourages exploration'. She also describes the importance of making the counselling process accessible and comprehensible, rather than mystifying and mysterious, and of a commitment to an egalitarian relationship rather than one based on a hierarchy.[16]

Lucy Goodison and Sheila Ernst[17] describe a variety of approaches which feminists may use and sum up the common outlook of 'feminist therapy' as follows:

The assumption which is shared by all feminists involved in therapy, however, is that as women we are brought up to be second-class citizens in a male-defined world, and that this deeply affects our emotional lives. It follows that the role of a feminist therapist, or a feminist self-help therapy group, is not to adjust us to being second-class citizens but to help us to explore how this experience has affected us, what a struggle it is to have your ways of seeing the world validated, and how we can make ourselves stronger.

If you go to a feminist therapist you could expect her to be aware that personal struggles are often connected with wider political issues. At the same time as helping you to work out personal problems in your own way, she would probably encourage you to understand these problems as occurring within

187

the context of a male-dominated society and as being shared by other women. You could also expect her to be aware of the need for women to experiment with new life-styles and forms of self-expression, including sexuality. At the same time, she should be aware of the forces which make change difficult, and of how risky it can feel to give up old ways of coping.

Many women who are both feminists and work in the 'caring professions' are meeting to discuss ways of working. This is how one feminist clinical psychologist, has described her work:

> In therapy the woman begins to identify the social values which she has internalised and come to consider her own. She realises that these may actually be alien to her and hinder development or self-fulfilment. By identifying them and their origins, it then becomes possible to externalise them. The woman is then free to explore what she actually feels and believes . . . her experience as a woman is validated. She may discover that she is not 'mad' or 'ill' and that some of her 'craziness' actually reflects the contradictions inherent in the society she lives in. As a therapist one has to constantly explore one's own values and attitudes concerning women and confront tendencies in oneself towards maintaining the status quo. The emphasis in feminist theory is on change rather than adjustment.[18]

Feminists are very aware of the power difference in the therapy relationship. During the last ten years there has been discussion and writing among feminist psychotherapists, counsellors and psychologists about establishing certain principles of feminist practice in therapy. The aim of these principles is to try to reduce the inequality of power in therapy. They include de-mystifying the therapy process by therapists being more explicit about the way they work; de-mystifying the therapist through therapists being more explicit about their training, areas of expertise and professional or personal values; and strengthening clients' rights in therapy and their active participation in therapy, through negotiating the aims of therapy and through involving clients in giving feedback about the therapy process and in evaluating the outcome at the end of therapy.[19]

An idea that has become important to feminist therapists is that of 'empowerment'. Gilli Watson and Jennie Williams have described the starting point of this process:

> Making explicit the social processes that delimit women's use of, and access to, power offers women a way of making visible these power processes. It may also lessen the shame or blame women may feel about the power they use – self-harm, alcohol, withdrawal.[20]

The process of empowerment means helping women find ways to use other sources of personal power that are not self-abusive. This may include finding our own voice: feeling safe to speak, finding ways to manage rage in a safe way, and many other aspects of becoming bigger, stronger and taking up more space.

An important aspect of the power difference within the therapy relationship is that most professionals are white, middle-class and heterosexual and have a great deal of privilege within society. Although it would not be possible or even a good thing for a therapist to have had exactly the same experiences as her client, wide differences in experience and status can cause problems.

Before choosing a therapist, whether feminist or otherwise, you might want to think about how important these differences are to you. The power differential and the possibility of its abuse within therapy has been one of the reasons for developing self-help groups.

> What is difficult about going into therapy as a lesbian, if your therapist is not a lesbian, is that she doesn't really know what it's like to have a lesbian identity. She can say she knows it's difficult – but she doesn't have the experience. I would like there to be more lesbian therapists. *Betsy*

There are some practising lesbian therapists who have written about their work.[21] There are many issues concerning the relationship between therapy and feminism which both lesbian and heterosexual therapists need to confront and which we have only touched on here. For example, we need to be aware of the contradiction between the way in which opportunities are determined by race and class, as well as sex, and the values of individual self-development which therapy tends to promote.

There are some feminist therapists who have worked in quite radical ways, to address these contradictions. For example, Sue

189

Holland has described her work as a community clinical psychologist in an urban multiracial housing estate in West London. In the programme she developed there, women are given the opportunity to move through individual psychotherapy into involvement in support groups and collective social action, which can be more empowering than the individual work alone.

Any psychotherapeutic intervention in their depression must address not only issues of loss and guilt, anger and reparation, but also the hidden rage and desire for justice provoked by years of poverty and oppression.[22]

Sue Holland has also discussed how her own transracial identity has influenced her work with mixed-race groups.

I have worked mostly with working-class, transracial and black people, trying to use psychotherapy in a way which would help them not only to change themselves but to change things around them. So I have had to struggle not only with psychotherapy itself, which has its limitations, but also to find other kinds of theories which would help me to achieve this.[23]

We have certainly not resolved all these issues for ourselves and we expect to continue discussing them with other women and learning from our own experiences.

Looking for a Therapist

Finding the right therapist is not easy. No matter what approach a therapist uses, it will be most important that you get on together as people. This is something which is hard to define. It does not mean that you have to agree about everything. But you need to be able to communicate about your disagreements. There may be quite small clues which lead one to feel comfortable with someone else's personality.

Ideally it would be best to 'shop around'. Find the names of several therapists that you can contact and make your decision on the basis of having talked with each of them. When you talk to a possible therapist you need to remember that you are interviewing them as much as they are interviewing you. You need to ask yourself 'Is this someone I could work with?' You may want to ask specific questions about her approach to therapy and what she would regard as being its aims. Therapists vary a great deal as to how much they will tell you about themselves but they should be able to discuss their way of working to some extent. It is important to trust your intuitive sense about the person according to how you feel when talking with them.

If you go to a therapist because you are in a crisis, you may not have time to think about finding the best person. If you desperately need to talk to someone, you are likely to accept the first person suggested to you. (This is why the anonymity and 'distance' of a phone line such as Samaritans, Rape Crisis Centre or Lesbian Line can in some ways be helpful when you are feeling desperate.) If a therapist helps you through a crisis, you do not have to stick with the same person if you want to continue on a long-term basis. You might want to consider various possibilities before committing yourself. Some therapists would suggest a break before deciding on long-term therapy.

It can however be very difficult to change your therapist once you have started. If you are not getting on well with your therapist it can be hard to tell whether this is because she (or he) is the wrong person for you or because it is your own problems with relationships which make you feel that way. In the end you have to trust your own judgement. You should be able to find out whether you basically trust this person but are feeling angry or dissatisfied at the moment or whether you really cannot trust them. As with other relationships, there is no perfect therapist and each therapist will have her own strengths and limitations in what she has to offer.

Because there is as yet no statutory registration for psychotherapists, anyone can call themselves a psychotherapist, however minimal their training. However there is now an organisation, the UK Council for Psychotherapy, which holds a voluntary National Register of Psychotherapists. In order to be registered, a psychotherapist must belong to one of the member organisations, which all conform to certain training standards as well as ethical guidelines, and have specific complaints procedures. We would therefore strongly advise women to choose a psychotherapist who is a registered member of UKCP.

The British Association for Counselling serves a similar function by producing a register of accredited counsellors, and for clinical psychologists there is a register of chartered clinical psychologists, which is held by the British Psychological Society. These professional bodies are important because they do provide some guarantee that a practitioner will have a reasonable level of training and experience, and their formal complaints procedures provide some protection from the risks of abuse within therapy.[24]

If you are referred to a therapist on the NHS there will be less possibility of choice. However, you should feel free to say if you don't like your therapist for any reason and to state your preference regarding the gender or racial background of your therapist, or a desire to be in women-only groups. These issues are frequently played down but are undeniably important. It may be difficult to negotiate but it is crucial that you feel comfortable and trusting of the person and the situation within which you are going to work.

> To a black woman that is depressed and looking for help, I would say that if you feel the need to see a black therapist, you should ask for one. You have a right to make that request. Even if you are seeing a white therapist, you have the right to put issues of racism, of oppression and about being a woman on the agenda. *Ayesha*

> It's all right to use whatever language you feel expresses your distress. You shouldn't feel that you have to say the right thing, or say things in a certain way. *Gita*

If your GP does not have access to a black psychotherapist, it is possible for them to make an extra-contractual referral to a service which does have a black therapist, and you can ask for this. It is also important to ask for information about local voluntary agencies which provide psychotherapy or counselling specifically for people from different ethnic groups.[25] You should try to ask as much as possible about what choices are available to you.

If you want to see a therapist privately and do not have much money, there are some therapists who operate a sliding scale according to income. It might be worth trying to find out about this rather than assume that you cannot afford it. Many women understandably dislike the idea of paying for an emotional relationship, but the advantage is that you do have more choice than within the NHS.

Other possibilities to consider are self-help groups, which we describe in the next section, and co-counselling, which we have already mentioned (see under *Counselling*). As well as the fact that you do not have to pay, both these approaches involve relationships with other women, in which time and attention are shared on an equal basis.

Self-help Therapy Groups

When women started meeting in consciousness-raising groups, the experience of being able to share doubts and dilemmas with other women was often found to be therapeutic or healing in and of itself. Women found that they could become more assertive, could pay more attention to their own needs and generally think better of themselves.

However, women also found it is very difficult to change fundamentally. The ways we have learnt to devalue ourselves go very deep and we can find that our own feelings seem to sabotage our conscious choices. Some women started to feel the need to go beyond the original format of consciousness-raising groups and try using therapy techniques within women's groups.

Sheila Ernst and Lucy Goodison have described the way self-help therapy groups developed.

Recognising that we needed to unlearn this conditioning, we started to bring to the surface some of our repressed feelings. This process should, perhaps have been called 'unconsciousness raising'. It is a pity that we called it therapy. Therapy suggests male therapists telling a women they are sick; it suggests a process aimed at adjusting women to conventional and restrictive roles; it suggests drug treatment to passify us, shock treatment to frighten and silence us. What we did was very different. We started to do therapy in small groups, without leaders, using our feminist understanding to help us develop in ways which we value, to increase our strength, creativity and confidence – in ourselves and in other women.[26]

Self-help therapy groups spring out of our need to share our experiences of trying to resolve difficulties. Whom better to talk to about depression than another woman who has experienced it as well? Together we can exchange ideas and information, practical suggestions, encouragement, support and insight.

> It was enormously reassuring to me to find out that other women had experienced the same sort of feelings as I had and that I did not have to pretend to be feeling all right. *Linda*

Self-help groups are an attempt to resolve the power imbalances other therapies create. Ideally they are groups of equals. Because of the inequalities inherent in society, this is a difficult ideal to accomplish, even in women-only groups. Often for this reason self-help groups are very focused and their membership is restricted to, for instance, certain age groups, racial groups, or sexual orientation.

In any group there must be a commitment to one another to work out differences, a mutual respect for and honesty with each other and an agreed structure. Self-help groups are supposed to be 'leaderless'. No expert is called in from outside to lead or guide the group each time it meets. It may be that one woman will take on this function at each meeting. How the group runs and what happens in the group is essentially determined by its members. Nevertheless, how the group deals with issues of leadership can be very important, as these are often a focus for both our needs for safety and nurturing, and our desire for structure and boundaries. As Jocelyn Chaplin and Amelie Noack have put it, 'We need to be mothered and nurtured, but we also need to focus and get on with business. It does not have to be one or the other.'[27]

Groups like Alcoholics Anonymous, Narcotics Anonymous and Weight Watchers started off as self-help groups. Many women have been helped by groups which address issues of dependency, such as Al-Anon and Co-dependents Anonymous. These groups often use the 12-step programme originally formulated for Alcoholics Anonymous, and may be particularly relevant to women who are caught up with taking responsibility for other peoples' problems.[28]

> I experienced depression, exhaustion and illness due to putting my partner's needs first and rescuing her. I am now trying to look at how I've colluded with my own loss of self. The process of extracting yourself from a compulsive helping relationship

is very painful, because it means saying 'no' and sticking to it, in the face of demands from the other person.

Sue, December, 1994

A feminist self-help group would incorporate basic feminist principles. These include a commitment to space for women to share their inner thoughts and feelings with other women, and a recognition of the oppression of women by men.

The difference between self-help therapy groups and consciousness-raising groups is difficult to describe. There is a large amount of overlap. Perhaps the most obvious difference is the methods used by self-help therapy to make issues conscious or readily available to our thinking selves. Self-help therapy groups employ 'exercises' and 'techniques' developed by the various psychological therapies for resolving personal difficulties. The point of using these techniques is to help women express feelings and find out more about their emotional roots. The aim is to go beyond intellectual discussion; to move towards exploring the more irrational parts of ourselves.

In consciousness-raising groups the method used is to allow each woman time to talk about how she has experienced a certain pre-arranged topic or theme (such as work, sexuality, mothers, fathers, self-image), in her life. The aim is for other women not to interrupt or intervene while one woman is talking but rather to learn from the process of listening and sharing. Consciousness-raising groups are less popular now than they were in the 1970s. The present-day equivalents are more likely to be called 'Women's support groups'. However we do know of several women's groups which have continued to run with the same membership for 15 to 20 years.

In practice each women's group, whatever its label, evolves its own sense of identity and tries to find the right level of communication to satisfy the needs of its members. It is becoming increasingly common for women to meet together in support groups focused on particular shared problems, such as those they face within a particular type of work or in coping with a particular disability or illness. The boundaries between therapy and support are not clear-cut.

I think it's like that for most people – they need to be talked to in a language they understand. Everyone has a different emotional language. My emotional language is to say things in a nice patient way and then I can talk through my problems.

Elizabeth

For some women it may be most helpful to join a group which is not specifically a therapy group.

Many black women have found it helpful, either during or after a period of depression, to join a group like a black women's creative writing group, or a black women's dance group. Especially in large cities, such as London, there are likely to be these opportunities. Being able to explore your difficulties within different creative media can be enormously empowering. It can help to create a link between where a black woman is now and her cultural past. Getting in touch with her sense of creativity can help to create a positive image about her own blackness, which she can then transmit to her children as well. *Gita*

The advantages of self-help therapy are first that it is free and second that as individuals we have more power and control over what we choose to discuss and how we choose to discuss it. It also encourages us to look to ourselves and each other for the answers. It can be frightening, as our very intimate feelings are often unknown to our outer selves. Our inner worlds still have a 'Pandora's box' aura about them – we have the idea that once we start talking and feeling from our 'innards', that we will unleash all manner of things, mostly horrible.

Your silence reinforces my fear that such behaviour is totally unacceptable. What a horrible feeling . . . loss of control, despair, clutching on to whatever is real – reeling, feeling nauseous . . . vomitting from the very pit of your stomach . . . getting rid of all the poison, all the badness – leaving me weak, defenceless and very isolated. *Marie, June 1980*

Can we trust each other that much? Can we know each other well enough to contain each other's experience in a safe, secure and comforting way? If we personally lose control can other women help us to regain it?

I have actually experienced 'a bout of depression' and for the first time felt able to bring it to the group. The support has altered not only how I dealt with this, but the nature of the experience itself.[29]

If you cannot find a self-help group in your area you might like to advertise for other women and start one yourself. The National Council for Voluntary Organisations offers some support to self-help groups and maintains a database and information service about self-help activities throughout the country.[30] If you are thinking of joining an existing group, it is important to think out what sort of questions you might want to ask the group members before deciding to join. You might want to ask about how they deal with issues of confidentiality, leadership, structure and commitment.[31]

In Our Own Hands[32] is a book which gives many creative ideas about techniques to use and things to do in a self-help therapy group. It also discusses all the dilemmas and difficulties involved in keeping such a group going. Another book which may be useful for self-help therapy, either on your own or within a group is *The Intimacy and Solitude Self-Therapy Book*.[33] There are also some books which may be helpful in working with issues of sexual abuse within self-help groups.[34]

You may find it useful to share and explore the meaning of dreams with other women in a group. There are some books which give ideas about how to do this.[35] Dreams can be a very powerful and immediate way of finding out about our unconscious selves.

I dreamt about having to look after two turtles who have lost their shells and are therefore very sensitive and vulnerable. They are like mischievous children who might get hurt. This dream showed me that it is the child in me which feels vulnerable and needs looking after. I realised that I get depressed when the child in me feels deprived. If I give more time and attention to this part of me, on my own and with other people, then I can feel more whole and more alive.

Lucie, October 1976

Depression and its intimate connection with sadness, misery and despair is a dreadful burden to carry alone. We must remember that self-help therapy is not about passing the burden to another woman (who no doubt would add it quite willingly to her own, as is our inclination), but about sharing the load more evenly between all of us. It may be that we must all walk a little stoop-shouldered for some time.

12
The Economy of Depression:
Social and Political Perspectives

'Coming Out' is a term used by the Gay Liberation Movement. It refers to the process of identification that a person goes through when they openly recognise and state their sexual attraction to same sex partners. It is multifaceted process. It can start by admitting your feelings to yourself and then stating them to others. It isn't easy because there are lots of reasons why we might feel safer keeping quiet about who we sleep with. Lesbians can, and do, lose their jobs, their children and perhaps some of their friends and family because they choose to share their sexuality with women.

As a process, 'coming out' can be usefully applied to depression. It is difficult for us to recognise and admit to feeling depressed.

> This is something I have never tried to say before. I didn't even know that this was how I felt until I sat down to write and this all poured out along with a lot of tears.[1]

By sharing our experiences we realise depression, the designated 'women's illness', is one of almost epidemic proportions. The complaints we are voicing are often justified and ought to be complained about. Sharing them can motivate women to get together and effectively organise around issues to improve the situation.

There are now many more collections of women's experiences available for us to read. Originally we singled out *Finding a Voice: Asian Women in Britain*[2]. There is also *The Heart of the Race: Black Women's Lives in Britain*[3] which outlines not only life issues for black women but also the organisation of black women's groups to become powerful lobbying bodies on behalf of black and asian women. The effectiveness of this lobbying can be seen in a number of high profile campaigns, such as the release of Kiranjit Aluwahlia who was gaoled for killing her husband following years of physical abuse from him.[4] The 1980s also saw the high profile Women against Pit Closures Campaign which demonstrated the key role women play in supporting and holding together not only their families but also their communities.

These accounts enable us to build up a collective strength with which we can protest about the situations that do make us more prone to depression.

Solidarity within the women's liberation movement grew not out of our strengths as women but out of our pain, suffering, doubts and dilemmas: feelings and confusion that in the past we bore and wrestled with in personal isolation.

There is enormous pressure on all of us to be happy or at least pretend to be; to keep miserable or worthless feelings quite separate from the rest of our lives. Even among our closest friends, it can be very difficult to share our morose thoughts. It is not really polite to discuss your suicide fantasies, or your most despairing points of view.

As a matter of habit, when we are asked how we are, we say fine, almost without hesitation or exception, regardless of how we actually feel. We assume this is what people expect to hear, or that they don't really care anyway. Many of us feel that our friends really are not interested in the depressed side of our character. This point of view only confirms our idea that depression is something nasty, maybe even catching!

We can worry about being a burden and cut ourselves off from the outside world further. We may fear alienating our friends or trying their patience. We can fear being rejected by them. We can feel angry that those who supposedly love and know us haven't recognised our depression; or frightened to admit to our depressed feelings for fear of being overwhelmed by them. We can feel that by fighting the feelings we will prevent them from getting worse.

Depression does not usually go away for good, so trying to plan a life free from the blues is unrealistic. It can be difficult to admit that you are going through yet another phase of being 'down'. Our own reaction is often 'Oh no, not again!' Trying to use depression as a passively creative phase may be a more realistic goal but not one to be tried alone.

Now I have phases of intense anxiety, more often than depression . . . I try to use this situation as a challenge to stay in touch with what my needs are and to find ways to meet those needs to some extent, rather than getting totally submerged. I have some ways of getting support. I have a session with a woman healer and counsellor about once a fortnight. I value this space where I can get some of the attention I need and can get help in identifying ways in which I am stuck and ways to move foreword. I find that writing down and discussing my dreams is very useful as they often give me a different perspective on what I am struggling with. I belong to a woman's support group, which does not meet very often, but provides a valuable source of continuity and connection with other women at a similar stage in life. *Lucie, November 1994*

Depression can help us to become more introspective or enable us to concentrate on taking care of ourselves for a while. Our emotions may also have a cycle that can manifest itself daily, monthly or seasonally. If we can recognise and accept it, we may be able to avert what in the past might have become another depressive episode.

Now, I'm not depressed: I'm just a normal person who has an up and a down – where one day is better than another. It doesn't last a day. I don't get worried any more if I feel down. It's lovely to know I can feel quiet. The girls at work sometimes say to me 'You all right?' and I can say, 'Yeah, it's just one of those days where I want to be quiet or something didn't go right.' It's lovely to know it's not depression. *Janice*

Networks
A small group of friends often operate as a support network. They can be women we work with, share a common interest with, classmates or neighbours. They may know each other, they may not. By talking more to each other about depression generally, we can begin to use our networks more supportively.

I know I can take care of myself and taking care of myself doesn't mean doing it on my own. It means other people helping me and helping other people. Whereas, before, I had totally isolated myself when I was depressed. *Betsy*

Together we can come up with solutions that individually would not be possible; the babysitting circle, the women's group, the so-called hen parties are all examples of a support network in operation.

I remember occasions when I have felt mentally hurt, helpless, alone and scared. I have been lucky because friends were there to help me through these journeys. *Jackie*

Female friendships are frequently based on our common, often painful, experiences. Women have gathered together around events like birth, the end of a relationship or death, not in a show of 'strength' but as a way of supporting each other and acknowledging the powerful feelings these experiences evoke.

We must remain committed to this ideal of female bonding – the mutual understanding that comes from our suffering and oppression.

My close friends help just by being around. They weren't around a lot, but made the occasional visit every couple of days. I would just sleep and sleep and occasionally they would bring some food in or talk to me and ask me how I was. I didn't need them to do more than just be there. *Sue*

Lovers will often be part of our support network.

My husband knows my moods and has always been very supportive to me both in the past and now with my present illness, but I find it is sometimes easier to talk to someone who is caring and not emotionally involved. I can then unburden myself without worrying about how it's going to affect them.

Chris

George Brown and Tirril Harris[5] noted that having a close confiding relationship (in their study predominantly with a husband or boyfriend) protected women from depression. The study of close confiding relationships and the role they play in mental health has continued to be well researched, including looking at the development of friendships in children and adolescents. There is clear link that close confiding relationships help individuals cope with difficult situations and adverse events.[6] Yet despite the benefits of an intimate relationship, sole dependence on one person for support makes us much more vulnerable to their feelings and behaviour. We may think what we have with a lover is a good solid base but in a crisis it can seem like a balance beam. It is perhaps ironic that lovers often halve our social networks rather than double them!

In sharing our doubts and dilemmas, we can begin to recognise what women collectively are up against and try to make our efforts to resist more effective. It is important to collect our individual experiences together and examine them for similiarities and differences. This will only strengthen our own identities and boundaries.

> If someone else is depressed at the same time as me, I can recognise now that their depression has a different root. So it doesn't have to be so symbiotic. We don't have to merge in a pit of despond. *Betsy*

Collections of personal histories and essays give all of us access to a richness of thought and experience that individually we could not otherwise achieve. They also demonstrate that 'coming out' is not a guilt-ridden self confession but a positive affirmation of a hitherto 'unacceptable' part of yourself. It is ultimately a creative experience that can make you feel more whole.

Recognising the connection between our own personal struggle and those of other women, puts the personal into the political. Understanding the nature of our oppression in this sexist society is essential in helping us assess our own needs and goals, and then communicate them to others.

It is still necessary for women to speak out about our individual needs. We have not yet learned a way of naturally understanding all of our different experiences. It is a measure of how much stronger all women are, that we are able to speak out for ourselves and cite our differences along with our needs.

> If I am to integrate myself so that I am no longer split between the 'normal' me and the 'ill' me then that 'ill' me must be acceptable not only to me but to other women as well. In fact, I

203

cannot accept it I think, until others do. And for other women to accept it means that those women must examine their unacceptable, inadequate, frightened, vulnerable parts of themselves. Then together we can try to find words for these experiences, to explore their origins and understand them in order to do something about them. What I am advocating is not some form of therapy. It is precisely the experience of pain as illness, a privatised personal problem that I want to get away from. I'm not asking for support so much as a sense of mutual recognition, a door through which I can come in from the cold, or through which you can come out into the storm.[7]

Over time we can begin to recognise the social values we have taken on board or internalised. We can see how often these values actually militate against a healthy coping image of ourselves. By identifying them and their origin we can begin to relieve ourselves of the burden.[8]

Consciousness raising validates our experiences as women and helps us take responsibility for some of them. It can help us feel confident about expressing our needs. If we have a commitment to seeing those needs fulfilled, we will begin to find the ways and means. It may be that we find some of our needs are unrealistic but in negotiating to have them met we may adjust our expectations. We may find that we value what we do get from a situation. We need to ask ourselves, is it enough?

I realise that no matter how we try to redefine our relationships with men, they become construed in traditional terms – a denial of the work, the pain that's gone into the relationship to make it different. *Fiona*

Learning to confront each other and challenge our assumptions is also very difficult.

I think, though, that it is respectful of autonomy to genuinely inquire into history and grounds of choices, and disrespectful or negligent of autonomy to let unfreedom masquerade as choice or let the declaration 'It's my choice' close off rather than open up inquiry.[9]

As we assume more control over our lives and try to exercise our choices, we are almost bound to become angry, frustrated and depressed. Learning to channel our emotional energy effectively, needs a lot of practice. Our anger, frustration and despair are related to the lack of *real* alternatives for women. Those that do exist often arise because of extreme situations. For instance, refuge is offered to women, only if they are being beaten by their male partners.[10] There are few places to go, just to get away from it all, unless we have access to money. Family holidays often mean more work for women, perhaps with only a change of scenery.

We need to hear about the alternatives women have tried to make for themselves. These can range from very simple things to more complex arrangements such as communal living or income sharing. We can discover that by pooling our resources we can achieve a higher standard of living for everyone involved.

By consciously sharing our novel solutions with each other we can bring life to the 'grapevine' and add new meaning to 'household hints' or 'old wives' 'tales' which have always been our heritage.

We are not only short of information about alternatives and their practical implications but also do not have images of strong women to identify with. In emphasising our ability to be strong and independent women we need to guard against not allowing space for sharing our anxieties, weaknesses and doubts.

I no longer feel the only unfeminine failure in a world of successful feminine women, but I still feel very much apart. Now I feel for most of the time like someone who 'cannot cope' in a movement full of women who can.[11]

By redefining strength, we can recognise it more clearly.

I think it does you good to realise you have been hurt and you have a right to feel sorry for yourself. So many people consider themselves hard because they can push it to the back of their minds. I consider myself strong because I have admitted to it . . . *Janice*

Our mothers, our grandmothers, our friends, ourselves . . . these are strong women. Women who have dealt with an infinite

205

number of problems quietly, efficiently and tenderly. We do pay a price for our understanding and strength.

'Understand?' he asked me silently . . . like my father – all men. And I understand only too painfully. 'You ask for too much', he said, when I have asked for nothing, only honesty. 'I need to negotiate my life from strength not weakness.' A luxury men can afford. Women must always negotiate from a position of weakness. I felt like saying to him, your weaknesses are your strengths. It was difficult – it was tense and it hurt like hell to understand. My strength is used against me. Men use it to ask me to put my own feelings aside. *Marie, August 1981*

In learning about ourselves, talking, reading, writing – alone and with other women, we will find obstacles to overcome. On this journey through, we do become stronger, more resilient and the obstacles seem to be more predictable. Knowing what compromises we make in our lives, can give us the possibility of choice. Feeling in control of our lives is a rare feeling for most women. It is precious for it can only be won by a lot of hardship and struggle, unless we fight standing on another woman's back.

This book is about different ways of dealing with depression. Throughout it, we have tried to emphasise that each one of us must make our own choices and take responsibility for them. There is no one prescription to 'cure' depression. There are many different ways of feeling it, living with it, preventing it, growing with it . . . We need to recognise that our choices, although made individually, will affect other women's choices. So we must remain responsible for sustaining our connectedness to other women.

Through knowing ourselves, we can begin to treat ourselves with the respect and love that will make any 'cure' most potent. It is important that we acknowledge our personal expertise. This book also emphasises that speaking from personal experience is not only helpful in and of itself but also to those women you choose to share your experience with. It enables others to speak of their lives and not feel disqualified.

We have written of the connection between depression and loss. In the face of loss, women respond with sadness not anger.[12] In some way, we as women are in a continual state of mourning

206

for something we have, but are stopped from using in a positive and personal way . . . power.

As Luisah Teish said in an interview with Gloria Anzaldúa,[13] 'We have become victims of our own benevolence.' We, unmindfully at times, sacrifice ourselves in the interest of *mankind*. We direct our energy to service others – men and male children first, daughters and other women next and finally ourselves. All women are deprived of the love of women. That neediness within each of us seeks fulfilment in many different ways. This twentieth-century epidemic of depression is not really an epidemic. It is the result of many years' famine. While we have fed the world we know with love, we have starved ourselves.

Adrienne Rich recounts this parable in her book *Of Woman Born*:

> A woman is trying to cross a deep fordless river into the land of freedom. She wants to carry with her the male infant suckling at her breast but she is told, No, you will lose your life trying to save him; he must grow into a man and save himself, and then you will meet him on the other side.[14]

In trying to carry on, to do the best by everyone else but ourselves, it is no wonder we are tired and despairing. Of the many battles we will fight in this life, perhaps the most significant will be the one with ourselves.

> This super-woman veneer also warded off internal self reflection needed to assess if indeed I was strong enough to carry such heavy burdens. The ever-growing intellect was an additional burden because the ability to think allows me to look at, if not truly see, options and truth. The open heart and forgiving soul stifled by righteous indignation, gagged my rage and forced my fears, my needs, my rage, my joys, my accomplishments, inward. The acceptance of total responsibility real, concrete or abstract for myself and others became my ultimate strait jacket, the last and strongest barrier to self.[15]

While many companies and professionals deal *in* depression as a means of social control and personal betterment, it is generally only women who truly deal *with* it. Our depression has a political meaning. Living as a woman in this society can be so desperately lonely that we may choose to poison ourselves and climb into the family freezer rather than carry on struggling. If that loneliness could find solace and that deadly courage become a fighting spirit, the trade in women's depression might come to an end.

Afterword

We know it is customary to begin with thanks; but we can honestly say that we are happy for the writing of this book to end, thankfully!

The women who helped with this project have all shared very private thoughts and agreed to have them printed. So we were able to use material from conversations, diaries, letters and taped interviews. The contents of any 'ordinary' person's diary, correspondence, conversations and therapeutic insights are rarely considered noteworthy. Yet personal ruminations and sometimes the therapeutic relationship, the content of which often remains secret, can unintentionally contribute to what Ruth Elizabeth has referred to as the 'privatisation of pain'. This book grows out of the personal experiences of many women who cared to share – our acknowledgement and thanks.

Tricia Graham and Wendy Simes typed, corrected, cut and pasted, photocopied and typed again, this manuscript. They watched it expand from an outline to a book. Any creeping pomposity on our part, they nipped in the bud.

Hannah Kanter asked for this book and having done so has stuck by us through the whole procedure. We have always found her suggestions useful and appreciated her thoughtfulness and concern. She added the finishing touches, editing and clarifying.

Ruth Elizabeth has read the manuscript at several important stages. Her individual perspective, coupled with her commitment to thinking beyond the purely personal to a wider political analysis, has helped to balance the book.

It is easy, given our psychological backgrounds, to over-emphasise the individual perspective. If this is done at the expense of recognising the social and political context of that individual, then the approach is ultimately reactionary. Although the current fashion in psychological treatment is 'family therapy', it is often offered without any attention being given to the political importance of the family as an institution of social control.

Ruth Elizabeth was not alone in helping us recognise our defensiveness of psychology as both a profession and a conceptual framework. Many times in writing this book we would slip into trying to provide THE ANSWERS or more rarely adopting a patronising tone. This comes from our genuine desire for change.

While emphasising the very real and potent social forces that keep women down, we try in our work to help individual women learn to strengthen themselves psychologically. We recognise that individual psychological change is not enough to liberate women; yet without inner strength, we will not realise the ideals of equality and freedom we strive for.

Women in the 'caring professions', like mothers, have a tendency to extend themselves until exhausted. When feeling needy, we often take on *more* work rather than less. The danger is that we come to live off the emotional satisfaction of being needed by others and the sense of power we get from being confided in. We can end up living vicariously through our work and spending the rest of the time recovering. Our own feelings and needs can get lost.

To avoid this pattern, we must take this danger seriously: to plan carefully to get the support we need at work and create spaces in our lives which are for ourselves alone. We try to foster a sense of personal potency and discover additional ways of getting our emotional needs fulfilled outside of our work. When we slip up on these personal prescriptions, our unflagging unconscious reminds us:

Just before Christmas I dreamt that I was walking along the road after work. I was on my way to buy myself a meal. Suddenly my legs collapsed. Two women helped me up but I told them I knew it was psychosomatic and that I would only collapse again.

I dreamt I was standing in the queue at a supermarket. In front of me are people I see at work. They are piling up a huge grocery order at the checkout counter. I can tell it is going to be a very expensive bill. Then I have this dawning realisation that they are going to use *my* cheque book to pay the bill. I am too far away to get it back and feel terribly panicky and out of control as the cashier continues ringing up the bill.

I dreamt of being asked as a psychologist to see a woman who has too much energy. This excess of energy comes out in destructive ways, I am told by the referring agent. I meet this woman and recognise that she is me. I tell her I cannot possibly treat her myself but not to worry because I will refer her to someone who can.

Finding a place to stop is very difficult but this is an appropriate one. We leave you then with our dreams.

Gerrilyn and Kathy
August 1983

Revising this book has been quite a shock to us both. When we wrote it, it served as an important benchmark in our friendship with each other, as a statement about our personal philosophies and politics and a measure of our professional development as clinical psychologists. Reading it ten years on could have been an excruciating experience where we were confronted with youthful optimism and the rhetoric that often accompanies it. But we both thought separately that we agreed with almost all of what we originally wrote and felt that our own politics had not deviated substantially from those stated in this book. What has changed enormously though is the growth in alternatives both therapeutically within the health service but also in terms of complementary medicine and the self-help movement. There are now many more books (an almost overwhelming number) detailing how to overcome, conquer, deal with, manage . . .

What we both liked most about this book were the women's voices. The contributions they made to the theoretical material was to put the practice back into the theory. Phyllis Chesler wrote in her re-released *Women and Madness* 'Not only am I "still out there"; so are many other feminists in psychiatry, psychology, social work, nursing and counselling. And so too is the book, which remains, unfortunately, up to date.' Reading that, in light of revising *Dealing with Depression*, we too were struck with how some of the major issues regarding women and depression have not really changed. Not that this is a cause for celebration or

211

indeed complacency on our part. Depression is, and will always be, an inevitable part of life. Perhaps if it was avoided less and spread more equally so that everyone could experience the deep inward contemplation that often accompanies depression it would not be seen as such a problem in need of treatment. Perhaps as a society we are happiest allowing a minority of the population to carry the majority of society's pain and distress.

In growing older, we have had to readjust our thinking about what changes are realistic within our lifetimes and to consider that we may never see the fruits of our labours. And yet there are moments when wider political and social changes remind us that the struggle is indeed having an effect. In 1990 the Berlin Wall came down, the USSR devolved into many nation states, Nelson Mandela was freed and the black people of South Africa voted . . . Each of these momentous historical events has then been followed by complex and perturbing reactions because life doesn't get magically better when the struggle has finally resulted in tangible change. Like the layers of an onion, there always seems to be another layer to peel.

Patience is necessary, as well as taking care of yourself to ensure that you can continue to struggle and to bear witness. The feminist struggle is not just about making things better for women but improving everyone's quality of life by valuing relationships and connectedness, by caring and nurturing those aspects of ourselves and each other that promote growth, curiosity and development, and by helping everyone learn that power that comes from within is preferable to that stolen from another.

Gerrilyn and Kathy
November 1994

Notes and References

Chapter 1: Depressing Business (pp. 3–14)

1. Oxford English Dictionary.
2. Mary Daly, *Gyn/Ecology*, The Women's Press, London, 1979.
3. Myrna Weissman & Gerald L. Klerman, 'Sex Differences and the Epidemiology of Depression', in *Archives of General Psychiatry*, no. 34, 1977, pp. 98–111.
4. Ruth Elizabeth, 'Deprivatising Pain', in *Catcall*, no, 14, pp. 4–8. A longer version of this article is in *Spare Rib*, no. 130, May 1983.
5. Martin Seligman, *On Depression, Development and Death*, W.H. Freeman, San Francisco, 1975.
6. David Burns, *Feeling Good: The New Mood Therapy*, Signet, New York, 1980, p. 28.
7. Shulamith Firestone, *The Dialectic of Sex*, Bantam, New York, 1972; The Women's Press, London, 1979. Some psychoanalysts, such as Karen Horney and Clara Thompson have reinterpreted the concept of 'penis envy'. For a more detailed discussion of feminism and psychoanalysis see, for example. *Psychoanalysis and Women* edited by Jean Baker Miller, Penguin, Harmondsworth, 1973 or *Psychoanalysis and Feminism* by Juliet Mitchell, Penguin, Harmondsworth, 1975.
8. See Florence Rush, *The Best Kept Secret*, Prentice-Hall, Englewood Cliffs, N.J., 1980.
9. George Brown and Tirril Harris, *Social Origins of Depression*, Tavistock Press, London, 1978.
10. B Andrews, GW Brown and L Creasey, 'Intergenerational Links Between Psychiatric Disorder in Mothers and Daughters: The Role of Parenting Experiences', in *Journal of Child Psychology and Psychiatry*, vol 31, 1990, pp.115–29.
11. *Op. cit.*, pp. 21–2.
12. For example Andrew Stanway, *Overcoming Depression*, Hamlyn, Feltham, Middlesex, 1981; Ross Mitchell, *Depression*, Penguin, Harmondsworth, 1975; Jack Dominian, *Depression*, Fontana, Glasgow, 1976.
13. Melba Wilson, *Crossing the Boundary: Black Women Survive Incest*, Virago, London, 1993.
14. Elizabeth Wilson, *Mirror Writing*, Virago, London, 1982, p. 156.
15. *Ibid.*, p. 155.

16. Michele Wallace, *Black Macho and the Myth of Superwoman*, John Calder, London, 1979, p. 107.

17. Marge Piercy, 'For Strong Women' in *The Moon is Always Female*, Alfred Knopf, New York, 1980.

18. bell hooks, *Sisters of the Yam: Black Women and Self Recovery*, South End Press, Boston, 1993.

19. Clarissa Pinkola Estes, *Women Who Run With the Wolves: Contacting the Power of the Wild Woman*, Rider, London, 1992.

20. *Ibid.*, p. 3.

Part One (pp. 27–28)

1. This difference has been observed in many epidemiological studies of depression. For a review of the evidence see S Nolen-Hoeksema, 'Sex Differences in Unipolar Depression: Evidence and Theory', in *Psychological Bulletin*, vol 101, 1987, pp. 259–82. Other relevant research reports include: Michael A Young, Louis F Fogg, William A Scheftner, Martin B Keller and Jan A Fawcett, 'Sex Differences in the Lifetime Prevalence of Depression: Does Varying the Diagnostic Criteria Reduce the Female/Male Ratio?', in *Journal of Affective Disorders*, vol 18, 1990, pp. 187–92; Andrew C Leon, Gerald L Klerman and Priya Wickramaratne, 'Continuing Female Predominance in Depressive Illness', in *American Journal of Public Health*, vol 83, 1993, pp. 754–57. The evidence from this research suggests that more women than men actually experience depression, rather than suggesting that more women than men get diagnosed and treated as depressed.

2. MIND, 'Stress on Women: Policy Paper on Women and Mental Health', MIND Publications, London, 1992. See also: Marian Barnes and Norma Maple, *Women and Mental Health: Challenging the Stereotypes*, Venture Press, Birmingham, 1992 and Jane Ussher, *Women's Madness: Misogyny or Mental Illness?*, Harvester Wheatsheaf, Hemel Hempstead, 1991.

3. Rachel Jenkins, 'Sex Differences in Minor Psychiatric Morbidity', in *Psychological Medicine*, monograph supplement 7, 1985 and K Wilhelm and G Parker, 'Is Sex Necessarily a Risk Factor for Depression?', in *Psychological Medicine*, vol 19, 1989, pp. 401–13.

4. See for example Tirril Harris, Paul Surtees and John Bancroft, 'Is Sex Necessarily a Risk Factor to Depression?', in *British Journal of Psychiatry*, vol 158, 1991, pp. 708–12.

5. See Gail Vines, *Raging Hormones: Do They Rule Our Lives?*, Virago, London, 1993 for a thorough critique of the belief, running deep in both scientific and popular culture, that hormones have the power to control how we feel and behave.

Chapter 3: Early Relationships (pp. 29–45)

1. For a feminist critique of the political implications of the use of psychoanalysis by feminists see Elizabeth Wilson 'Psychoanalysis: Psychic Law and Order?', *Feminist Review*, no. 8, 1981; Janet Sayers, 'Psychoanalysis and Personal Politics', *Feminist Review*, no. 10, 1982. See also: Rachel T

Harve-Mustin and Jeanne Mavecek, 'Gender and the Meaning of Difference: Postmodernism and Psychology', in Rachel T Harve-Mustin and Jean Maracek (eds.), *Making a Difference: Psychology and the Construction of Gender*, Yale University Press, London, 1990.

2. Vivienne Welburn, *Postnatal Depression*, Fontana, Glasgow, 1980, p. 171.

3. Dale Spender and Elizabeth Sarah (eds.), *Learning to Lose: Sexism and Education*, The Women's Press, London, 1980. Dale Spender, *Invisible Women: The Schooling Scandal*, Writers and Readers, London, 1982.

4. Amrit Wilson, *Finding a Voice: Asian Women in Britain*, Virago, London 1978. It is also remarkable that woman's role in the economy as producer of labour and servicer of it, as well as labourer herself, is never recognised.

5. Helen O'Connell, *Women and the Family*, Zed Books, London, 1994, p. 76.

6. Cambridge Centre for Family Research Survey 1993, referred to by G Greer in the *Guardian*, 21 March 1994, in the context of a discussion about whether parents should be allowed to choose the sex of their child.

7. Rachel Billington in 'About Men, About Women', *Observer*, 22 May 1994. Rachel Billington is also the author of *The Great Umbilical*, Hutchinson, London, 1994.

8. Statistics quoted by Victor Keegan in the *Guardian*, 9 April 1994.

9. Harriet Harman in *The Century Gap*, Vermillion, London, 1993 argues that the implications of the changes in women's lives and their struggles to combine work and family responsibilities have not yet been addressed by men, employers and government.

10. Michael Rutter, *Maternal Deprivation Reassessed*, Penguin, Harmondsworth, 1972.

11. More recently some researchers have begun to study the relationships between men and children. See, for example, Nigel Beail and Jacqueline McGuire (eds.), *Fathers: Psychological Perspective*: Junction Books, London, 1982; L. McKee and M. O'Brien, (eds.) *The Father Figure*, Tavistock, London, 1982. We do not yet know whether this research will benefit women. For a feminist critique of new approaches to fathering see Jo Sutton and Scarlet Friedman, 'Fatherhood: Bringing it all Back Home' in Scarlet Friedman and Elizabeth Sarah (eds.), *On the Problem of Men*, The Women's Press, London, 1982.

12. Eleanor Maccoby and Carol Jacklin, *The Psychology of Sex Differences*, Stanford University Press, Stanford, California, 1974. A Lake, 'Are we Born into our Sex Roles or Programmed into them?' in *Woman's Day*, January, 1975, pp. 24–25.

13. bell hooks, *Sisters of the Yam: Black Women and Self-Recovery*, Turnaround, London, 1993.

14. Phyllis Chesler, *Women and Madness*, Doubleday, New York, Allen Lane, London, 1972.

15. Nancy Chodorow, *The Reproduction of Mothering*, University of California Press, Berkeley, Cal., 1978. Susie Orbach and Luise Eichenbaum have also discussed in depth the difficulties women have in separating from their mothers in *Understanding Women*, Penguin, London, 1985.

215

16. Barbara M. McCandish, 'Therapeutic Issues with Lesbian Couples' in J.C. Gonsiorek (ed.), *Homosexuality and Psychotherapy*, The Haworth Press, New York, 1982.

17. Adrienne Rich, 'Compulsory Heterosexuality and Lesbian Existence' in *Signs: Journal of Women in Culture and Society*, vol. 5, no. 4, 1980.

18. George Brown and Tirril Harris found in their study that one of the factors which made a woman more vulnerable to depression was the loss of her mother before the age of eleven years.

19. Dorothy Dinnerstein, *The Rocking of the Cradle: and the Ruling of the World*, Souvenir Press, London, 1978. First published as *The Mermaid and the Minotaur; Sexual Arrangements and Human Malaise*, Harper and Row, New York, 1976. We are focusing in this section on Dorothy Dinnerstein's theory about the perception of women's power. However, more recent work has been done exploring women's perception of power, both as mothers and in other ways. For example: Jean Baker Miller, 'Women and Power', in Marjorie Braude (ed), *Women, Power and Therapy*, Harrington Park Press, New York and London, 1988; Kathryn A Pederson, Bonita C Long and Ruth Linn, 'Relationships and the Meaning of Power for Disadvantaged Women' in *Feminism and Psychology*, vol 4, 1994, pp. 229–49: Elly Singer has also discussed issues of power in the parent–child relationship. See Elly Singer, *Child-care and the Psychology of Development*, Routledge, London, 1992. Another interesting book giving a feminist and psychoanalytic discussion about power and domination in relationships is Jessica Benjamin, *The Bonds of Love: Psychoanalysis, Feminism and the Problem of Domination*, Virago, London, 1990.

20. *Ibid.*, p. 51.

21. Adrienne Rich, *Of Woman Born*, Virago, London, 1977.

22. Jane Lazarre, *On Loving Men*, The Dial Press, New York, 1980; Virago, London, 1981.

23. Florence Rush, *The Best Kept Secret: The sexual abuse of children*, Prentice-Hall, Englewood Cliffs, N.J., 1980. See also: Moira Walker, *Surviving Secrets*, Open University Press, 1992 and Carolyn Ainscough and Kay Toon, *Breaking Free: Help for Survivors of Child Sexual Abuse*, Sheldon Press, 1993.

24. See Patricia Hewitt and Penelope Leach, 'Social Justice, Children and Families' published by the Institute for Public Policy Research.

25. Harriet Harman, *The Century Gap*, Vermillion, London, 1993.

26. See Susan Hemmings (ed.), *Girls are Powerful*, Sheba Feminist Publishers, London, 1982.

27. A recent Panorama programme, The Future is Female, discussed the fact that girls are now doing better than boys educationally at all ages. Although the programme did not suggest any connection with feminism, we cannot help thinking that girls today may be influenced by the increasing support for them to be more assertive and have higher expectations. On the other hand, Carol Gilligan and other members of the Harvard Project on the Psychology of Women and the Development of Girls, have published research showing that girls tend to lose confidence in themselves at adolescence, when they are faced with the pressures to take on a feminine role

in relationships and with the dilemma about how to be true to themselves while still maintaining relationships. See: Carol Gilligan, Annie Rogers and Deborah L Tolman, *Women, Girls and Psychotherapy: Reframing Resistance*, Harrington Park Press, New York, London and Sydney, 1991.

Chapter 4: Images of Women (pp. 46–59)

1. Much of feminist literature and art is, at least in part, an attempt to do this. See Jane Rule, *Lesbian Images*, The Crossing Press, Trumansburg, N.Y., 1982; Elizabeth Wilson, *Mirror Writing*, Virago, London, 1982; Rozsika Parker and Griselda Pollock, *Old Mistresses: Women, Art and Ideology*, Routledge and Kegan Paul, London, 1981; Lisa Tickner, *The Spectacle of Women: Imagery of the Suffrage Campaign 1907–1914*, Chatto and Windus, London 1987.

2. Inge Broverman, Donald Broverman, Frank Clarkson, Paul Rosenkrauts and Susan Vogel, 'Sex-Role Stereotypes and Clinical Judgements of Mental Health' in *Journal of Consulting and Clinical Psychology*, 34, 1970, pp. 1–7, reprinted in Elizabeth Howell and Marjorie Bayes (eds.), *Women and Mental Health*, Basic Books, New York, 1981. This is a classic study, which has been referred to many times in discussions about mental health and gender stereotypes. As far as we know it has not been repeated more recently. It would be interesting to find out what answers psychotherapists or mental health professionals would give now. It is possible that the answers would conform less to the stereotypes. However even if this were so, the original study still gives us a vivid illustration of the traditional stereotypes which may still be operating unconsciously, even if they are now less likely to be overtly expressed.

3. Naomi Selig, 'Ethnicity and Gender as Uncomfortable Issues; in Shulamith Ramon, Maria Grazia, and Gianna Chedda, *Psychiatry in Transition*, Pluto Press, London, 1988, chapter 7, p. 94.

4. For a discussion of the way black women are affected by the politics of skin colour and other aspects of appearance such as hair texture, see bell hooks, *Sisters of the Yam: Black Women and Self-recovery*, Turnaround, London, 1993, and particularly chapter 6. See also: Margo Okazawa-Rey, Tracey Robinson, and Janie Victoria Ward, 'Black Women and the Politics of Skin Colour and Hair', in Marjorie Braude (ed), *Women, Power and Therapy*, Harrington Park Press, New York and London, 1988.

5. Melba Wilson, *Crossing the Boundary: Black Women Survive Incest*, Virago, London, 1993. pp. 66–8.

6. Jean Baker Miller, *Towards a New Psychology of Women*, Beacon Press, Boston, 1976; Penguin, Harmondsworth, 1978.

7. Sheila Shulman, 'Lesbian Feminists & the Great Baby Con' in *Spinster*, no. 4. See also Stephanie Dowrick and Sibyl Grundberg (eds.), *Why Children?*, The Women's Press, London, 1980; Jane Bartlett, *Will You Be Mother? Women Who Choose to Say No*, Virago, London, 1994.

8. See Rosie Jackson, *Mothers Who Leave: Behind the Myth of Women Without Their Children*, Pandora, London, 1994.

9. Various writers and researchers have explored the issues involved in

women's efforts to combine living up to the ideal of motherhood while maintaining a sense of their own identity through work or in other ways. See for example: Rosalind Coward, *Our Treacherous Hearts*, Faber and Faber, London, 1992; Tuula Gordon, *Feminist Mothers*, Macmillan, London 1990; Adrienne Katz, *The Juggling Act*, Bloomsbury, London, 1992; Kate Mosse, *Becoming a Mother*, Virago, London, 1993.

10. 'The Real Estate Industry in Women', in *War on Rape*, published by Women against Rape Collective, Melbourne, Australia, p. 7.

11. bell hooks, *op. cit.*, p. 119.

12. Susan Griffin, *Pornography and Silence*, Harper & Row, New York, 1981; The Women's Press, London, 1981.

13. See also Andrea Dworkin, *Pornography: Men Possessing Women*, The Women's Press, London, 1981; Catherine Itzin (ed), *Pornography: Women, Violence and Civil Liberties: A Radical New View*, Oxford University Press, Oxford, 1992.

14. Susan Griffin, *op. cit.*, p. 215.

15. A useful book is Anne Dickson, *The Mirror Within: A New Look at Sexuality*, Quartet, London, 1985.

Chapter 5: Recognition and Reward (pp. 60–76)

1. United Nations, 1980. We do not know of any report which gives more recent equivalent figures. However, two World Surveys on the role of women in development, produced by the United Nations (1986 and 1989) have both shown that to a large extent development has not benefited women. For a summary of these surveys and of what the United Nations has been doing to tackle women's issues, see Hilkka Pietila and Jeanne Vickers, *Making Women Matter: The Role of the United Nations*, Zed Books, London, 1990; revised and updated edition, 1994.

2. Ann Oakley, *Housewife*, Allen Lane, London, 1974 and *The Sociology of Housework*, Martin Robertson, London, 1974.

3. Hazel Seidal, unpublished M. Phil thesis, University of London, 1978. See also: S Sharpe, *Double Identity*, Penguin Books, Harmondsworth, Middlesex, 1984 and Agnes Miles, *Women and Mental Illness* Wheatsheaf Books Ltd, Brighton, 1988, pp. 50–51, for further discussion of the relationship between housework and depression.

4. The 1992 British Social Attitudes survey found that over two-thirds of women with full-time jobs still took on the main responsibility for general domestic duties. Women with part-time jobs took on almost the same responsibility as women outside the home; for example, 82 per cent did all the household cleaning. For a fuller discussion of these issues, see Harriet Harman, *The Century Gap*, Vermillion, London, 1993.

5. Linda, quoted in Jane Smith, *Little Box Living* in *Spare Rib*, no. 121, August 1982.

6. For a discussion of the ways in which part-time flexible work exploits rather than benefits women, see Kate Figes, *Because of Her Sex: The Myth of Equality for Women in Britain*, Macmillan, London, 1994, chapter 5.

7. Report by Isobel Wolff in the *Observer*, 20 November 1994.

8. Vivienne Welburn, *Postnatal Depression*, Fontana, Glasgow, 1980, p. 113.

9. B J Elliott and FA Huppert, 'In Sickness and in Health: Associations between Physical and Mental Well-being, Employment and Parental Status in a British Nationwide Sample of Married Women,' *Psychological Medicine* 1991, vol 21, pp. 515–24.

10. *Op. cit*

11. George Brown and Tirril Harris, *Social Origins of Depression*, Tavistock, London, 1978, p. 282.

12. *Ibid.* There have been other studies more recently looking at whether employment outside the home protects women from depression, some of which have found more complicated effects, in which other factors such as class and parental status are also important. For example: EJ Costello, 'Married with Children: Predictors of Mental and Physical Health in Middle-aged Women', *Psychiatry*, vol. 54, 1991, pp. 292–305; BJ Elliott and FA Huppert, In Sickness and in Health: Associations between Physical and Mental Well-being, Employment and Parental Status in a British Nationwide Sample of Married Women', *Psychological Medicine*, vol. 21, 1991, pp. 515–24. For a study which looks at similar issues about the protective effects of work outside the home with Indian women, see SS Nathawat and Asha Mathur, 'Marital Adjustment and Subjective Well-being in Indian-educated Housewives and Working Women', *Journal of Psychology*, vol 127, 1993, pp. 353–8.

13. Ann Oakley, *Women Confined: Towards a Sociology of Childbirth*, Martin Robertson, London, 1980.

14. Anna Coote and Beatrix Campbell, *Sweet Freedom: The Struggle for Women's Liberation*, Pan, London, 1982, p. 49. For a more recent discussion of these issues, see Kate Figes, *Because of Her Sex: The Myth of Equality for Women in Britain*, Macmillan, London, 1994.

15. Cynthia Cockburn, 'Do the Unions only look after their own?' in the *Guardian*, 22 February 1983. See also Cynthia Cockburn *Brothers: Male Dominance and Technological Change*, Pluto Press, London, 1983. There have been quite extensive changes in attitudes within Unions over the last 10 years, and most Unions do now recognise issues around discrimination against women and organise campaigns accordingly. There are however still far more men in positions of leadership within the Unions.

16. Rights for Women Unit Newsletter, National Council for Civil Liberties, London, January 1983.

17. Kate Figes, *Because of Her Sex: The Myth of Equality for Women in Britain*, Macmillan, London, 1994.

18. A study prepared by Dr David Owen of Warwick University, drawing on answers given in the 1991 census which for the first time asked for ethnic details. Published by the Equal Opportunities Commission, 1994.

19. For example, 'Sexual Harassment is a Trade Union Issue', National and Local Government Officer's Association (NALGO), 1 Mabledon Place, London WC1H 9AJ; and 'Sexual Harassment: A Trade Union Issue', MSF, 64–66 Wandsworth Common, Northside, London SW18 2SH.

20. Ann Sedley and Melissa Benn, 'Sexual Harassment at Work', 1982.

Available from the National Council for Civil Liberties, 21 Tabard St, London SE1 4LA; 0171 403 3888.) A more recent booklet, also produced by the NCCL in association with Southwark Black Sisters and Changes, which gives information about women's legal rights in relation to sexual harassment and many other work-related issues is 'Women's Rights, Human Rights, Report 5,' 1994. You can also get legal advice and counselling in relation to sexual harassment from Women Against Sexual Harasssment (WASH). See Appendix 3 for contact details.

21. Based on figures taken from the Department of Education. Table B12, 1992.

22. Information taken from the survey 'Sex in the Professions', carried out by MORI for Hays Personnel Services, 1994.

23. Barbara Ehrenreich and Deidre English, *Witches, Midwives and Nurses: A History of Women Healers*, Writers and Readers Publishing Co-operative, London, 1973; Mary Chamberlain, *Old Wives' Tales: Their History, Remedies and Spells*, Virago, London, 1981.

24. Abayomi McEwen, in an interview with Penny Junor in the *Guardian*, 17 June 1982.

25. Margaret Ghilchik, in an interview with Penny Junor in the *Guardian*, 15 June 1982.

26. Report by Madeleine Bunting in the *Guardian*, 9 April 1991.

Chapter 6: Process and Points (pp. 77–98)

1. Gail Sheehey, *Passages*, Bantam, New York, 1977.

2. Elizabeth Wilson, *Mirror Writing*, Virago, London, 1982.

3. Reported in the *Guardian*, 14 December 1994, from figures provided by the OPCS.

4. Gail Sheehy, *The Silent Passage*, HarperCollins, London, 1993.

5. Germaine Greer, *The Change: Women, Ageing and the Menopause*, Penguin, Harmondsworth, Middlesex, 1992.

6. Kate Millet, *The Loony Bin Trip*, Virago, London, 1991.

7. Further research of the original Brown and Harris study has elaborated their original findings, proposing a path model where earlier experiences are seen to shape our choices later in life. See for example A Bifulco, G Brown and T Harris, 'Childhood Loss of Parent, Lack of Parental Care and Adult Psychiatric Disorder: A Replication', in *Journal of Affective Disorder*, vol 12, 1987, pp. 115–28 or B Andrews, G Brown and L Creasey, 'Intergenerational Links Between Psychiatric Disorder in Mothers and Daughters. The Role of Parenting Experiences', *Journal of Child Psychology and Psychiatry*, vol 31, 1990, pp. 1115–1129.

8. See for example Colin Murray Parkes, *Bereavement*, Tavistock Press, London, 1972, for a more detailed discussion on loss through death.

9. Jo Campling, *Images of Ourselves: Women With Disabilities Talking*, Routledge and Keagan Paul, London. There has been a high profile campaign to get the UK government to address the issue of disability rights. To date it has refused to pass equal opportunities legislation that would, amongst other things, ensure that disabled access is a statutory right.

220

10. See Vivienne Welburn, *Postnatal Depression*, Fontana, Glasgow, 1980; Ann Oakley, *Women Confined: Towards a Sociology of Childbirth*, Martin Robertson, Oxford, 1980; Katharina Datton, *Depression After Childbirth: How to Recognise and Treat Postnatal Illness*, Oxford University Press, Oxford, 1989; and Kate Mosse, *Becoming a Mother*, Virago, London, 1993.

11. See for example, Stephanie Dowrick and Sibyl Grundberg (eds), *Why Children?*, The Women's Press, London, 1980 and N Pfeffer, *The Stork and the Syringe: A Political History of Reproductive Medicine*, Polity Press, London, 1993.

12. See for example Gillian Hanscombe and Jackie Forster, *Rocking the Cradle: Lesbian Mothers*, Sheba, London, 1982 and Phyllis Burke, *Family Values: A Lesbian Mother's Fight for Her Son*, Vintage, New York, 1994. There are also support groups for lesbian mothers that will also help out witth information regarding custody battles. They can be contacted through Lesbian Line or ROW (see Appendix 3 for contact details).

13. See for example Andrea Dworkin, *Pornography: Men Posssessing Women*, The Women's Press, London, 1981; Suzanne Kappeler, *The Pornography of Representation*, Polity Press, Cambridge, 1986; and Catherine MacKinnon, *Only Words*, HarperCollins, Glasgow, 1994.

14. Liz Kelly, Linda Regan and Sheila Burton, 'An Exploratory Study of the Prevalence of Sexual Abuse in a Sample of 16–21 Year Olds', Polytechnic of North London: Child Abuse Studies Unit, 1991.

15. See for example Gerrilyn Smith, *The Protector's Handbook: Reducing the Risk of Child Sexual Abuse and Helping Children Recover*, The Women's Press, London, 1995 and Laura Bass and Ellen Davis, *The Courage to Heal: A Guide for Women Survivors of Childhood Sexual Abuse*, Cedar Publishing, London, 1990.

16. This refers to Michael Fagan who managed to break into the Queen's bedroom in Buckingham Palace in 1982. He was detained at Her Majesty's Pleasure and sent to a special hospital to receive psychiatric treatment.

17. W Barnard, H Vera, M Vera and G Newman, 'Till Death Do Us Part: A Study of Spouse Murder', Bulletin of the American Academy of Psychiatry and the Law, no 10, 1982, pp. 271–80.

18. J.C. Fraser, *Battered of course I was*, 1978, words written in love & peace.

19. See Majorie Bayes' article in Elizabeth Howell and Marjorie Bayes (eds)' *Women and Mental Health*, 'Wife Battering and the Maintenance of Gender Roles: A Socio-psychological Perspective', Basic Books, New York, 1981.

20. L J F Smith, 'Domestic Violence: An Overview of the Literature', Home Office Research and Planning Report, *HMSO*, 1989.

21. L B Rosewater and LEA Walker (eds.), *Handbook of Feminist Therapy: Women's Issues in Psychotherapy*, Springer, New York, 1985.

22. See London Rape Crisis Centre Reports available by post, P.O. Box 69, London WC1.

23. Women's Aid will provide women with refuge. See Appendix 3 for address details.

24. Audre Lorde, *The Cancer Journals*, Spinsters Ink, New York, 1980.

25. Caroline Halliday, 'The Birth', in *Spinster*, no. 3.

26. See for example Ellen Goudsmit, 'All in Her Mind! Stereotypic Views and the Psychologisation of Women's Illness', in Sue Wilkonson and Celia Kitzinger (eds.), *Women and Health: Feminist Perspectives*, Taylor & Francis, London, 1994.

27. Reported by Wendy Moore in 'Born of Choice', *Guardian*, 7 December 1994. See also 'Where to be Born? The Debate and the Evidence' from the National Perinatal Epidemiology Unit, Radcliffe Infirmary, Oxford OX2 6HE.

28. See for example J.S. Scott, 'Obstetric Analgesia', in *American Journal of Obstetrics and Gynecology*, no. 106, 1970, p. 959. Also some studies in Cardiff looked at the amount of Pethadine women used in childbirth when they controlled their own intake. This is referred to in *Childbirth*, Elliot Philipps, Fontana, Glasgow, 1978, p. 81.

29. See for example T. Garrett, 'Sexual Contact Between Psychotherapists and Their Patients', in P. Clarkson and M. Pokorny (eds.), *The Handbook of Psychotherapy*, Routledge, London, 1994.

Chapter 8: A Way of Life (pp. 115–126)

1. Ruth Cooperstock. 'A Review of Women's Psychotropic Drug Use' in Elisabeth Howell and Marjorie Bayes (eds), *Women and Mental Health*, Basic Books, New York, 1981, p. 131. See also the chapters 'What can she depend on? Substance Use and Women's Health' by Elisabeth Ettore and 'Surviving by Smoking' by Hilary Graham both in *Women and Health: Feminist Perspectives* edited by Sue Wilkinson and Celia Kitzinger, Taylor & Francis, London which address issues of dependency in women and the wide range of substances they come to depend on to manage their lives.

2. L. Guse, G. Morier and J. Ludwig, *Winnipeg Survey of Prescription (Mood Altering) Use among Women*. Technical Report NMUDD Manitoba Alcoholism Foundation, Oct. 1976.

3. See for instance Hazel Seidal's unpublished M. Phil. Thesis, University of London, which discusses the effect of housework on women's mood; Ann Oakley, *The Sociology of Housework*, Martin Robertson, London, 1974; L. Morris, *The Workings of the Household*, Polity Press, Oxford, 1990; and also S. Berk, *The Gender Factory: The Apportionment of Work in American Households*, Plenum, New York, 1985.

4. J.A. McRae and C.J. Brody, 'The Differential Importance of Marital Experiences for the Wellbeing of Women and Men: A Research Note', *Social Science Research*, 18, 3, 1989, pp. 237–48.

5. Emile Durkheim, *Suicide*, Routledge & Kegan Paul, London, 1952.

6. P. Nicholson, 'Counselling Women with Postnatal Depression: Implications from Qualitative Research', *Counselling Psychology Journal*, 2, 2, 1989, pp. 123–32.

7. Brown and Harris, *op. cit.*, p. 189. See also H. Smith, 'Caring for Everyone? The Implications for Women of the Changes in Community Care Services', *Feminism and Psychology*, 1, 2, 1991, pp. 279–92.

8. Dr Judith Grey, a specialist in community medicine in Manchester

researched sex differences in doctors' behaviour towards their patients. The results of her study were summarised in a newshort in *Over 21*, December 1982. The complete study was published in the *Journal* of the Royal College of General Practitioners.

9. Ellen Goudsmit, 'All In Her Mind! Stereotypic Views and the Psychologisation of Women's Illness', in S. Wilkonson and C. Kitzinger, (eds.), *Women and Health: Feminist Perspectives*, Taylor & Francis, London, 1994, pp. 7–12.

10. MIND, 'The Hidden Majority', MIND Publications, London 1992. See also 'Stress on Women', Policy paper on women and mental health, also published by MIND, 1992.

11. J. Williams and G. Watson, 'Mental Health Services that Empower Women: The Challenge to Clinical Psychology', *Clinical Psychology Forum*, no. 64, pp. 6–12.

12. Phyllis Chesler, *Women and Madness*, Doubleday, New York, 1972; Allen Lane, London, 1972.

13. See Virgina Davidson's review article 'Psychiatry's Problem with no Name: Therapist–Patient Sex' in *Women and Mental Health*. The specific study cited is Kardener, S. Fuller, M. and I. Mensh. 'A Survey of Physician's Attitudes and Practices regarding Erotic and Non-erotic Contact with Patients', in *American Journal of Psychiatry*, 130, pp. 1077–81. See also D. Jehu, *Patients as Victims: Sexual Abuse in Psychotherapy and Counselling*, Wiley, Chichester, 1994.

14. T. Garrett, 'Sexual Contact Between Psychotherapists and their Patients', in P. Clarkson and M. Pokorny (eds.), *The Handbook of Psychotherapy*, Routledge, London, 1994.

15. J. Marzillier and D. Gardner, 'Boundaries in Professional Relationships: Conference Workshop', *Clinical Psychology Forum*, no. 72, 1994, pp. 20–25.

16. Laura Brown, *Beyond Thou Shall Not: Thinking About Ethics in the Lesbian Therapy Community*, Haworth Press, London, 1989.

17. Laura Brown, 'Harmful Effects of Post Termination Sexual and Romantic Relationships Between Therapists and their Former Clients', *Psychotherapy*, vol. 25, 2, 1988, pp. 249–55.

18. Ruth Elizabeth, 'Deprivatising Pain', in *Catcall*, no. 14.

19. See Frank Pittman and Kalmen Flomenhaft, 'Treating the Doll's House Marriage', in *Family Process*, 9, 1970, pp. 143–55. The summary to the article states: 'Therapy seems more successful when the therapist respects the basically unequal framework the couple has chosen [!] and works towards greater understanding and respect for unique individual needs within that framework'. A blatant example of how therapy seeks not to promote real change but sometimes actively encourages the oppression of women. For a more recent discussion of some of these issues see Gwyn Daniel and Charlotte Burck, 'Abuses of Power: Working with Physical and Sexual Violence', in *Gender and Family Therapy*, Karnac, London, 1995.

20. See for example ads in MIMS or publications aimed directly at doctors like the *General Practitioner*. You can complain about the images of women used in advertising by writing to the Advertising Standards Authority.

21. Women's Liberation Song Sheet.

Chapter 9: Coping with Depression (pp. 129–148)

1. A book which explores the connections between women's anger and depression in more detail is Lois P. Finkel, *Women, Anger and Depression: Strategies for Self-Empowerment*, Health Communications Inc., Florida, 1992.

2. See Harriet Goldhor Lerner, *The Dance of Anger; A Woman's Guide to Changing the Pattern of Intimate Relationships*. This is a very helpful book, explaining how to turn your anger into a constructive force, particularly within intimate relationships.

3. Clare Weeks, *Agoraphobia: Simple, Effective Treatment*, Angus and Robertson, London, 1977; Muriel Frampton, *Agoraphobia: Coming to Terms with the World Outside*, Thorson's, Wellingborough, 1990; Robyn Vines, *Agoraphobia: The Fear of Panic*, Fontana, London, 1987. Many women have also found *Feel the Fear and Do it Anyway* by Susan Jeffers (Fawcett Columbine, New York, 1987) very helpful although it is not specificially about agoraphobia. An organisation which can give information about local self-help groups is Phobic Action, (0181–559–2459).

4. M. Vaughan, 'The Relationships Between Obsessional Personality, Obsessions in Depression and Symptoms of Depression', in *British Journal of Psychiatry*, no. 129, 1976, 36–9.

5. For example: Jane Madders *Stress and Relaxation*, Martin Dunitz (Positive Health Guide Series), London, 1979; Maxine Tobias and Mary Stewart, *Stretch and Relax*, Dorling Kindersley, London, 1985; Paddy O'Brian, *A Gentler Strength: The Yoga Book for Women*, Thorsons, London 1991.

6. There are many books on aromatherapy that may be useful. For example: Maggie Tisserand, *Aromatherapy for Women*, Thorsons, Wellingborough, 1985; Daniele Ryman, *Aromatherapy: The Encyclopedia of Plants and Oils and How they Help You*, Piatkus, London, 1991. A good book about general massage is *The Complete Book of Massage* by Clare Maxwell-Hudson, Dorling Kindersley, London.

7. Many surveys of sex ratios in suicide attempts are summarised in Myrna Weissman and Gerald Klerman, 'Sex Differences and the Epidemiology of Depression' in *Archives of General Psychiatry*, 34, pp. 98–111. Since the 1970s, male suicide rates have been rising, while female suicide rates have been falling. This is the first time since 1911 that the trends for male and female suicide rates have moved in opposite directions. For more details, see John Charlton, Sue Kelly, Karen Dunnell, Barry Evans, Rachel Jenkins and Ruth Wallis, Trends in Suicide Deaths in England and Wales, *Population Trends*, 69, Autumn 1992, pp. 10–16.

8. Paula Weideger, *Female Cycles*, The Women's Press, London, 1978. First published as *Menstruation and Menopause*, Alfred A. Knopf, New York; 1975. Since Paula Weideger wrote her book, various other women writers have challenged the taboo around discussing menstruation and menopause. For example: Gail Sheehy, *The Silent Passage*, HarperCollins, London, 1993;

Germaine Greer, *The Change: Women, Ageing and the Menopause*, Penguin, London, 1992. See also: Jane Ussher, *The Psychology of the Female Body*, Routledge, London, 1989.

9. Penelope Shuttle and Roger Redgrove, *The Wise Wound: Menstruation and Everywoman*, HarperCollins, London, 1994.

10. *Ibid.*, p. 29.

Chapter 10: Looking for Help – Medical Approaches (pp. 149–174)

1. Kate Millett, *The Looney Bin Trip*, Virago, London 1991.

2. See Susan Nolen-Hoeksema, Sex Differences in Unipolar Depression: Evidence and Theory', *Psychological Bulletin*, vol 101, 1987, pp. 259–82; P.J. Clayton, "The Epidemiology of Bipolar Affective Disorder', *Comprehensive Psychiatry*, vol 22, 1981, pp. 31–43.

3. See Susan Nolen-Hoeksema, *Ibid*, pp. 259–82; M.M. Weissman, The Myth of Involutional Melancholia', *Journal of the American Medical Association*, vol 242, 1979, pp. 742–4.

4. See Malkah T. Notman, 'Midlife Concerns of Women: Implications of the Menopause' in *Women and Mental Health*. A helpful book about ageing and menopause is Rosetta Reitz, *Menopause: A Positive Approach*, Unwin, London, 1981. An interesting book about women in midlife is Caroline Bailey, *Beginning in the Middle: Women in their Prime*, Quartet, London, 1982. See also Lillian Rubin, *Women of a Certain Age: The Midlife Search for Self*, Harper and Row, New York, 1979. Other books which may be helpful are Linda Ojeda, *Menopause without Medicine – How to Cope with 'The Change'*, Thorsons; Anne Dickson and Nikki Henriques, *Menopause: The Women's View*, Grapvine, Thorsons, London, 1987.

5. Gail Sheehy, *The Silent Passage: Menopause*, HarperCollins, London, 1993, pp. 84–92.

6. Germaine Greer, *The Change: Women, Ageing and the Menopause*, Penguin, London, 1992, p. 274.

7. Since the term 'postnatal depression' covers a range of types of distress, it is sometimes considered useful to divide it into four categories: maternity blues, postnatal exhaustion, postnatal depression and puerperal psychosis. See Katharina Dalton, *Depression after Childbirth*, Oxford University Press, Oxford, 1989.

8. Sandra Elliot, personal communication. For examples of such research, see S.A. Elliot 'Psychological Strategies in the Prevention and Treatment of Postnatal Depression', in M.R. Oates (ed) 'Psychological Aspects of Obstetrics and Gynaecology', *Balliere's Clinical Obstetrics and Gynaecology*, vol. 3, no. 4, 1989, pp. 839–56.

9. *Trouble with Tranquillisers*, Release Publications, 1982. Available from Release, 388 Old St, London EC1V 9LT (0171–729 9904). MIND has also produced a Special Report called Minor Tranquillisers – Hard Facts, Hard Choices', available in several different languages, from MIND Publications. A useful guide to groups and services offering support to people who want to come off minor tranquillisers is 'Tranquillisers: The MIND Guide to where to

get Help', by Russel Murray, Donna Hurle and Anthony Grant, MIND/ Bradford University, 1991.

10. *Ibid.*, p. 18.

11. For example: Louise Roddon, *Am I a Monster or is this PMS? Self Help for PMS sufferers*, Headline Book Publishing, London, 1994; Dr. Caroline Shreeve, *Premenstrual Syndrome: Curing the Real Curse*, Thorsons, 1983, new edition 1992. (This book advocates the use of Evening Primrose Oil).

12. See, for example, a study of mental health issues in the Asian Community in one London Borough: Jayanthi Beliappa, Illness or Distress? Alternative Models of Mental Health', Confederation of Indian Organisations, 1991 (obtainable from MIND Publications); see also: Carolyn Baylies, Ian Law, and Geoff Mercer (eds), The Nature of Care in a Multi-Racial Community: Summary report of an Investigation of the Support for Black Ethnic Minority Persons After Discharge from Psychiatric Hospitals in Bradford and Leeds', Social Policy and Sociology Research Working Paper 8 (available from the School of Sociology and Social Policy, University of Leeds). A summary of this report is published by the Joseph Rowntree Foundation as 'Social Care Findings 58' and is available free of charge from the Joseph Rowntree Foundation, The Homestead, 40 Water End, York YO3 6LP.

13. Katy Gardner and Lynda Birke, *Why Suffer? Periods and their Problems*, Virago, London, 1979.

14. Ruth Elizabeth, 'Deprivatising Pain', in *Catcall*, no. 14.

15. L.R. Squire and P.L. Miller, 'Retrograde Amnesia and Bilateral Electro-convulsive Therapy', in *Archives of General Psychiatry*, no. 38, 1981, pp. 89–95.

16. J. Heshe and A. Theilguard, 'Unilateral and Bilateral ECT', *Acta Psychiatrica Scandinavica*, suppl. 275, 1978. MIND have produced a special report, ECT – Pros, Cons and Consequences'. This is a leaflet which suggests questions which it would be useful to ask, if someone is advised to have ECT. (Obtainable from MIND Publications.)

17. L.R. Frank, 'Electroshock: Death, Brain Damage, Memory Loss, and Brainwashing', *Journal of Mind and Behavior*, vol 11 (3/4), 1990, pp. 489–512; H. Buchan, E. Johnstone, K. McPherson, R. Palmer, T.J. Crown, and S. Brandon, Who Benefits from Electroconvulsive Therapy? Combined Results of the Leicester and Northwick Park Trials', *British Journal of Psychiatry*, vol 160 1992, pp. 355–9.

18. Ginny Cook, news item in *Spare Rib*, no. 116, 1982.

19. The Institute for Complementary Medicine holds The British Register of Complementary Practitioners. They can provide you with lists of qualified local practitioners in any particular field of complementary medicine. Institute for Complementary Medicine, Unit 4, Tavern Quay, London, SE16 1AA (0171–237 5165). Send sae for information.

20. There are various books now available about acupuncture. One that may be helpful is *Traditional Acupuncture: The Law of the Five Elements* by Diane Connelly.

21. Carola Beresford Cook, personal communication.

22. See, for example, *The Joy of Feeling* by Iona Marsaa Teeguarden, Japan

Publications, 1987. This book is about a kind of acupressure and particularly discusses the treatment of emotional problems.

23. See Rima Handley, *Homeopathy for Women*, Thorson's, London, 1993.

24. See Judy Howard, *Bach Flower Remedies for Women*, The C.W. Daniel Company Ltd, Saffron Waldon, 1992.

25. *Aromatherapy for Women* by Maggie Tisserand, Thorson's, Northamptonshire, 1985 is a helpful book, which has a short section on depression. Other useful books are: Daniele Ryman, *Aromatherapy: The Encyclopedia of Plants and Oils and How They Help You*, Piatkus, London, 1991; Patricia Davis, *Subtle Aromatherapy*, C.W. Daniel Co Ltd, Saffron Walden, 1991.

26. For a guide to a variety of different treatment options, see Patsy Westcott, *Alternative Health Care for Women*, Thorson's, Northamptonshire, 1987 or Liz Grist, *A Women's Guide to Alternative Medicine*, Fontana.

Chapter 11: Looking for Help – Psychological Approaches (pp. 175–198)

1. Anuradha Sayal, 'Black Women and Mental Health', *Clinical Psychology Forum*, no 22, August 1989, pp. 3–6.

2. Sue Holland, 'Psychotherapy, Oppression and Social Action: Gender, Race and Class in Black Women's Depression', in Rosine Jozef Perelberg and Ann C. Miller, *Gender and Power in Families*, Routledge, London and New York, 1990, p. 261.

3. Jean Baker Miller, *Towards a New Psychology of Women*, Beacon Press, Boston, 1976; Penguin, Harmondsworth, 1978.

4. C.B. Truax and R. Carkhuff, *Towards Effective Counselling and Psychotherapy*, Aldine, Chicago, 1967.

5. Dennis Brown and Jonathan Pedder, *Introduction to Psychotherapy: An Outline of Psychodynamic Principles and Practice*, Tavistock, Routledge, London, 2nd edition, 1991.

6. Dennis Brown and Jonathan Pedder, *Introduction to Psychotherapy: An Outline of Psychodynamic Principles and Practice*, Tavistock, London, 1979.

7. Luise Eichenbaum and Susie Orbach, *Understanding Women*, Penguin, Harmondsworth, London, 1985. See also: Charlotte Krause Prozan, 'An Integration of Feminist and *Psychoanalytic Theory*', in Marjorie Braude (ed), *Women, Power and Therapy*, Harrington Park Press, New York and London, 1988. Janet Sayers, 'Phallic Illusions, Feminist Therapy: a Freudian story' in *Clinical Psychology Forum*, no 64, February 1994. This article is based on a forthcoming book of the same name; Janet Sayers, 'Feminism, Psychoanalysis and Psychotherapy' in Jane Ussher and Paula Nicholson (eds.) *Gender Issues in Clinical Psychology*, Routledge, London 1992.

8. Anthony Ryle, *Cognitive Analytic Therapy: Active Participation in Change*', Wiley, Chichester, 1990.

9. Alison Culverwell, Roxane Agnew, Michael Boukham, Gillian Hardy, Anne Rees, David Shapiro, Shirley Reynolds, Jeremy Halstead, William Stiles and Veronica Harrington, The Second Sheffield Psychotherapy Project, Collaborative Project: Some Initial Findings and their Clinical Implications', *Clinical Psychology Forum*, no. 72, October 1994.

10. See William C. Schutz, *Joy: Expanding Human Awareness*, Penguin, Harmondsworth, 1973.

11. There is still a London Marriage Guidance Council, and in most parts of the country there are Catholic Marriage Advisory Councils, which offer similar help to Relate. (You do not have to be a catholic to go to them for help, and they do not impose catholicism on their clients.)

12. Sheila Ernst and Lucy Goodison, *In Our Own Hands: A book of Self-Help Therapy*, The Women's Press, London, 1981.

13. Examples are: Petrushka Clarkson and Michael Pokorny (eds), *The Handbook of Psychotherapy*, Routledge, London, 1994; Lesley Knight, *A Consumer's Guide to Therapy*, Fontana, London, 1986; Ann France, *Consuming Psychotherapy*, Free Associations Books, London, 1988; and Nini Herman, *Why Psychotherapy?*, Free Associations Books, London, 1988.

14. For an example of such a challenge, see Shulamith Firestone, *The Dialectic of Sex*, The Women's Press, London, 1979. Celia Kitzinger and Rachel Perkins have more recently written critically about the use of psychology and psychotherapy in relation to lesbian women. Celia Kitzinger and Rachel Perkins, *Changing our Minds: Lesbian Feminism and Psychology*, Onlywomen Press, London, and New York University Press, New York, 1993.

15. For examples see Sheila Ernst and Marie Maguire (eds), *Living with the Sphinx*, The Women's Press, London, 1987; M.A. Dutton-Douglas and L.E.A. Walker (eds), *Feminist Psychotherapies: Integration of Therapeutic and Feminist Systems*, Ablex, Norwood, New Jersey, 1988.

16. Moira Walker, *Women in Therapy and Counselling: Out of the Shadows*, Open University Press, Buckingham, 1990; especially pp. 73–6. See also: Jocelyn Chapman, *Feminist Counselling in Action*, Sage, London, 1988.

17. Sheila Ernst and Lucy Goodison, *In Our Own Hands*, The Women's Press, London.

18. Naomi Selig, 'Therapy with Women in the NHS, in *Medicine and Society*, vol. 9, no. 2, 1983.

19. Gilli Watson and Jennie Williams, Feminist practice in therapy', in Jane Ussher and Paula Nicholson, *Gender Issues in Clinical Psychology*, Routledge, London and New York, 1992; Liz Harlow, 'Politicizing the Personal and Subverting Power: The Principles and Practices of Feminist Therapy and Counselling', *Clinical Psychology Forum*, no. 64, February, pp. 28–30.

20. Gilli Watson and Jennie Williams, *op. cit.*, p. 226.

21. For example, Barbara McCandlish, 'Therapeutic Issues with Lesbian Couples'; Bronwyn Anthony, 'Lesbian Client – Lesbian Therapist: Opportunities and Challenges in Working Together'. Both articles are in J. C. Gonsiorek (ed), *Homosexuality and Psychotherapy*, The Haworth Press, New York, 1982. See also: Laura Brown, 'Power Responsibility, Boundaries: Ethical Concerns for the Lesbian Feminist Therapist', *Lesbian Ethics* vol. 2, no. 4, 1985, pp. 9–16; Rachel Perkins, Therapy for Lesbians? The case against', *Feminism and Psychology*, vol. 1, no. 3, 1991, pp. 325–328; Norren O'Connor and Joanna Ryan, *Wild Desires and Mistaken Identities: Lesbianism and Psychoanalysis*, Virago, London, 1993.

22. Sue Holland, 'Psychotherapy, Oppression and Social Action: Gender, Race and Class in Black Women's Depression', in Rosine Jozef Perelberg and Ann Miller, *Gender and Power in Families*, Tavistock/Routledge, London and New York, 1990. p. 256.

23. Sue Holland, *op. cit.*, p. 259.

24. There is a new organisation called 'Separate', which has been set up to find out more about problems of sexual abuse of clients by psychotherapists and counsellors, and to disseminate information about the problem and its consequences. Details obtainable from UKCP (address in the resources section). Additionally contact Prevention of Professional Abuse Network. (address in the resources section).

25. For example, Nafsiyat Intercultural Therapy Centre. For more details of this and other existing services for black communities, see: Melba Wilson, *Mental Health and Britain's Black Communities*, published by the King's Fund Centre, 1993. (The King's Fund Centre, 126 Albert St, London NW1 7NF; 0171-267 6111.)

26. Sheila Ernst and Lucy Goodison, *In Our Own Hands*, p. 4

27. Joceyln Chaplin and Amelie Noack, 'Leadership and Self-help Groups', in Sue Krzowski and Pat Land, (eds), *In Our Experience: Workshops at the Women's Therapy Centre*, The Women's Press, London, 1988, chapter 13. This provides a very useful discusson of leadership issues in self-help groups and also proposes a model for the group process in self-help therapy.

28. Al-Anon organises groups for family members or friends of problem drinkers. Families Anonymous is a similar organisation for family members and friends of problem drug-takers. Co-dependents Anonymous is for anyone who recognises a problem of co-dependency and is seeking to grow from it. (People who are co-dependent are people who get all their self-esteem and sense of identity from looking after others. A useful book about codependency is *Codependency: How to break Free and Live Your Own Life* by David Stafford and Liz Hodgkinson, Piatkus, London, 1991.

29. Ruth Elizabeth, 'Deprivatising Pain', in *Catcall*, no. 14. Ruth Elizabeth also has published an extended version of this article, 'Deprivatising Depression' in *Spare Rib*, no. 130.

30. Women's Therapy Centres, which exist in some big cities, are also likely to have information about existing self-help groups or about how to set one up. Alternatively, it might be useful to contact a local council for voluntary service. A publication which may also be useful is 'Self-help Alternatives to Mental Health Services' also by Vivien Lindow, MIND Publications, London, 1994. This book is not about therapy groups but about a wide range of other types of self-help mental health projects.

31. There is a useful article about this by Katrina McCormick, 'Questioning self-help groups', in MASH (*Mutual Aid and Self Help*), no 27, Spring 1993. MASH was the bulletin of The Self-Help Centre at NCVO, which was funded by the Department of Health for 3 years, but which was due to close in April 1995. The NCVO will be carrying on some of the work of this centre.

32. Sheila Ernst and Lucy Goodison, *In Our Own Hands*. See also Anne Kent Rush, *Getting Clear: Body Work for Women*, Wildwood House, London, 1974.

33. Stephanie Dowrick, *The Intimacy and Solitude Self-Therapy Book*, The Women's Press, London, 1993.

34. Ellen Bass and Laura Davis, *The Courage to Heal: A Guide for Women Survivors of Child Sexual Abuse*, Harper and Row, New York, 1988: Cedar, Mandarin Paperbacks, London, 1990; also Carolyn Ainscough and Kay Toon, *Breaking Free: Help for Survivors of Child Sexual Abuse*, Sheldon Press, London, 1993.

35. Ann Faraday, *The Dream Game*, Penguin, Harmondsworth, 1976; Lucy Goodison, *The Dreams of Women: Exploring and Interpreting Women's Dreams*, The Women's Press, London, 1995.

Chapter 12: The Economy of Depression – Social and Political Perspectives (pp. 199–208)

1. Ruth Elizabeth, 'Deprivatising Pain', in *Catcall*, no. 14.

2. Amrit Wilson, *Finding a Voice: Asian Women in Britain*, Virago, London, 1978.

3. Beverley Bryan, Stella Dadzie and Suzanne Scafe, *The Heart of the Race*, Virago, London 1985.

4. This campaign was organised and co-ordinated by Southall Black Sisters whose address is listed in Appendix 3.

5. George Brown and Tirril Harris, *Social Origins of Depression*, Tavistock Press, London, 1978; G. Brown, B. Andrews, T. Harris, Z. Adler and L. Bridge, 'Social Support, Self Esteem and Depression', *Psychological Medicine*, vol. 16, pp. 813–31.

6. Elizabeth Monck, 'Patterns of Close Confiding Relationships Amongst Adolescent Girls', *Journal of Child Psychology and Psychiatry*, vol. 32, no. 2, 1991, pp. 333–45.

7. Ruth Elizabeth, 'Deprivatising Pain'.

8. Jane Ussher, 'Women's Conundrum: Feminism or Therapy?', *Clinical Psychology Forum*, vol. 64, pp. 2–6.

9. Marilyn Frye, Speak on 'Lesbian Perspectives on Women's studies', printed in *Sinister Wisdom*, no. 14, p. 6.

10. Funding for refuges often remains precarious and despite an obvious and now well accepted need, the actual number of refuges has not grown substantially over the last ten years.

11. Ruth Elizabeth, 'Deprivatising Pain'.

12. Phyllis Chesler, *Women and Madness*, Harcourt Brace Jovanovich, London, 1989.

13. Luisah Teish, 'O.K. Momma, Who the Hell Am I?' in *This Bridge Called My Back*, p. 227.

14. Olive Schreiner quoted by Adrienne Rich in *Of Woman Born*, Virago, London, 1977, p. 215.

15. Andrea Canaan, 'Brownness' in *This Bridge Called My Back*, p. 233.

Appendix 1
Guide to the NHS
Complaints: The Mental Health Act;
Who's Who in the NHS

The way that the NHS is organised radically changed in 1990. It is now divided into provider organisations, most of which have now become NHS Trusts, and purchasing organisations, which are sometimes still called health authorities, but are more often now called commissioning agencies. More recently the FHSAs (Family Health Service Authorities), which were the funding and supervising bodies for GPs, have amalgamated with the health commissioning agencies or health authorities in most areas. Other changes include the introduction of the 'Internal Market' in which providers have to compete for contracts, and budget-holding GPs, who may be very conscious of the cost to them of prescribing different treatments to you.

Complaints

If you feel dissatisfied with the treatment you receive within the NHS you can complain about it. If it occurs within a hospital or mental health centre you can complain directly to the service manager, usually in writing, outlining your complaint. Anybody who works in the Mental Health Service should be able to tell you or find out for you what sort of complaint procedures they have. You can also approach the **Community Health Council** who can offer you support and more detailed information about how to proceed with your complaint. (**Citizen's Advice Bureaux** may also help with complaints.) Community Health Councils will vary from one area to another but they were set up with the intention of providing the community with information and advice regarding the health service. If they receive numerous complaints

231

about a particular service or doctor they can approach management structures and request further investigations into the matter. There are Community Health Councils for each area and they are listed in the phone book.

If you want to complain specifically about your GP you can write to the **Family Health Services Authority** (FHSA) or the **Health Commissioning Agency** in your area. The type of response you get may vary. These organisations should be listed in the phone book.

There is also the **General Medical Council** (44 Hallam Street, London W1; (0171 580 7642). The GMC is the organisation that is responsible for the registration of doctors and psychiatrists, and acts as a formal disciplinary committee. For serious offences, for example sexually assaulting a patient, doctors and psychiatrists may be struck off the register. This register is kept by the GMC.

If you have complained and are not satisfied with the replies you have received you can then complain to the **Health Service Commissioner**. This must be done in writing. The Health Service Commissioner publishes a leaflet outlining its practice. This can be obtained by writing to:

Health Service Commissioner
Church House
Great Smith Street
London SW1P 3BW

A very useful publication to refer to is *A to Z of Your Rights Under the NHS and Community Care Legislation* by Catherine Grimshaw, published by MIND, 1993.

Making a complaint is a time-consuming procedure. It is often very complicated and so it is best to seek advice of some sort before beginning. Trying to complain about issues regarding mental health is especially difficult because the label itself and popular misconceptions imply that your judgement is not to be taken seriously. The organisation MIND can be very helfpul and campaigns around issues relating to mental health.

The Mental Health Act

Sections

There are various sections of the Mental Health Act which define the circumstances in which people may be taken into hospital against their will. The new Mental Health Act became effective on 30 September 1983 and involved some changes in the sections as they were in the Act of 1959.

If you are 'sectioned' two people will be involved in making the decision. One of these must be a consultant psychiatrist and the other must be either your nearest relative or an approved social worker. 'Nearest relative' is defined by the Act as being husband, wife, parent (either mother or father, who have equal rights), brother and sister. With cohabiting couples, your partner will count as your nearest relative if you have been together for more than six months if you are heterosexual, or five years if you are homosexual. (A blatant example of discriminating against lesbian and homosexual couples.) An approved social worker is one who is considered to have enough experience in assessing mental illness. Procedures for becoming a 'warranted officer' vary from place to place.

With regard to the issue of consent it is possible that your family could be overruled by a social worker or vice versa. It only takes one of the listed people to consent to your being sectioned. This is very frightening for women as it puts us at tremendous risk. The Mental Health Act is a very powerful tool of social control. It is important that you know your rights should you ever be in the position of being sectioned. After you have been sectioned you have the right to appeal to the **Mental Health Review Tribunal** (MHRT) within a certain period of time. Hospital managers have a duty to inform you about your section and about your right of appeal. If you are sectioned for a certain length of time, it does not necessarily mean that doctors will keep you in hospital for all of that time. You can still be discharged sooner, but during that time they retain the right to bring you back into hospital, if they think it is necessary. Once your section expires, you can either leave hospital or become an 'informal' patient; that is one who can discharge herself at any time.

Section 2 Admission for Assessment

This used to be Section 25 of the old Mental Health Act. It can

233

include compulsory treatment and it lasts for 28 days. Your nearest relative or approved social worker may apply for admission. Your nearest relative may request discharge. You can appeal to the MHRT during the first 14 days of your section. If a relative applies for admission, the local social services will provide a report on your social circumstances.

Section 3 Admission for Treatment
This used to be Section 26. It lasts for six months. It can then be reviewed for a further six months, and then for a year. Your nearest relative or approved social worker applies for admission. As with Section 2, a report on your social circumstances must be provided. You can apply to the MHRT once during the first six months, then again during the next six months and then every year. This section is sometimes used to enable nurses to give compulsory treatment, such as injections of drugs, without intending that you remain in hospital for six months.

Section 4 Emergency Admissions
This was Section 29 in the old Act. It lasts for three days and nights. Your nearest relative or an approved social worker can apply for emergency admission. You must be seen by a psychiatrist within 24 hours of the application and admitted within another 24 hours. People are often brought into hospital in this way and then become 'informal' patients. It is also possible that a treatment section will be made when the emergency admission section expires.

Section 5 Application for Compulsory Admission of Informal Patient already in Hospital
This used to be Section 30. It enables a doctor to detain you in hospital against your will, if it is felt that it would be dangerous to allow you to leave. The section lasts for three days and nights. A registered nurse has the right to hold you for up to six hours until a doctor with the power to officially detain you arrives.

Sections cannot be renewed, except for a Section 3 (Admission for Treatment). However you can be admitted on one Section and it can be changed into another. For example, you could be admitted on a three-day Section and before going home they could change it to a 28-day Section even if they really only wanted you to stay one day longer.

234

The police also have the power to section people. This pow...
used in London with alarming frequency.

Voluntary Admission

If you feel so distressed that you, your family and friends can no longer cope and hospital seems to be the only alternative, it would be better if you go in as an informal patient. This will enable you to have more control over how long you stay and what happens to you. Sections deprive you of this control. In retrospect, a voluntary admission will be associated with less stigma. Many psychiatric hosptials or wards of general hospitals have emergency admission procedures. You, a member of your family or a friend can ring up beforehand to find out if this is a service offered by your local hospital.

With a voluntary admission you do run the risk of a Section 5 being made on you (a restraining order to keep you in hospital). However if you can try to plan an admission and keep the support of friends and family you may avoid being detained against your will.

See also a leaflet, produced by MIND, *Mental Health Act 1993 – An Outline Guide*, obtainable from MIND Publications, Granta House, 15–19 Broadway, Stratford, London E15 4BQ. 0181–519 2122.

Who's Who in the National Health regarding your Psychological Health

1. G.P. Your local doctor. They can be very helpful although the quality of care varies a lot. Many women doctors choose general practice. Studies seem to indicate that female GPs offer a different sort of care to their patients. They are said to spend more time listening and talking to you. If you are being seen elsewhere in the NHS your GP is usually told, unless you specifically request otherwise. GPs will prescribe tablets and can refer you to on for more specialised help. This will usually be a psychiatrist, although they can refer directly to psychologists and psychotherapists within the health service.

2. Psychiatrists are also doctors. They have done a general medical training and then specialised in mental illness. They are usually male. They almost always have junior staff under them. The order of seniority is Consultant, Senior Registrar, Junior Registrar, Senior House Officer, Junior House Officer.

As psychiatry is a specialty, most doctors will have already been a house officer before starting their training in psychiatry. The hierarchy is frequently concealed as they are all called doctors. Psychiatrists do not necessarily have any training in 'talking' therapies. Their training will be based in organic medicine (i.e. mental 'illness'). They can prescribe drugs and if need be do home visits (for which they are paid extra).

3. Psychotherapists   Psychotherapists are registered with the **UK Council of Psychotherapists**, and any complaints should be sent to this body. Registration with the UKCP is voluntary so there may be professionals who practise as psychotherapists who are not registered. At present only psychotherapists who work with children require registration. They are predominantly women and registration means they must have done a recognised training in child psychotherapy. Otherwise anyone can practise as a psychotherapist, although many have done specific trainings. Psychotherapy is usually talking aimed at helping you to understand your feelings. It is based on the belief that insight helps you to change. There are many different types of psycho-therapy depending on which model of change they are based on. Most psychotherapists work privately although there are some who work within the NHS. A lot of other professionals psychiatrists, psychologists and social workers do psycho-therapy. A medical background is not necessary.

4. Psychologists.   There are two main types of psychologists, educational and clinical. (There are also industrial or occu-pational psychologists as well.) Psychology means the study of the mind.

Educational psychologists work with school-age children. They are employed by local authorities or county councils to assess educational need. They have been teachers and then specialised in educational psychology. They make recommendations regarding special educational placement.

Clinical psychologists work within the health service although they sometimes work in other settings. They do all sorts of

236

therapies to help with psychological problems. They cannot prescribe drugs. They are predominantly women although at higher levels there are more men than women. They have no statutory responsibilities, unlike educational psychologists. Until recently there were four grades of psychologist: basic, senior, principal and top grade. Now there are only two grades: 'A' grade, which incorporates the old basic, senior and principal grades, and 'B' grade, often called 'consultant clinical psychologist'. The old grade titles are still sometimes used.

There is now a register of Chartered psychologists administered by the **British Psychological Society**. It will detail the qualifications, specialisms and geographical areas where the psychologist practices. Any complaints regarding psychologists should be addressed to the BPS. The register is only for those psychologists who are also members of the BPS as there is still no statutory requirement for registration.

5. *Social Workers* usually work for local government social services departments although some work in hospitals. However regardless of where they are based they are almost always paid by a local authority and are accountable to that authority. With the recent changes in the health service, it is now possible for social workers to be directly employed by a hospital trust. The professional body that oversees the profession is the **British Association of Social Workers** (BASW). Social Workers can do different types of therapy. They also have access to practical information about your rights and state benefits. They have statutory responsibilities, such as the power to remove your children and to section you. They frequently have very large caseloads so the opportunity of doing intensive work is often difficult to find. As in psychology, the more senior positions are held most often by men.

6. *Nurses* are frequently involved in psychological treatments, especially if you are an in-patient. Community Psychiatric Nurses and Health Visitors both do home visits. They have specialised within the nursing profession and are usually very experienced.

The nursing profession has undergone significant restructuring since this book was originally written. There are now many more nurses in managerial positions, and midwifery is no longer closed to men. Nurses are not routinely trained to do psychiatric intensive work unless they have specialised in psychiatry. Many are however very experienced counsellors. All nurses are registered with the **Royal College of Nursing**.

7. Occupational Therapists The traditional idea of an OT as someone who teaches you basketwork is no longer usually true. OTs now have training which includes a variety of creative therapies particularly those using art and drama. They are often involved in psychological treatment programmes such as social skills training. They are also trained to assess people's domestic and work skills. They are usually women.

8. Psychoanalyst This is someone who has trained in a specific type of psychotherapy usually Freudian, Jungian or Kleinian (all named after the person who formulated the theories on which the therapy is based). In order to do this type of work, individual analysts will have had treatment themselves. In America you must also be a trained psychiatrist. This is not the case in Britain. They rarely work within the NHS, doing most of their work in private practice. Some child psychotherapists are also analysts. This type of therapy, called an analysis, is long-term intensive work usually involving attendance four to five times per week over several years.

9. Family Therapists This is a relatively new professional group. Family therapists will usually have another professional qualification and then have specialised in systemic approaches. They are registered with the UKCP and accredited by the **Association of Family Therapy**. Family Therapists are most likely to work with family groups in child and adolescent mental health settings, although it is becoming a more common practise amongst adult client groups especially when helping families come to terms with issues that will impact on more than one family member such as bereavement, chronic illness or disability. The sessions are rarely more than weekly, usually occurring fortnightly to monthly for a limited number of sessions.

10. Counsellors The last few years have seen a big expansion in the number of trained counsellors. They are registered by the **British Association of Counsellors** although this is voluntary. Counsellors often have specific skills around a topic area or specialism such as mediation, bereavement and addictions. They often work with a client for a limited number of sessions.

Appendix 2
Guide to Drugs
Anti-Depressants; Tranquillisers, Lithium, and Antipsychotics

When this book was first published, many women thought it particularly helpful that we had included information about the colour of tablets, since people often think of their drugs in terms of colour rather than name: 'the little blue ones' etc. More recently, doctors have been advised whenever possible to prescribe according to the non-proprietary or generic names of drugs, rather than specify patented brand names which are usually more expensive. This means that a pharmacist can then dispense any one of a variety of makes of the drug, and these could be a number of different colours. It is therefore not possible to specify the colour of tablet for non-proprietary names of drugs.

Anti-depressants

Until recently there were two main types of anti-depressant drugs; the tricyclic anti-depressants, such as amitriptyline and imipramine, and the monoamine-oxidase inhibitors (MAOIS), such as phenelzine and tranylcypromine. The tricyclics remain by far the most commonly prescribed. Now however there is a third type of anti-depressant, called serotonin uptake inhibitors, the most well-known of which is Prozac (generic name Fluoxetine). These are considerably more expensive, and their use is still to some extent controversial.

1. Tricyclics (and related anti-depressant drugs)

These are the drugs most often used in the treatment of depressive

239

illness. They are preferred to MAOIs because they are thought to be more effective and less dangerous.

Tricyclics are considered to be most effective for treating moderate to severe depression, when there are physical changes such as loss of appetite and disturbance of sleep. Being able to sleep better is often the first benefit of these drugs. It may be two to three weeks before the anti-depressant effect becomes noticeable. The tricyclic anti-depressants can be roughly divided into those which are more or less sedative in their effects. If you seem to be agitated or anxious as well as depressed you will be likely to be prescribed one of the more sedative anti-depressants. Sometimes the whole dose is given at night before you go to sleep to help with insomnia and to avoid drowsiness in the daytime.

Side-effects The most common side-effects include drowsiness, dry mouth, blurred vision, nausea, constipation, urinary retention, tremor, rashes, sweating, and dampening of sexual feelings. You are not likely to get all of these side-effects. Which ones you experience and how severely varies a great deal from person to person. The side-effects are supposed to become less severe if you persist with taking the medication. This is because the body adapts to the presence of the drug. Tricyclics can also occasionally produce abnormal heart beat rhythms and so they should not be given to people who have had recent heart problems. The side-effects can be much greater in elderly people who must therefore be given lower doses.

2. Monamine-Oxidase Inhibitors (MAOIs)

These are less often prescribed than tricyclics, because they can be dangerous in combination with certain foods or drugs. They may be prescribed if tricyclic anti-depressants have failed to work. They can take three weeks or more before having an effect.

With these drugs you are not allowed to eat cheese, pickled herrings or broad bean pods. You must not eat or drink Bovril, Oxo, Marmite or any similar meat or yeast extract. You must not take any other medicines (including cough mixtures, pain relievers, etc.) without consulting your doctor.

Side-effects The most common side-effects are dizziness and postural hypotension (feeling faint or dizzy when you stand up). Less common side-effects are agitation, headache, tremor, constipation, dry mouth, blurred vision, difficulty in urinating,

240

liver damage, rashes, psychotic episodes in those susceptible to them, and severe hypertensive reactions to certain drugs and foods.

Reversible MAOIs A new anti-depressant, called MACLOBEMIDE, is used only for very serious depression. (Brand-name MANERIX). *Side-effects* sleep disturbances, dizzyness, nausea, headaches, restlessness, agitation, confusion; on rare occasions, raised liver enzymes.
Dose range 150–600mg per day.
Colour yellow tablets – 150mg each.

3. Other anti-depressant drugs

FLUPENTHIXOL (Brand name FLUANXOL) is a major tranquilliser, normally used for psychoses, which in very low doses sometimes has an anti-depressant effect. Because of the low doses, side effects are fewer.
   Side-effects restlessness, insomnia. Rarely there may be abnormal face and body movements, and a syndrome similar to Parkinson's disease with lack of control over body movements.
   Dose range 1mg–3mg.
   Colour Red tablets – 500 micrograms or 1mg

4. Serotonin Uptake Inhibitors

These are a relatively new type of anti-depressant, which are less sedative than the tricyclics, and are much less likely to have effects on the heart. They are often very effective anti-depressants, but are less often prescribed because they are much more expensive.
Side-effects gastro-intestinal (diarrhoea, nausea and vomiting), headaches, restlessness and anxiety.

FLUXOETINE (Brand Name PROZAC)
Side-effects As above. There are various other reported side-effects, including allergic reactions, mania and sexual dysfunction.
Dose range 20–60mg per day.
Colour Green/off-white capsules – 20mg each.

CHEMICAL NAME	BRAND NAMES*	SIDE-EFFECTS
AMITRIPTYLINE	TRYPTIZOL	See p.240.
	LENTIZOL	ditto
DOTHIEPIN	NON-PROPRIETARY	See p.239.
DOTHIEPIN	PROTHIADEN	See p. 239.
DOXEPIN	SINEQUAN	As above, but effects on heart are less than with amitriptyline.
MIANSERIN	NON-PROPRIETARY	See p. 239. Fewer and milder effects on the heart, but other possible effects include jaundice, arthritis, arthralgia and an influenza-like syndrome.†
MIANSERIN	BOLVIDON	As above.
	NORVAL	ditto
TRAXODONE	MOLIPAXIN	Fewer and milder. Sometimes quite strongly sedative.
TRIMIPRAMINE	SURMONTIL	As above, but more sedating. Often prescribed for depression with insomnia.
MAPROTILINE	LUDIOMIL	Less frequent, except for rashes, which often occur.

*You are more likely to know your drugs by their **Brand Name** and **colour**.
† Your doctor should do a full blood count regualrly.

WITH SEDATIVE PROPERTIES

DOSE RANGE PER DAY	COLOUR* OF TABLETS	QUANTITY IN EACH
50–200mg	**Orange** capsules	75mg
	Blue tablets	10mg
	Yellow tablets	25mg
	Brown tablets	50mg
ditto	**Pink** capsules	25mg
	Pink-red capsules	50mg
	(sustained-release)	
75–150mg	Colour varies	25mg
		or 75mg
75–150mg	**Red-brown** capsules	25mg
	Red tablets	75mg
30–300mg	**Orange** capsules	10mg
	Orange-blue capsules	25mg
	Blue capsules	50mg
	Yellow-blue capsules	75mg
30–90mg	Colour varies	10mg
		20mg
		or 30mg each
30–90mg	**Yellow** tablets	10mg
	Tablets **(film coated)**	20mg
	Tablets **(film coated)**	30mg
ditto	**Orange** tablets	10mg, 20mg
		30mg each
100–600mg	**Violet-green** capsules	50mg
	Violet-fawn capsules	100mg
	Pink tablets	150mg
	Liquid, sugar free	
50–300mg	**Green-white** capsules	50mg
	Tablets (compression coated)	10mg
		or 25mg each
25–150mg	**Pale yellow** tables	10mg
	Greyish-red tablets	25mg
	Light orange tables	50mg
	Brownish-orange tablets	75mg

CHEMICAL NAME	BRAND NAMES*	SIDE-EFFECTS
IMIPRAMINE	NON-PROPRIETARY	See p. 239. Less sedating, but other side-effects occur more frequently.
	TOFRANIL	ditto
CLOMIPRAMINE	NON-PROPRIETARY	As above.
CLOMIPRANINE	ANAFRANIL	As above, mildly sedative (N.B. this drug is often used for obsessional or phobic problems associated with depression)
DESIPRAMINE	PERTOFRAN	Most commonly – insomnia, tremor, constipation, nausea, urinary retention, dry mouth, blurred vision.
IPRINDOLE	PRONDOL	Fewer and milder – but jaundice very rarely may occur.
NORTRIPTYLINE	ALLEGRON	Less sedating – but other side-effects occur more frequently.
	AVENTYL	ditto
VILOXAZINE	VIVALAN	Fewer and milder but nausea and headaches may occur.
†ZIMELDINE	ZELMID	Most common side-effects are headache, gastro-intestinal disturbances and sweating.

*You are more likely to know your drugs by their **Brand Name** and **colour**.
† This drug has recently been withdrawn from the market.

WHICH ARE LESS SEDATING

DOSE RANGE PER DAY	COLOUR* OF TABLETS	QUANTITY IN EACH
75–300mg	Colour varies	10mg 25mg
ditto	**Red-brown** tablets	10mg or 25mg
10–250mg	Colour varies	10mg 25mg or 50mg
10–15mg	**Yellow-caramel** capsule **Orange-caramel** capsule **Grey caramel** capsules Pink tablets (modified release)	10mg 25mg 50mg 75mg
75–200mg	**Pink** tablets	25mg
45–180mg	**Yellow** tablets	15 or 30mg
30–100mg	**Yellow** tablets **Orange** tablets	10mg 25mg
ditto	**Yellow-white** capsules **Yellow-white** capsules	10mg 25mg
100–400mg	**Yellow** tablets	50mg
200–300mg	**Film-coated** tablets	100mg or 200mg

MONOAMINE-OXIDASE INHIBITORS (MAOIs)

CHEMICAL NAME	BRAND NAMES*	DOSE RANGE PER DAY	SIDE EFFECTS	COLOUR* OF TABLETS	QUANTITY OF EACH
PHENELZINE	NARDIL	45–60mg	See above	Orange tablets	15mg
ISOCARBOXAZID	MARPLAN	10–30mg	As above; very occasionally can lead to anemia, hepatitis, peripheral oedema and rashes.	Pink tablets	10mg
TRANYLCYPROMINE	PARNATE	10–30mg	More common – insomnia, dizziness, dry mouth, hypotension, muscular weakness, hypertensive crises with throbbing headache. Less common – liver damage.	Red tablets	10mg

*You are more likely to know your drugs by their **Brand Name and colour.**

FLUVOXAMINE (Brand Name FAVERIN)
Side-effects As above, plus bradychardia, convulsions; on rare occasions, increase in liver enzymes.
Dose range 100–200mg per day.
Colour Yellow tablets – 50 or 100mg.

PAROXETINE (Brand Name SEROXAT)
Side-effects As above, plus sexual dysfunction and some other possible reactions.
Dose range 20–50mg per day.
Colour 20mg tablets – colour uncertain; Blue tablets – 30mg.

SERTRALINE (Brand Name LUSTRAL)
Side-effects As above, plus tremor, increased sweating, dyspepsia.
Dose range 50mg–200mg.
Colour 50mg or 100mg tablets – colour uncertain.

Tranquillisers, Lithium, and Antipsychotics

1. Tranquillisers (Anxiolytics: Benzodiazepines)

These are drugs which are used to lessen anxiety. They will not help depression but may be prescribed for you if you seem anxious as well as depressed. In the past, some doctors tended to overprescribe them, giving them to anyone who complained of being unhappy. This led to many women becoming addicted to valium, librium, ativan, etc. These days, doctors tend to prescribe tranquillisers less often because of the publicity and attempted legal action about their adverse addictive properties.

If you have been taking these drugs for a long time and wish to stop, you will need to do so very gradually as you may get unpleasant withdrawal symptoms if you stop too quickly. It should be possible to obtain help and advice about how to withdraw from tranquillisers from your GP or local mental health service or from your local branch of MIND.

The most common anxiolytics are called *Benzodiazepines*. The other main group is *Barbiturates*, but these are seldom prescribed now because they are considered to be more dangerous.

Side-effects of Benzodiazepines drowsiness, dizziness, ataxia (feeling dizzy and unsteady – particularly in the elderly); occasionally confusion, dry mouth, headache, hypersensitivity reactions. Sometimes there may be a morning hangover feeling.

Names of Benzodiazepine drugs (brand names in brackets)

Diazepam (Valium, Alupram, Atensine, Evacalm, Solis, Tensium, Valrelease)

Lorazepam (Almazine, Ativan)

Benzoctamine (Tacitin)

Bromazepam (Lexotan)

Chlordiazepoxide (Librium, Tropium)

Chlormezanone (Trancopal)

Clobazam (Frisium)

Clorazepate (Tranxene)

Hydroxyzine (Atarax)

Meprobamate (Equanil, Meprate, Miltown, Tenavoid)

Oxazepam (Serenid-D, Serenid Forte)

Prazepam (Centrax)

2. Sedatives:
Benzodiazepines prescribed for Insomnia (Hypnotics)

These can cause hangovers with drowsiness, dizziness, confusion, dry mouth, hypersensitivity. Using them for a long time can lead to dependence (not being able to stop taking them), tolerance (the effect of the drug gets less), and rebound insomnia when you stop taking them. They can also inhibit dreaming. Commonly used drugs of this type are (brand names in brackets):

Flurazepam (Dalmane)

Nitrazepam (Mogadon, Remnos, Somnite, Surem, Unisomnia, Nitrados)

Flunitrazepam (Rohypnol)

Temazepam (Euhypnos, Euhypnos Forte, Normison)

Lormetazepam (Noctamid)

Triazolam (Halcion)

3. Lithium

This is an element which is similar to potassium and sodium and is prescribed in the form of simple salts. How it produces psychiatric benefit is not known, but it has been found to control or prevent severe mood swings in manic-depressive illness, or in severe depression that seems to occur in regular cycles. It has quite dangerous long-term side-effects including possible damage to the kidneys, so the exact dose and its effects have to be monitored very carefully, using blood tests. Immediate side-effects can include nausea, vomiting, diarrhoea, tremor of the hands, mild dryness of mouth or slight thirst, muscular weakness and fatigue. There are two forms of Lithium:

Lithium carbonate (brand names – Camcolit 250, Camcolit 400, Liskonum, Phasal, Priadel)

Lithium citrate (Litarex)

4. 'Major Tranquillisers'
Antipsychotic drugs (phenothiazines)

These are not used for depression, but you might be prescribed a low dose if you are very anxious or agitated. They are strong drugs with unpleasant long-term side-effects which include abnormal face and body movements, stiffness of arms and legs, loss of facial mobility and expression, and restlessness. If used to control anxiety, you should only be on them for a very short time. Names of Phenothizaines include (brand names in brackets):

Chlorpromazine   (Largactyl, Chloractil, Dozine)
Flupenthixol   (Depixol)
Haliperidol   (Haldol, Seranace)
Perphenazine   (Fentazin)
Pimozide   (Orap)
Thioridazine   (Melleril)
Trifluoperazine   (Stelazine)

Most of this information on drugs and their side-effects was obtained from the *British National Formulary*, no. 26 (September 1993), published by the British Medical Association and the Pharmaceutical Society of Great Britain. A good layperson's guide to psychiatric drugs is *The Complete Guide to Psychiatric Drugs: A Layman's Handbook* by Ron Lacey (Ebury Press/ MIND, London, 1991).

Appendix 3
Resources

The following is by no means comprehensive. It includes a range of services and organisations that may help you to get the help you need. When contacting an organisation be sure to check whether you will need to pay for the service they are offering; whether or not you will be offered a helper of the same gender and race as yourself if that is what you want; how accessible the service is; and whether they have childcare facilities. You may also want to check what training the staff have to provide the service they are offering and what their policy is on confidentiality.

Accept provides a range of services for people who are experiencing difficulties with alcohol including a phone line and a women only drop in group. Contact Anne Hunter, 724 Fulham Road, London SW6 5GE (0171 371 7477).

Afro-Caribbean Mental Health Association offers counselling both one to one and group work for black men and women. Contact the Clinical Manager 35–37 Electric Avenue, London SW9 (0171 737 3603).

Al Anon Family Groups offers support for people with alcohol problems and their families. Contact 61 Great Dover Street, London SE1 4YF (0171 403 0888).

Big Issue runs a weekly newspaper on the issue of homelessness and a helpline. Contact the office nearest to you. In the West Midlands, 5 Shaw's Passage, Digbeth, Birmingham B5 5JF (0121 643 4535), in the South West, 4 Peirpont, Bath BA1 ILE (01225 312951); in Brighton, 23 Preston Street, Brighton BN1 3YE (01273 737795); in Cymru, 22 St Mary Street, Cardiff, South

Glamorgan CF1 2AA (01222 224606); and in London, 57/61 Fleet House, London ECIM 5NP (0171 418 0418).

Birmingham Women's Counselling and Therapy Centre is the only women's therapy centre wholly funded by the NHS. They provide individual and group therapy. Access is by self referral for women in South Birmingham. Contact Mary Robinson, The Lodge, 52 Queensbridge Road, Moseley, Birmingham B13 8QD (0121 442 2241).

Black Mental Health Resource Centre provides counselling for black users of mental health services. Contact Ms H Samuels, 277 Chapeltown Road, Chapeltown Leeds LS7 3HA (0113 2374229).

British Association For Counselling 1 Regent Place, Rugby CV21 2PJ (01788 578328). Send an sae for information.

British Psycho-analytical Society, 63 New Cavendish Street, London W1M 7RD (0171 580 4952). This is for individual Freudian therapy.

British Psychological Society (BPS), St Andrew's House, 48 Princess Road East, Leicester LE1 7DR (0116 2549568).

Bristol Crisis Service for Women specifically offers help for women who are self harming. This includes not only self injury but also other destructive addictions such as alcoholism, anorexia and bulimia. The main service is a phone line. Contact Hilary Lindsey, PO Box 654, Bristol BS99 1XH (0117 9251119).

Camden Black Sisters offers counselling for black women survivors of sexual abuse. Contact 2c Falkland Road, London NW5 2PT (0171 284 3336).

Cardiff Institute of Family Therapy, 105 Cathedral Road, Cardiff, CF1 9PH (01222 226532/371020).

Centre 33 provides counselling and information to any woman under 25. Contact Elaine Short, 33 Clarendon Street, Cambridge CB1 1JX (01223 314763).

Co dependents Anonymous for help with co-dependent relationships. Contact PO Box 1292, London N4 2YX.

Good Practices in Mental Health, 380–384 Harrow Road, London W9 2HU (0171 289 2034/3060). This group in collaboration with the European Regional Council and World Federation for Mental Health have produced an information pack specifically on Women and Mental Health which contains 8 Pamphlets each outlining services for women that are considered examples of good practice. The 8 areas include: All women; women with children; women of specific racial and ethnic origin; women with long term recurring mental health problems; lesbians and bisexual women; women who have experienced sexual abuse and violence; women in middle or later life; and women who self harm or misuse food, alcohol or drugs. Available for £14.95.

Institute of Complementary Medicine, PO Box 194, London SE16 1QZ (0171 237 5165). Send a large sae and they will send you a list of practioners in your area.

Institute of Family Therapy, 43 New Cavendish Street, London W1M (0171 935 1651). Works with families and couples together. There are special projects which focus on bereavement, safety in families following violence and sexual abuse, working with issues of sexual orientation and disability.

Lambeth Women and Children's Health Project is a community health project that offers a wide range of services including counselling. They also offer support to mothers of children who have been sexually abused. Contact Pat Agana or Femi Anyabwile, Angel Town Estate, 8 Hollis House, Overton Road, London SW9 (0171 737 7151).

Lesbian and Gay Bereavement Project provides a range of services for lesbians and gay men experiencing grief through the loss of someone special to them. They run a help line from 7pm to midnight every evening. Contact Vaughan Williams Centre, Colindale Hospital, London NW9 5HG (0181 200 0511).

252

Maya Project/Young Women's Project offers a service for young women up to the age of 17. Contact 45 New King's Road, Fulham Broadway London SW6 4SD (0171 731 4907).

The Mental Health Foundation, 37 Mortimer Street, London W1N 7RJ (0171 580 0145).

MIND (National Association for Mental Health), Head Office Granta House, Broadway, London E15 4BQ (0181 519 2122). There are many local associations that will be listed in your local directory. MIND also publishes some excellent reports on women and mental health.

Miscarriage Association offers befriending, group therapy advice and information to anyone affected by a miscarriage. Contact Morag Kinghorn, 15 Clerwood Bank, Edinburgh EH12 8PZ (0131 334 8883).

Mothers for Mothers provides support for women who are suffering from post-natal depression. Contact Sonia Hilder, c/o 50 Avenue Road, Trowbridge, Wilts (01225 763598).

NAFSIYAT Intercultural Therapy Centre, 278 Seven Sisters Road, Finsbury Park, London N4 2HY (0171 263 4130).

National Association for Mental Health see MIND above.

National Council for Voluntary Organisations, Regent's Wharf, 8 All Saints Street, London N1 9RL (0171 713 6161).

National Family Mediation and Conciliation Services, 5 Tavistock Place, London WC1H 9SN (0171 983 5993/5994).

Off Centre is counselling service for adolescents. 25 Hackney Grove, London E8 3NR (0181 985 8566); Helpline: 0181 985 0044.

Phobic Action, Hornbeam House, Claybury Grounds, Manor Road, Watford Green, Essex IG8 8PR (0181 559 2551); Helpline: 0181 559 2459.

Pink Practice offers one to one counselling for lesbian and bisexual women (as well as gay and bisexual men). All practitioners are gay or lesbian themselves. Contact Pink Practice, London WC1N 3XX (0181 809 7218).

POPAN (Prevention of Professional Abuse Network) provides a service for women who have been sexually abused by their therapists. Contact Jenny Fasal, Flat 1, 20 Daleham Gardens, London NW3 5DA (0171 794 3177).

Positively Women provides counselling and advice for women with HIV/AIDS. Contact 5 Sebastian Street, London EC1V 0HE (0171 490 5501).

Powerhouse is a group of both disabled and able bodied women who are setting up a refuge for women with learning difficulties who have been threatened or abused. They can be contacted by post c/o Didsbury Close, Melbourne Road, London E6 2RX.

Register of Chartered Psychologists available from the British Psychological Society. This register lists all chartered psychologists who are members of the BPS. To be registered you must have done a recognised training in psychology. Areas of interest are identified as well as where the professional practices are located.

Relate (formerly Marriage Guidance) Find your nearest centre in your telephone directory.

Shanti is a service provided by the National Health Service which aims to provide psychotherapy including group work and consultancy within a multicultural framework. Contact 1a Dalebury House, Ferndale Road, London SW9 8AP (0171 733 8581).

Southall Black Sisters Women's Centre runs a safe house, counselling and support services for black and Asian women. Contact 86 Northcote Avenue, Southall, Middlesex UB1 2AZ (0181 843 0578).

Women's Aid Federation now called **Refuge** co-ordinates the national work of women's refuges. They run a 24-hour crisis line on 0181 995 4430; their office telephone number is 0181 747 0133.

Women's and Girls Network provides a counselling service for women and girls through a phone line as well as face to face. Contact London Women's Centre, Wesley House, 4 Wild Court, London WC2B 5AU. (0171 404 1234); Phone line: 0171 978 8887.

Women Against Sexual Harassment (WASH) can offer legal advice and counselling in relation to sexual harassment. Contact 305 The Chandlery, 50 Westminster Bridge Road, London SE1 7QY (0171 721 7592).

Women in Learning Difficulties Network (WILD) is a network of both service users and professionals who campaign to ensure that issues regarding women and learning disabilities are addressed. Contact Ruth Townsley, North Fry Research Centre, University of Bristol, 32 Tyndall's Park Road, Bristol B58 1PY (0117 9238137).

Women's Therapy Centre offers individual and group work for women. They also have a database of services offered beyond London and will try to put women in touch with a service in her area. Contact 6–9 Manor Gardens, London N7 6LA (0171 281 7879).

UK Council for Psychotherapy, Regents College, Inner Circle, Regents Park, London NW1 4NS (0171 487 7554). Send a sae for names of registered practitioners in your area. Includes a range of psychotherapies including family therapists which may be confusing.

Appendix 4
Useful Reading

Self-help Books on Depression

Atkinson, Sue, *Climbing Out of Depression*, Lion Publishing, Oxford, 1993.

Finkel, Lois, *Women, Anger and Depression: Strategies for Self Empowerment*, Health Communications Inc, Florida, 1992.

Rowe, Dorothy, *Depression: The Way Out of Your Prison*, Routledge, London, 1989.

Saunders, Dierdre, *Women and Depression: A Practical Self Help Guide*, Sheldon Press, London, 1984.

Other Useful Books

Andrews, Catherine, Nadirshaw, Zenobia, Perkins, Rachel and Copperman, Jeanette, eds, *Women and Mental Health in Context*, Pavillion, London, 1994.

Barnes, Marian, and Maple, Norma, *Women and Mental Health: Challenging the Stereotypes*, Venture Press, London, 1992.

Chesler Phyllis, *Women and Madness*, Harcourt Brace Jovanovich, London, 1989.

Estes, Clarissa Pinkola, *Women Who Run with the Wolves: Contacting the Power of the Wild Woman*, Rider, London, 1992.

hooks, bell, *Sisters of the Yam: Black Women and Self Recovery*, South End Press, Boston, 1993.

King's Fund Centre, *Mental Health in Britain's Black Communities*, King's Fund Centre, London, 1993; distributed by

Bournemouth English Book Centre.

Ussher, Jane and Nicolson, Paula, eds, *Gender Issues in Clinical Psychology*, Routledge, London, 1992.

Williams, Jennie, Watson, Gillig, Smith, Helen, Copperman, Jeanette, and Wood, Daphne, *Purchasing Effective Mental Health Services for Women: A Framework for Action*, MIND Publications, London, 1993.